THE FIVE AGES
SWEDENBORG'S VIEW OF S...

A new book by Swedenborg? Well not exactly, but ... ~~ ..e the nearest thing to it. Swedenborg died in 1772, aged 85, not long after having completed his extensive *The True Christian Religion*, but, had he lived on, what might he have published next? Actually the last unpublished manuscript of any length he left behind was *The Coronis* which sadly is no longer extant, except for an imperfect and incomplete copy. It describes five ages or 'churches', as he calls them. A world history, but a spiritual or psychological history, not a political or social history, although it does touch on social matters.

In *The Coronis*, and also in earlier works, Swedenborg explores a theme that can be found in most mythologies, the idea of the 'world ages'. The Greeks and Romans called them the Golden Age, the Silver Age, the Bronze Age and the Iron Age. Hindu mythology talks of the four 'yugas'; an idea developed by Buddhism. In the structure of the Bible one can discern similar periods initiated by Adam, Noah, Moses, Christ and a new age foretold in the Book of Revelation. Mohammed had a very similar pattern of six 'great prophets' and St Augustine had seven ages. You will find more versions in Norse, Persian, Aztec and other myths. Nowhere, however, will you find a treatment of the theme as extensive and detailed as Swedenborg's.

Swedenborg's thoughts on these matters are scattered through several of his books, but are here brought together in one volume. We are told of mankind's psychological development through the ages and how God accommodated His revelation to suit us. You will learn nothing about kings and battles, but will come to understand the underlying spiritual basis of the developing pattern of world history.

The passages from Swedenborg have been compiled by P L JOHNSON who has added a commentary to help continuity. He also offers notes showing how well Swedenborg's ideas fit in with historical and archaeological knowledge gathered since his time. Patrick Johnson has been interested in History and Swedenborg all his life and has been the editor of two Swedenborgian Magazines. A retired architect, he was fortunate to spend the latter years of his career with English Heritage, exploring and caring for the structures people inhabited through the ages.

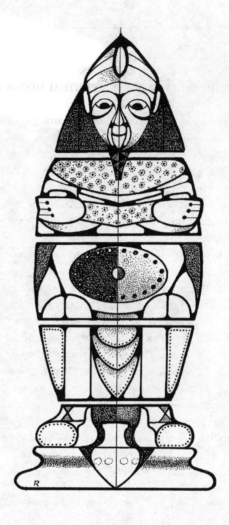

You looked, O king, and there before you stood a large statue... The head of the statue was made of pure gold, its chest and arms of silver, its belly and thighs of bronze, its legs of iron, its feet partly of iron and partly of baked clay. (Daniel 2:31-3)

The Five Ages:
Swedenborg's View of Spiritual History

Extracts from Emanuel Swedenborg
with commentary by P L Johnson

Swedenborg House
20-21 Bloomsbury Way
London WC1A 2TH

—

2009

All rights reserved. No part of this publication may be reproduced, stored in a retrieval system, or transmitted, in any form or by any means, without the prior permission in writing of The Swedenborg Society, or as expressly permitted by law, or under terms agreed with the appropriate reprographics rights organization. Enquiries concerning reproduction outside the scope of the above should be sent to The Swedenborg Society, at the address below.
The author's moral rights have been asserted.

Published by:
The Swedenborg Society
Swedenborg House
20-21 Bloomsbury Way
London WC1A 2TH

© 2009 The Swedenborg Society
2nd edition

Cover Illustration: G R Smith
Frontispiece Illustration: G R Smith
Book Illustrations: P L Johnson
Book Design: Stephen McNeilly

Typeset at Swedenborg House
Printed and bound in Great Britain by
Hobbs the Printers Ltd, Totton, Hampshire

ISBN 978-0-85448-155-2
British Library Cataloguing-in-Publication Data
A catalogue record for this book is available
from the British Library

| Acknowledgements |

My thanks to Ian Johnson, Norman Pettersen, Richard Lines and John Elliott for their help reading and commenting on the text, and especially to John Elliott and Ian Johnson for their revised translations of some of the older quotations. Also to G Roland Smith, James Wilson and Stephen McNeilly for their work on the book's production and finally to my wife Hilda for not throwing that horrible computer out of the window.

DEDICATION

To my father the Rev Philip H Johnson BA BSc
whose booklet *Revelation Through the Ages*
first launched my interest in the subject.

Contents

	Page no.
Acknowledgements	v
List of Illustrations	ix
Introduction	xi

1—The Five Ages	3
2—The Nature of the Church	17
3—The Most Ancient Church	31
Marriage Love in the Golden Age: Conjugial Love §75	57
4—The Ancient Churches	65
Marriage Love in the Silver Age: Conjugial Love §76	90
5—The Second Ancient Church	97
Marriage Love in the Bronze Age: Conjugial Love §77	105
6—The Israelite and Jewish Churches	111
Sexual Relations in the Iron Age: Conjugial Love §78	138
7—The Christian Church	145
Sexual Relations in Later Times: Conjugial Love §79	175
8—The New Church	183

Contents

Endnotes..219
Appendix: World Age Patterns..223
Index of Quotations from the Works of Swedenborg.............................227
Select Bibliography..231
Index...233

List of Illustrations

Frontispiece. Nebuchadnezzar's Statue

Fig. 1.   Comparisons of five age concepts, p. 12.

Fig. 2.   Uluru or Ayers Rock, p. 34.

Fig. 3.   Palaeolithic 'Tents', p. 37.

Fig. 4   Palaeolithic Village, p. 41.

Fig. 5.   Aborigine Turinga, p. 51.

Fig. 6.   The Extent of the Ancient Church, p. 67.

Fig. 7.   Ahura Mazda, p. 71.

Fig. 8a.   Greek Temples, p. 75.

Fig. 8b.   Roman Temples, p. 75.

Fig. 9.   Great Tartary, p. 81.

Fig. 10.   A Neolithic Long Barrow, p. 83.

Fig. 11.   Canaanite Gods, p. 88.

Fig. 12.   A reconstruction of the Ziggurat of Ur, p. 89.

Fig. 13.   Limited Extent of the Second Ancient Church, p. 98.

Fig. 14.   The Phoenician Alphabet, p. 99.

Fig. 15.   A Canaanite Altar, p. 101.

List of Illustrations

Fig. 16. An Egyptian Princess, p. 119.
Fig. 17. List of Clean and Unclean Animals, p. 124.
Fig. 18. Hebrew Script, p. 128.
Fig. 19. Solomon's Temple, p. 131.
Fig. 20. The Jewish Diaspora, p. 137.
Fig. 21. The Empires of Alexander and Rome, p. 146.
Fig. 22. Canon of the Bible, p. 152.
Fig. 23. The Spread of Islam, p. 160.
Fig. 24. Access to the Bible in the Eighteenth Century, p. 166.
Fig. 25. Emanuel Swedenborg, p. 186.
Fig. 26. Divine Influx to the World, p. 190.
Fig. 27. Christ in Majesty, Coventry Cathedral, p. 195.
Fig. 28. Post 1757 Religious Developments, p. 201.
Fig. 29. 'Map' of the World of Spirits shortly after 1757, p. 206.
Fig. 30. Bryn Athyn Cathedral, p. 212.

Introduction

There is an overall pattern to Swedenborg's output of theological works. Information seems initially to have flooded into his mind and in *The Spiritual Diary* he could only write it down as fast as it came. Next, in the many volumes of *Arcana Caelestia*, he is writing a commentary on the biblical books of Genesis and Exodus and so the biblical text dictates the structure of the work. Nevertheless, as he proceeds, he also adds 'inter-chapter' material, most notably the 'memorable relations' of his psychic experiences in the other world, but also other essays on various themes. Having completed *Arcana Caelestia*, however, he then took the opportunity to extract from its vast text some of these secondary themes and publish them separately in more easily digested volumes, such as *Worlds in Space* or re-present the material as in the case of *Heaven and Hell*. This general pattern was repeated with the six volume *Apocalypse Explained* and the short works which followed it.

In this way many interesting themes were published in a more convenient form than the many volumed *Arcana Caelestia*. One intriguing theme, that covers many pages of *Arcana Caelestia* and other major works, which was 'ripe' for similar treatment was his concept of the 'Five Churches'. Swedenborg did in fact draft a manuscript of both existing and new material which he entitled *The Coronis*. A 'coronis' is an ornamental flourish printers put at the end of a chapter or book. Perhaps Swedenborg was indicating that the book would complete his work. Unfortunately, it was indeed almost his last work and the draft was never finalized. Its list of contents and the actual written text do not tie up. Worse still, the original manuscript was borrowed by Swedenborg's friend Dr Messiter in order to make a copy. Before he had completed the copy, the Doctor mislaid the original document, and so we only have a 'copy' and lack the latter chapters. They would have contained material about the Christian and New churches—not much explored in Swedenborg's other books. The main content of *The Coronis* consists of commentaries on key passages in the Word relating to the critical stages of these five 'churches' or 'ages'. It also includes the reports of Swedenborg's visits to the heavens populated by the peoples from those ages, which he had already published in *Conjugial Love*. But it does not attempt to gather up the numerous references to the five churches scattered elsewhere in *Arcana Caelestia* and other volumes.

I feel *The Coronis* has a further disadvantage. In practically all Swedenborg's theological writing he is the master of his subject. His knowledge of the Bible, the Hebrew language, the spiritual world, astronomy and other sciences referred to is quite adequate for the task he sets himself. In the case of *The Coronis*, however, the subject is 'world history'; if only the spiritual aspects of it. Unfortunately history as we know it today was still in its infancy and not much studied in the eighteenth century. This was partly due to lack of interest and of properly sorted information, but also to over-reliance on the Bible and the Greek and Roman 'Classics', which were assumed to contain most, if not all, the information necessary for an understanding of the past. As a mining engineer, familiar with geological strata, Swedenborg probably had some appreciation of the extent of 'the past'; but one doubts if he, or anyone else, then appreciated its true magnitude, or realized how little of it was covered in the Hebrew and classical writings. Similarly, although the coastlines of the continents had just about been established in the eighteenth century, the nature of the people who lived beyond the coast was mostly unknown to Europeans. Under these circumstances Swedenborg could hardly be the 'master of his subject'.

I do not think the gaps in Swedenborg's knowledge have led to any serious inaccuracies in his writing on this subject; nevertheless, had he possessed the knowledge of archaeology, history, geography or anthropology that we have today, he might well have written a

Introduction

much longer and more comprehensive book than *The Coronis*. It would be an interesting task to attempt to contrive such a book, but although we have many volumes of modern information, we lack Swedenborg's spiritual insight and sources and so might not achieve very much.

In any case it must be borne in mind that, for Swedenborg, the 'history' of the five churches corresponds at another level to five stages of development we pass through in our psycho-spiritual lives from infancy through childhood, youth and adulthood to maturity. That spiritual development was always the essence of his message is clear when one reads the early chapters of *Arcana Caelestia*. The church exists as a general body within society, but there is also a personal church in each one of us. I had originally felt that I should present the development of the general (historic) and the individual (psycho-spiritual) churches in parallel in this text. For the sake of simplicity, however, I have concentrated on the theme of the general church as pictured in history.

What I have brought together in this book is a selection of quotations from Swedenborg's many books which I hope cover all the main points he makes about his five churches, adding my own comments to give continuity and add relevant recent knowledge. He makes mention of these churches in more than two thousand of the numbered paragraphs in his writings, so to print them all would produce a very unwieldy volume. However, these paragraphs often repeat the same information, so the number of them we need to mention is much reduced. In very many—quite possibly most—cases the mentioned 'church' is not the main subject under discussion, so that only a sentence or two of the paragraph needs to be quoted for our purposes. This does mean that points are taken out of context, but to introduce the 'context' of the passages, from which the passing comments are taken, would lead the mind of the reader off at a tangent to subjects other than our theme. Swedenborg's holistic approach inevitably means he can be very discursive. It has therefore been desirable to edit the quotations somewhat drastically, starting quotations off in mid sentence, making considerable omissions and inserting my own words for continuity—the latter should all be in [square brackets].

I must remind new readers that Swedenborg wrote the books, from which the passages have been taken, in eighteenth-century Latin (sometimes called Neo-Latin). They have been translated into English by many different scholars (mostly educated in classical Latin) at different times over the past century. If the passages are at times obscure, one should not necessarily blame Swedenborg, or the translators, but rather the tortuous process of translation. In the main I have used current Swedenborg Society translations, but occasionally, where it seemed desirable, other translations. I have sometimes found it useful to use passages from *The Swedenborg Concordance* as it too had to lift quotations out of their context and the editor, J F Potts, made judicious modifications to allow quotations to stand alone. Most of the translations were prepared in recent decades, but some, such as those of *Apocalypse Explained* and *The Coronis* (for this book rather important alas!), were quite old and tended to show their years. Fortunately, however, the Revd John Elliott has kindly made new translations of the pertinent passages and also pointed out where passages from recent translations paralleled the quotations I had chosen from older translations.

In a physical or technical sense, however, the translations have been taken from the NewSearch computer software program which has conveniently placed all of Swedenborg's writings 'on disk'. It has occasional typing errors I may not have noticed, but without the facility NewSearch provided to 'copy and paste' passages from Swedenborg, I doubt that I would ever have found time to compile this book and so a large share of the credit for it should be given to the creators of the software, and its publishers, the Academy of the New Church. It is to be hoped that at some time in the future a more capable scholar than I, with more time and resources at their disposal, may compile a better and more complete version of this book.

I trust that the comments I have added alongside the quotations will be considered of value. Their intended function is twofold: to help to tie quotations from various sources together; and also to add new historical, archaeological and anthropological information which was not available to Swedenborg, where I feel it helps to complete or amplify the picture. I am aware of the dangers of mixing theology and history, and the need to keep them distinct in one's mind. Nevertheless, like Swedenborg, I feel there is much to be said for comparing them and letting each illuminate the other. He was a cheerful advocate of the holistic approach. However, the layout is such that you can read the Swedenborg

Introduction

quotations without interruption, if this is preferred. The Swedenborg quotations are in Book Condenced type and the comments in Roman.

I hope that what I have selected does justice, if not full justice, to this theme of the five ages; a theme which does much to put history into spiritual perspective. Also, as I have noted in the Appendix, because the 'five age' theme is common to many faiths, it could do something to help inter-religious understanding.

Patrick Johnson
London 2007

Chapter One—The Five Ages

Since the creation of this earth there have been, to speak in general terms, four churches, each succeeding the one before. This can be established from the historical as well as the prophetical books of the Word, especially the book of Daniel. Here the four churches are described by the statue Nebuchadnezzar saw in a dream (Daniel 2:31-36), and later by the four beasts coming up out of the sea (Daniel 7:1-7).

The first church, which may be called the Most Ancient Church, came into existence before the flood, and its ending or departure is described by the flood.

The second church, which may be called the Ancient Church, was in Asia and in parts of Africa; this came to an end and perished as the result of idolatrous practices.

The third was the Israelite Church, begun by the proclamation of the Ten Commandments on Mount Sinai, and continued through the Word written by Moses and the Prophets. The fourth is the Christian Church founded by the Lord by means of the Evangelists and the Apostles.

The True Christian Religion §760

These statements define one of Swedenborg's grandest visions, his concept of the Five Churches, presenting our Lord, not just as the God of the Jews or Christians, but as the God of all peoples throughout all time. He identifies four churches that are past but not the fifth new one about to begin.

Initially these statements may seem somewhat improbable; particularly the mention in the first quotation of the quaint-sounding 'Most Ancient' and 'Ancient' churches, as they seem not to appear in history books. The same applies to his 'new church' although a 'new age' is not an uncommon idea now.

The Latin words Swedenborg used, *Ecclesia Antiquissima* and *Ecclesia Antiqua*, could have been translated by the more familiar-sounding terms, the 'Oldest Religion' and the 'Old Religion'. As we shall see, Swedenborg's use of the word 'church' and his concept of the 'Church' do not necessarily involve the material sort of organization that would interest historians or figure in archaeological evidence. His 'church' is a state of mind, an all pervading psycho-spiritual body of affection and thinking expressed in the whole way of life of the people of these periods.

> **The succeeding states of the church [...] are described in the Word by the four seasons [...] and by the four times of day, morning, midday, evening and night. Since the present-day Christian Church is in night, it follows that morning is at hand, that is, the first state of a new church.**
>
> *The True Christian Religion* §764

Swedenborg is writing about 1770 when the state of the Church was moribund.

It is perhaps strange that Swedenborg hardly ever lists all five churches together, but as he was writing before the new church had begun, it is understandable. We today can look back on evidence that suggests a new age or new church and so see five entities. For Swedenborg, however, the new church, although he confidently expected it, was in the hazy future.

Swedenborg also describes the 'four churches' in *Arcana Caelestia* §1551 and §10355, *Heaven and Hell* §327, *Last Judgment* §46, *Conjugial Love* §§75-9 and *Apocalypse Explained* §176 and briefly 'six churches' in *Apocalypse Explained* §948.

The terms Most Ancient, Ancient, Israelite (or Jewish), Christian and New are those normally used by Swedenborg, but he does present them in other patterns using other terms as the following pages show.

BIBLICAL PERIODS

> **Four churches have existed on our planet since it was created—**
> **a first, which should be called the Adamic Church;**
> **a second, the Noachian;**
> **a third, the Israelite;**
> **and a fourth, the Christian.**
> **The fact that four Churches have come to exist on our planet is made very plain in Daniel, by the image which Nebuchadnezzar saw in a dream, and by the vision of the four beasts rising up out of the sea, seen by the prophet himself. [Daniel Chapters 2 and 7]**
>
> *Coronis* §2

Here, in Swedenborg's unpublished and last book, he uses different terms although they clearly refer to the same entities mentioned above. It is the first time he uses the terms Adamic and Noachian, nevertheless from the beginning of his first major theological work, the *Arcana Caelestia*, he identifies Adam and Noah with his Most Ancient and Ancient Churches. All the churches or periods he is speaking of do relate to sections of the Word. The Jewish Church is presented in the Old Testament and the Christian in the New. The New Church is introduced in the Book of Revelation. His ecclesiastical history is derived from the general historical structure of the Bible as well as individual passages, such as that in the Book of Daniel.

TWO PERIODS WITHIN THE ANCIENT CHURCH

> **The story of the Churches after the Flood is as follows: There were three Churches which receive specific mention in the Word—the first Ancient**

Church which took its name from Noah, the second Ancient Church which took its name from Eber, and the third Ancient Church which took its name from Jacob, and subsequently from Judah and Israel.

Arcana Caelestia §1327

Here we have a further variation. Commenting on the text of Genesis in the *Arcana Caelestia*, Swedenborg tells us that each of the numerous patriarchs mentioned represents 'a church'. However, these many churches are grouped under the names of the major patriarchs. Adam symbolizes the whole period down to Noah and Noah the period until the establishment of the Jewish Church. But Swedenborg also names the latter part of the Noachian period after the patriach Eber (or Heber—the nominal father of the Hebrews). He divides his Ancient Church into two, or even three churches, although the third would be the same as the Jewish Church of his five-church system.

This may initially seem an unnecessary complication, but it does in fact help, as in some contexts the five-age pattern does seem to have six ages caused by a subdivision in the second part of the five. We will find that the Second Ancient Church is comparable with the Bronze Age. I hope that the chart on page twelve will help to explain this.

THE GOLDEN, SILVER, BRONZE AND IRON AGES

Furthermore, in the Word there are countless places where gold, silver, bronze, or iron is used to picture some state of the Church. Gold is used to picture the spiritual state of the Church in respect to the good of love, silver to picture its spiritual state in respect to the truth of wisdom, bronze the natural state of the Church in respect to the good of charity, and iron its natural state in respect to the truth of faith. For this reason people in earliest times who were wise and knew about the spiritual meanings of metals also compared succeeding ages, from first to last, to those four metals, calling the first age the golden; the second, the silver; the third the copper; and the fourth the iron.

Coronis §2 (see also *Apocalypse Revealed* §§913; *Apocalypse Explained* §70)

Here, a little later in the passage from *Coronis* mentioned above, Swedenborg relates his four Churches to the four classical ages he was familiar with from the classical education he had received, one that was normal throughout Europe in his time. These four ages are found in both Greek and Roman literature and may well go back to earlier mythologies.

Although Swedenborg seems not to have been aware of it, the concept is also to be found in his native Norse mythology and in the legends of the Celts, Persians and Hindus. From the Hindus it passed into Buddhism and from the Persians it was adopted by astrology. It can also be found in several forms in Amerindian mythology. From the biblical pattern the idea was carried on by St Augustine and Mohammed.

Like the Flood or Tree of Life it is one of those universal myths you will find in many places. However, I do not know where you will find the subject treated as extensively as in pages of Swedenborg's Writings (see Appendix I).

THE CHURCHES CATEGORIZED BY DISCRETE DEGREES

Swedenborg employs the concept of 'discrete degrees' in various contexts, three distinct levels one above another. Things on separate planes which can be interrelated, but cannot be merged. Examples are love, wisdom and power, or end, cause and effect. For Swedenborg these degrees come in trines, the highest of which he calls 'celestial', the middle 'spiritual' and the lowest 'natural'. He uses these terms frequently and with them describes the whole structure of the spiritual and physical universe.

> **The Most Ancient Church was celestial.**
>
> *Arcana Caelestia* §4454
>
> **Good that originated in the will existed among the most ancient people who belonged to the celestial church, whereas good that originated in the understanding existed among the ancients who belonged to the spiritual church.**
>
> *Arcana Caelestia* §6065
>
> [The] Jewish nation [. . .] did not know what any of the symbolism [in the Word] signified; for they were altogether natural people, and therefore

they were neither able nor willing to know anything about the spiritual person and his faith and love.

On the Sacred Scripture §19

Thus of necessity every church must be both internal and external, as was the Ancient Church, and as at this day is the Christian Church. The internals of the Christian Church are exactly like the internals of the Ancient Church, but other externals have succeeded in their place [. . .] the Ancient Church did not differ one whit from the Christian Church as to internals, but only as to externals.

Arcana Caelestia §1083

'And he carried me away in the spirit above a great and high mountain, and showed me the great city, the holy Jerusalem, coming down out of heaven from God' signifies John transported into the third heaven [the celestial heaven], and his sight opened there, before whom was made manifest the Lord's New Church as to doctrine in the form of a city.

Apocalypse Revealed §896

To understand Swedenborg's five churches it helps to relate them to his concept of three discrete degrees, noted above. He also uses the terms spiritual and natural in the usual way as in 'spiritual world' and 'natural world' for heaven and earth, which can confuse.

He uses 'celestial', 'spiritual' and 'natural' to identify three levels relating to love, wisdom and service, which could be termed emotional, intellectual and practical. They describe three mental environments in which people are motivated either by affections, by beliefs, or by obedience to rules. Heaven is divided into three such levels and Swedenborg's churches were primarily related to one or other of those heavens.

The relationship between the celestial and the Most Ancient, and the spiritual and the Ancient, are frequently mentioned. He never calls the Jewish church a 'natural church' but we are usually told that the character of the biblical Jews was such. Neither is the Christian Church called 'spiritual', yet we are told that in essence it was 'exactly like' the Ancient Church. In that both were based on teachings from the Word, they had a 'spiritual' character.

That the new church will be 'celestial' seems more doubtful; its current earthly organizations are always being accused of being too intellectual. Nevertheless Swedenborg says that in order to see the Holy City New Jerusalem, the symbol of the New Church, John was taken up to the third or celestial heaven. Presumably the people of the New Church will in time have the potential to reach that level. The revival of the nuclear family and the growing respect for feminine values and the needs of children—all features of the Golden Age—do give cause for hope.

AN ORDERLY PATTERN,
... FOR TIMES, HISTORY, OR THE HUMAN LIFESPAN

The rise on this earth of four churches since the creation of the world is in accordance with Divine order. This demands that there should be a beginning and an end to it, before a new beginning can arise. This is why every day begins with the morning, advances, and ends in night, after which a new day begins. Likewise every year begins with spring, advances through summer to autumn, and ends in winter; and after this the year begins again. It is to produce this result that the sun rises in the east, and then travels through the south to the west, and ends in the north, from which it rises again. It is much the same with churches. The first of these, the Most Ancient Church, was like morning, spring and the east. The second, the Ancient Church was like the day, summer and the south. The third was like evening, autumn and the west, the fourth like night, winter and the north.

These ordered progressions gave the wise men of antiquity the idea of the four ages of the world. They called the first golden, the second silver, the third copper and the fourth iron. These metals were also used to represent the churches themselves in Nebuchadnezzar's statue. Moreover, in the Lord's sight the church looks like one person; and this person on the grand scale will pass through the same stages in his life as one on the small scale, progressing, that is, from childhood to adolescence, from that to young adulthood, and finally to old age; and then after death he will rise again.

The True Christian Religion §762

The fourfold pattern of the ages is not a one-off arrangement but a conception which the Creator of the world seems to have used in many contexts. A creative mode employed in the schematic design of a day, a year, a whole lifetime or the whole of history. Swedenborg also says that each 'age' passes through a morning, noon, evening and night phase.

Nevertheless the concept is not rigid and is modified where necessary. One notes that at the end of the first paragraph Swedenborg prefers to say third and fourth instead of Jewish and Christian. The end of the First Christian Church may have been like night, but its beginning was a new dawn or spring.

Elsewhere he notes that the night has good as well as bad portents. As a Swede he was familiar with the phenomenon of 'the midnight sun' and he reminds us of the promise it gives of a new dawn. One also recalls God's promise to Noah in Genesis 8:22:

While the earth remains,
Seedtime and harvest,
And cold and heat,
And winter and summer,
And day and night shall not cease.

There will always be a new beginning, so that the fourfold pattern extends into a fivefold pattern. Further the fifth stage is a restoration of the first stage.

Finally we are reminded that interesting although this historical pattern is, essentially it is the pattern of our lives. It is not just the pattern of our material lives, so much as the programme for our spiritual life and development.

The more interior contents of the Word are such that whatever statement is made about the Church is a statement about the individual member of the church.

Arcana Caelestia §82

Chapter One—The Five Ages

As I noted in the Introduction the story of the five churches can be presented as *history* or as human psycho-spiritual development. The latter might have greater spiritual value, but would greatly increase the scope of this text. In the quotations below, however, Swedenborg often switches between these themes; for him they are one theme. I have concentrated on the *historical* theme, but this need not prevent readers from reflecting on its application to their personal experience.

TIME AND SPIRITUAL MATTERS

> It is known in the world, that there is no time in heaven, for people say of those who die that they leave the things of time and that they pass out of time, meaning by this, out of the world. [...] Some also know that times in their origin are states, for they know that times are entirely in accordance with the states of the affections in which they are, short to those who are in pleasant and joyous states, long to those who are in unpleasant and sorrowful states [...] This leads learned men to enquire what time and space are, and some of them know that time belongs [only] to the natural man.
>
> *Heaven and Hell* §168.3

It is probably best that we should not go deeply into this matter here, but readers should nevertheless be reminded of Swedenborg's enlightening statement that there is no time in heaven or in spiritual matters. In our earthbound minds we are prone to think of the Five Ages as progressing through time, but we should also think of them as progressing through states. In this respect the concept of the passage through the various states from infancy to maturity may be most helpful. We may think of the ages in a linear pattern, but to God they may appear more as a vertical progression. Our awareness may be likened to the content of a daily newspaper whereas His awareness is like the instantaneous comprehension of a complete world history book. As we will note later, the life of the Lord is recorded in the deepest sense of the Word from Genesis to Revelation, it thus appearing that some of it was recorded before it even happened, but it is simpler to accept that it occurred outside time; or happens *all the time*. See also *Heaven and Hell* §§162-9 and *Arcana Caelestia* §4813.

SUMMARY

Swedenborg found within the Bible rich symbolical meanings; he called them 'correspondences'. He found them within the general text and also within specific passages such as the visions of Daniel. Like the Jews, he regarded the stories of Genesis as a history of mankind, though a history of spiritual development rather than political, economic or social development. He saw a pattern of five or six churches or dispensations which he names in different ways. He related these to the classical Golden, Silver, Bronze and Iron Ages and his 'celestial', 'spiritual' and 'natural' degrees.

We have yet to mention the items in the latter two columns which will be introduced in later parts of the text.

Most Ancient Ch.	Ancient Church		Jewish Church	Christian Ch.	New Ch.
Most Ancient Ch.	1st Ancient Ch.	2nd Ancient Ch.	3rd Ancient Ch.	Christian Ch.	New Ch.
Adamic Church	Noachian Ch.		Israelite Ch.	Christian Ch.	New Ch.
Adam	Noah	Heber	Abraham/ Israel	New Testament	Book of Revelation
Golden Age	Silver Age	Bronze Age	Iron Age	Age of Religions	New Age
Childhood	Adolescence		Adulthood	Maturity	Resurrection

Relative historical periods and approximate dates:

Palaeolithic	Neolithic	Bronze Age	Iron Age	Age of Religions	Industrial Age
Pre-8000 BC	8000-3000 BC	3000-1500 BC	1500 BC-AD 1	AD 1-1750	1750-

Fig. 1. Chart showing comparisons of five age concepts

Overlaps in the Ages

While it is most helpful and agreeable to use the five/six-age pattern to give a structure to the vast extent of history, it must be accepted from the start that there will nevertheless be complications. The five/six ages are nice tidy compartments, but it must be realized that one did not stop one year and another start in the next year as our centuries do. Although the Golden Age lost its perfection and was superseded by the Silver Age in certain lands, it kept going elsewhere. Indeed it was arguably still doing reasonably well in Aboriginal Australia, Bushman South Africa and other tribal areas before Western influence polluted its innocence. Neolithic culture is still alive today in the peasant countryside of many lands. The warlike ethos of the Iron Age can be found in remote areas such as central Asia and is frequently being revived in military dictatorships. It is helpful to realize that chapters 2, 3 and 4 of Genesis each tell the complete history of the Most Ancient Church through different symbolisms. Thus the Cain and Abel story encapsulates the whole period of the Most Ancient Church. Genesis 4:3 can be translated: 'And it happened at the end of days that Cain brought some fruit of the ground, a gift for Jehovah', suggesting that the event occurred at the end of the Adamic age. Cain represents the intellectual man, more interested in truth than goodness, who will be typical of the coming Ancient Church. He is therefore appropriately cast as a Neolithic farmer.

There are Adam and Eve, and Cain and Abel type stories going right back into Palaeolithic times, but the biblical version of the Adam and Eve story was obviously 'fleshed out' in the Neolithic or Bronze Age periods. Indeed as early as chapter 4 of Genesis we are hearing about Tubal-Cain who was described as a 'craftsman in bronze and iron' (long before those metals were discovered), indicating that that particular version of the text of the Bible was compiled at least as late as the Iron Age.

Dates

Until the nineteenth century we had very little knowledge of prehistoric chronology and historians are still reassessing dates and will continue to do so. Swedenborg can give us little guidance on dating. Please do not take any dates I offer for granted, nevertheless they are mostly a reliable indication of the sequence in which things happened.

Similarly we in the West cheerfully label the last two millennia as the Christian age, but in the East it was equally the Islamic, Buddhist or Confucian age. A period when international religions spread across frontiers becoming of greater long term importance than national rulers or religions. Therefore our Christian age might better be called 'the Age of Religions'.

Chapter Two—
The Nature of the Church

Alternative concepts:

The Church's relation to Heaven and to the Ages;

The Universal and the Specific Churches;

The Church of the Gentiles;

The Internal and External Churches;

Representative Churches.

THE CHURCH AND HEAVEN

The Church on earth is the foundation on which heaven rests, for goodness and truth flow from the Lord—by way of the heavens—into forms of goodness and truth residing with a member of the Church [. . .] the Lord always provides for some vestige of the Church to be left and when the old Church perishes a new one is established.

Arcana Caelestia §4060.4

There can be no linking with heaven, unless somewhere on earth there is a church which possesses the Word, and the Lord is known through its means, because the Lord is the God of heaven and earth, and without Him there can be no salvation. It is enough for a church possessing the Word to exist somewhere on earth, even though it has relatively few members.

On the Sacred Scripture §40

This is the ideal design, but God can also work through other methods such as the 'universal church' described below. Swedenborg was obviously at home with the Latin word *ecclesia*, which it is normal to translate as church, but one feels at times that 'religion' or 'faith' would convey his meaning better. He certainly did not have an *exclusive* group of *believers* in mind.

CHURCHES AND AGES

> By Adam and his wife there is meant [. . .] the Most Ancient Church, which was the golden age, the time of Saturn [. . .]
>
> *De Conjugio* §119
>
> The golden age is the same as the age of the Most Ancient Church.
>
> *Coronis* §37
>
> The golden age was the time of the Most Ancient Church.
>
> *Arcana Caelestia* §1551
>
> The names of metals were used by people in ancient times to refer to ages. They called them the Golden, Silver, Copper, and Iron Ages—the Golden Age because of the most ancient peoples who led lives in keeping with the goodness belonging to love; the Silver Age because of the ancients after them who led lives in keeping with the truths springing from that goodness; the Copper Age because of those who came after the Ancients who led lives in keeping with outward or natural goodness; and the Iron Age because of those who succeeded these, who led lives in keeping with natural truth alone devoid of goodness.
>
> The consecutive states of the Church down to the Lord's Coming are meant by the gold, silver, bronze and iron composing the statue that Nebuchadnezzar saw in a dream.
>
> *Apocalypse Explained* §176

I am not aware of any extensive passage in which Swedenborg discusses with precision the relationship between his 'churches' and 'ages', but these short quotations may help. It is clear that the concepts were closely related in his mind. The implication above in *De Conjugio* and the *Coronis* is that they were one and the same thing. This is modified by the slight distinction in the *Arcana Caelestia* quotation where the church existed during the age. It is probably more accurate to see the churches as set within the culture of the ages. This distinction certainly applies to the Jewish Church and the Iron Age; the Jewish case being different in a number of ways.

To extend these distinctions between churches and ages, I would suggest that the Most Ancient Church was a spiritual culture, set in the psychological culture of the Golden Age, which was set against the physical culture of the Palaeolithic Age. However, everyone living in Palaeolithic times may not have experienced the Golden Age culture or have been part of the Most Ancient Church. But as Swedenborg would point out, the 'Church' has several forms and there are many, more or less intimate, degrees of *membership*, as discussed below. One could suggest that the Most Ancient Church was what Swedenborgians call a 'specific church' while the Golden Age was part of what Swedenborg calls the 'universal church'.

EACH CHURCH PASSES THROUGH A CYCLIC PATTERN

There have been four periods, or successive states, of each church, which in the Word are meant by 'morning', 'day', 'evening', and 'night'.

Each Church has passed through four consecutive changes of state, the first state being when the Lord appeared, which time was its morning or rising. The second state was when it received instruction, which time was its midday or advancement. The third state was when it declined, which time was when it reached its evening or devastation. The fourth state was when it reached its end, which time was its night or termination. After its end or termination the Lord Jehovih comes to execute judgment on members of the former Church. He separates those who are good from those who are bad, raising up the good towards Himself, into heaven, and moving the bad away from Himself into hell.

After all this he forms a new heaven out of the good [. . .] and a new hell out of the bad. From this new heaven the Lord Jehovih brings a new Church into being on earth, which he accomplishes through revelation from His own mouth or else from His Word and through inspiration.

Coronis, Summaries II-III

The five churches do not just succeed each other, but proceed through the cycle described above. The church begins well, but eventually has to be 'wound up' or judged. Such an event was the Last Judgment referred to in the Book of Revelation, which should have been translated as 'Consummation of the Age'. Similar terminations or 'consummations' occurred at the end of the Most Ancient Church—symbolized by the Flood—and at the end of the Jewish Church, at the time of our Lord. Swedenborg seems less clear about the judgment made on the Ancient Churches. In *Last Judgment* §46 he implies that the Ancient Churches were 'judged' at the same time as the Jewish Church, at the time of our Lord's resurrection. In *Arcana Caelestia* §2323.2 and *Coronis* §41.3, however, he seems to indicate that the destruction of Sodom and Gomorah symbolized the end of that Ancient Church. I assume that the judgment required at that time was of a less radical nature. I would suggest that even today echoes of the Ancient Church live on in oriental religions.[1]

We will learn more about 'judgments' in the chapter on the New Church.

THE SPECIFIC AND UNIVERSAL CHURCHES

The Lord in his Providence ensures that on earth there is always a Church where the Word is read, and the Lord is known by means of it.

Doctrine of the Sacred Scripture §110

Those outside the church who acknowledge one God and who in accordance with their religion live in some sort of charity towards the neighbour are in communion with those who belong to the church. For no one is damned who believes in God and lives a good life. From this it is plain that the Lord's church exists throughout the whole world, although it is especially located where the Lord is acknowledged and the Word is known.

The New Jerusalem §244

From this passage it is clear that Swedenborg sees the church in two ways. Especially or specifically it is where 'the Word' is understood, usually in organized forms. But also it exists in the hearts of all people of goodwill, perhaps in quite informal groupings. Swedenborg calls the latter group the 'universal church' or the 'Church of the Lord', but has no distinguishing term for the former group. For convenience Swedenborgians have adopted the term 'church specific'. This is convenient, but it should not be thought that the two are completely separate, rather, they are two ends of a spectrum. He conceived the 'universal church' as truly universal, covering Muslims, Africans and Orientals. Today the terms *universal religion* or *faith* might carry his meaning better. The following passages define the matter further.

> The name *church* [my emphasis] is given where the Lord is acknowledged and where the Word is known. For the essential elements of the church are love and faith directed to the Lord and coming from the Lord; and the Word teaches how a person must live, in order to receive love and faith from the Lord.
>
> For a church to exist, there must be teaching from the Word, since the Word is not intelligible without teaching. But it is not teaching alone that makes the church in the case of a person, but living in accordance with that teaching. From this it follows that it is not faith alone which makes the church, but the life of faith, which is charity. The true teaching is the teaching of charity and faith together, not faith without charity. For the teaching of charity and faith together is teaching how to live one's life; but the teaching of faith without charity is not.
>
> *The New Jerusalem* §§242-3

As regards the Lord's spiritual Church it should be realized that it exists throughout the whole world, for it is not confined to those who possess the Word and from the Word have knowledge of the Lord and of some truths of faith. It also exists among those who do not possess the Word and therefore do not know the Lord at all, and as a consequence have no knowledge of any truths of faith—for all truths of faith regard the Lord. That is, it exists with gentiles remote from the Church. For among those people there are many who know from the light of reason that there is one God, that He has created and preserves all things; and also that He is the source of everything good, and consequently of everything true; and that being the likeness of Him makes a person blessed. And what is more, they live up to their religion, in love to that God and in love towards the neighbour.

Arcana Caelestia §3263.2

Although I am not aware that Swedenborg specifically mentions the idea, I would suggest we should also consider the other side of the coin. The 'specific church' envisaged above is always a small enlightened group leading the greater church, but in the decaying stages of a church, it may be that the greater church is led by a perverse group with false ideas. Our Lord's condemnation of the Jews was primarily aimed at the Sadducees, Pharisees and scribes. Similarly I think Swedenborg's condemnation of the Jews and Christians was aimed at the leading priests and theologians in the first or the eighteenth centuries and those who supported them, rather than at the simple good who were their nominal followers. *Last Judgment* §69, which I quote in Chapter Eight says that the judgment was only made on a specific group of people, not on Christians in general.

Swedenborg also uses the term 'Church of the Gentiles' to describe something similar to the 'universal church'. He says that in the Bible the words 'gentiles' and 'nations' usually symbolize the 'universal church'. There is more on the Church of the Gentiles in Chapter Six dealing with the Jewish Church.

PERFECTION IN VARIETY

In describing a 'universal church', Swedenborg is not saying that the Lord wishes to gather everyone together in one consistent amorphous lump, he welcomes the different religions and cultures. In the following passages Swedenborg advocates variety and talks of 'The Lord's church in all varieties of religion in the world' being represented by Solomon's many wives.

Heaven is where the Lord is recognised, trusted and loved. The different ways he is worshipped—in variations that stem from the difference of activity from one community to another—do not cause harm but bring benefit, because variety is the source of heaven's perfection.

We can say the same of the church as we have of heaven [...] It has many components and yet each is called a church and is a church to the extent that the qualities of love and faith rule within it. In it the Lord forms a single whole out of the varied elements and therefore makes a single church out of many churches.

Heaven and Hell §§56-7

Solomon was permitted to establish idolatrous worship. This was done that he might represent the Lord's kingdom or the Church with all forms of religion in the whole world. For the Church established with the nation of Israel and Judah was a representative Church, and therefore all the judgments and statutes of that Church represented the spiritual things of the Church, which are its internals. The people themselves represented the Church, the king represented the Lord, David representing the Lord who was to come into the world and Solomon the Lord after His Coming. Because the Lord after the glorification of His Human had power over heaven and earth, [...] therefore Solomon who represented Him appeared in glory and magnificence, and possessed wisdom above all the kings of the earth, and also built the temple. Moreover, he permitted and established the forms of worship of many nations, by which were represented the various religions in the world. His wives, who numbered seven hundred and his concubines who numbered three hundred had a similar signification; for a 'wife' in the Word signifies the Church and a 'concubine' a form of religion. Hence it may be evident why it was granted to Solomon to build the temple [...] and why he was permitted to set up idolatrous forms of worship, and to marry so many wives.

Divine Providence §245

THE INTERNAL AND EXTERNAL CHURCHES

Perhaps one of the most obvious variations in the nature of churches and in church membership is the degree of spirituality. Swedenborg categorizes such variation with the terms 'internal' and 'external'.

Some people consider Divine worship to consist in going to church, listening to sermons, attending the Holy Supper, and doing these things in a devout manner, yet do not think of them except as duties to be done regularly because they have been instituted and commanded. Those people belong to the external Church. Others however likewise believe that such duties should be attended to, but that nevertheless the essential element of worship is the life of faith, which is charity towards the neighbour and love to the Lord. These people belong to the internal Church. Consequently those also belong to the external Church who do good to the neighbour and worship the Lord, but solely in a spirit of obedience born of faith, whereas those belong to the internal Church who do good to the neighbour and worship the Lord out of love. And so on with all else exemplifying those two aspects of the Church.

But with every member of the Church both aspects must be present, the external and the internal. Unless both are present spiritual life does not exist with him; for the internal is so to speak the soul, and the external so to speak the body housing the soul. Those however who belong to the external Church are plainly concerned with external things of the Church and only vaguely with internal ones, whereas those belonging to the internal Church are plainly concerned with internal things and vaguely with external ones. But those concerned only with external things and not at the same time with internal do not belong to the [true] Church.

Arcana Caelestia §8762

Members of the internal Church are those who are led to do good to the neighbour by an affection rising out of charity, whereas members of the external Church are led to do it by a sense of obedience. Every person who is being regenerated first becomes a member of the external Church, then later on a member of the internal Church.

Arcana Caelestia §7840

DECLINE OF CHURCHES AND DIVINE PROVIDENCE

All this talk of rise and decline in the history of churches may give the impression that one's eternal destiny is totally dependent on where and when and into what environment one is born. From a worldly point of view this may well seem to be so, but in his book *Divine Providence* Swedenborg assures us that the Lord provided safeguards to ensure that a path to heaven has always been open to everyone who genuinely follows a heavenly life. The matter is discussed at length in *Divine Providence* §§327-9, but to avoid deflecting from our main theme only a few passages are quoted here.

> Every religion declines and is consummated by the *inversion* [my emphasis] of the image of God in man. It is well known that man was created in the image of God [. . .]
>
> The image and likeness of God are not actually destroyed in man, though they may be seemingly destroyed; for they remain inherent in his two faculties called liberty and rationality. They have become seemingly destroyed when man has made the receptacle of Divine Love, that is his will, a receptacle of self-love, and the receptacle of Divine Wisdom, that is, his understanding, a receptacle of his own intelligence. By doing this he has inverted the image and likeness of God, for he has turned these receptacles away from God and has turned them towards himself. [. . .] Hence arose in the Churches the worship of men in place of the worship of God, and worship based on doctrines of falsity in place of worship based on doctrines of truth, the latter from one's own intelligence and the former from love of self. From this it is clear that religion in process of time declines.
>
> This takes place from the continual increase of hereditary evil in successive generations. Hence there now proceeds a gradual destruction of good and desolation of truth in the Church until its consummation is reached.
>
> Nevertheless it is provided by the Lord that everyone may be saved. It is provided by the Lord that there should be a religion everywhere; and

that in every religion there should be the two essentials of salvation, namely, to acknowledge God and to refrain from evil because it is against God.

Further, there is granted to everyone after death the opportunity of amending his life, if that is at all possible. All are instructed and led by the Lord by means of angels; and as they by then know that they live after death, and that there is a heaven and a hell, they at first receive truths.

Divine Providence §328

Swedenborg also assures us that the decaying church can, despite the moral weakness of its establishment, still be effective in leading people towards heaven. In the following passage he is talking about power-loving priests he came across in the world of spirits in the eigteenth century, which presumably has a general application to all churches or religions at the end of their eras.

The reason why they have been tolerated there up to the day of the Judgment was that God's order ensures that all are preserved who could possibly be preserved, and this until they could no longer be among good people. All therefore are preserved who can put on a pretence of spiritual life in externals and display it in their morality, as if it underlay it, no matter what they are like in internals as regards faith and love. Those too are preserved who make an external show of holiness, even if without any internal content. Many of those people were like this, able to conduct pious conversations with the common people, to adore the Lord in holy fashion, to implant religious belief in people's minds and bring them to think about heaven and hell, and make them continue to do good by preaching about good works. Many have thus been led to a life devoted to good, and so into the way to heaven. As a result many [people of the church] have been saved, though few of those who led them are.

Last Judgment §59.1

REPRESENTATIVE CHURCHES

Since all things in nature are representative of spiritual and celestial things, therefore, in ancient times, there were Churches wherein all the externals or rituals were representative; wherefore those Churches were called representative Churches. The Church which was instituted among the sons of Israel was a representative Church. All the rituals in it were externals which represented the internal things belonging to heaven and the Church. The representatives of the Church and of worship ceased when the Lord came into the world, because the Lord laid open the internal things of the Church [...]

The New Jerusalem §261

Generally the minds of the angels and the people of the church on earth are thinking on the same levels and are both spiritually aware (although not consciously in contact with one another). Around the time of the Bronze Age and Iron Age, however, earthly people's minds were less spiritually aware and could only conceive material thoughts; although these could by symbolism, or representation, embody higher thoughts. In such a situation Swedenborg says the church on earth was not fully one with the heavens, but it could nevertheless be linked through symbolic rituals. The material rituals represented the ideas of the spirit. The matter is discussed in detail in *Arcana Caelestia* §4288, and was also illustrated in the passage on Solomon above (*Divine Providence* §245).

Chapter Three—
The Most Ancient Church

Alternative concepts:
The Golden Age;
The Palaeolithic Age;
Adam; Paradise;
Spring; Morning; Infancy;
A Celestial Church.

PRE-ADAMITES

It was shown me what the Pre-adamites were like, who were regenerated by the Lord and called 'Adam': a certain one spoke with me in a speech not swiftly articulated, as speech usually is, yet in the words there was a little of life, so that one could hear [from the speech] what kind of life. I heard him speaking when I awoke in the night.

The Spiritual Diary §3390

Before we examine the Most Ancient or 'Adamic' Church, it should just be noted that Swedenborg did make a few notes about 'Pre-adamites' in his diary, which is now published as *The Spiritual Diary* (see §§3390, 3397, 3399). He did not develop the notes in his later works. The notes suggest that their minds had not been much developed.

I would suggest that all we need to know is that the Most Ancient Church had a definite divinely initiated beginning, rather than having gradually coalesced out of chaos.[1]

GENERAL CHARACTER

The Most Ancient Church was, in Swedenborg's terminology, 'celestial', inspired by love, rather than wisdom, or simple obedience.

> This Church, more than all other Churches in the whole world, was in origin Divine, for the good of love to the Lord was present in it. Will and understanding with them made one, and so one mind, and on that account they had from good a perception of truth. For the Lord was flowing in by an internal route into the good present in their will and from this into the good present in their understanding, that is, into their truth, as a consequence of which that Church more than all others was called Man [Adam], and also the Likeness of God.
>
> <div align="right"><i>Arcana Caelestia</i> §4454</div>

Compared with later times the Most Ancient Church and early religions had quite unique qualities: their closeness to the Lord and a special psychology. The people of the time were 'celestial', inspired by the Lord's love rather than wisdom, which gave them perception or insight into moral questions. Their pure and innocent wills were allowed uninhibited control over their understandings, thus operating without any need for the restraint of conscience.

In time, however, this delightful uncontrolled spontaneity turned out to be a serious weakness as well as an advantage. Humankind had to move on from infancy and innocence.

BELIEF IN ONE GOD

> The Most Ancient Church was of one mind in acknowledging the Lord and calling Him Jehovah, as is clear from the early chapters of the Word and elsewhere.
>
> <div align="right"><i>Arcana Caelestia</i> §1343.1 (<i>The True Christian Religion</i> §9 is similar)</div>
>
> [. . .] the men of most ancient times, who were celestial, understood by Jehovah no other than the Lord.
>
> <div align="right"><i>Arcana Caelestia</i> §3035</div>

I cannot find a passage where Swedenborg actually discusses the most ancient's concept of God, but when considering the concepts of later religions he often makes comparisons such as those above. The purist may object that the most ancients would not have used the word 'Jehovah', but I assume Swedenborg intended to convey that they used a word with a similar meaning. The etymology of Jehovah or Yahweh is not known, but for the Jews it appeared to mean something like 'I am'. Swedenborg's understanding of the matter is stated as follows:

> The reason why 'I am Jehovah' means that the Lord is the only God, is that Jehovah means He Is, that is, the Source of the Being and Coming-into-Being (*Esse et Existere*) of all things, which must necessarily be unique and one.
>
> *Arcana Caelestia* §7636

The impression we are offered is of a simple and straightforward monotheistic concept of God. It used to be assumed that primitive peoples were all polytheists, but opinion has tended to change and it is now realized that they mostly believe in one supreme 'high god' and that their other 'gods' originally represented particular aspects of his character. They may also be the names given to spirits who have had contact with them. Sadly the more distant high god has often become a shadowy background figure, such as the Australian Aborigine's Baiame or Ungud, or the Greek Uranus. Nevertheless the belief in a Father Creator, such as Swedenborg suggests, seems once to have been universal.[2]

RELIGION AND WORSHIP

> [...] those who belonged to the Most Ancient Church were internal people and had no external forms of worship, while those who belonged to the Ancient Church were external people and did have them. For the former saw external things in the light of internal ones, [...] whereas the latter saw internal things in the light of external ones.
>
> *Arcana Caelestia* §4493.3

> For the member of the Most Ancient Church there was no other worship than the internal such as is offered in heaven, for among those people heaven so communicated with man that they made one. [...] Thus, being

Fig. 2 **Uluru or Ayers Rock**. This mountain in Australia has been used as a holy place by the Aborigines from time immemorial. Many mountains all over the world, such as Mount Olympus, Fuji-yama or Snowdon have been similarly revered for centuries.

> angelic people, they were internal men. They did indeed apprehend with their senses the external things that belonged to the body and to the world, but they paid no attention to them. In each object apprehended by the senses they used to perceive something Divine and heavenly. For example, when they saw any high mountain they did not perceive the idea of a mountain but that of height, and from height they perceived heaven and the Lord. That is how it came about that the Lord was said to 'live in the highest', and was called 'the Most High and Lofty One', and how worship of the Lord came at a later time to be celebrated on mountains.
>
> *Arcana Caelestia* §920

It is interesting that primitive tribes are sometimes said to have no religion, or alternatively that everything they do is religious. They are rarely seen to sit down in rows and sing and pray, they have 'no external worship'. On the other hand they will pray before setting out hunting and will dedicate the animal killed. They may insist that the earth or the forest is their mother. As Swedenborg puts it 'In each object they perceive something Divine and heavenly'.

These most ancients, like the Aborigines and Bushmen of today, had a holistic vision of life. The earth, the plants, the animals and people are all one system and the physical and spiritual are intimately intertwined. Reading Laurens van der Post on the Bushmen, Colin

Turnbull on Congo pygmies or the reports of other students of hunter-gatherer tribes, one is surely in the 'most ancient' world, albeit a fading and even decadent example of it.[3]

> **In the Word 'tent' is used to mean the holiness of worship and the good of love, because in most ancient times worship took place in tents; and because the source of people's worship in those times was the good of celestial love, 'tent' is also used to mean that good. And since celestial good holds peace within itself, it is said [in Job 5:24], you will know that peace [resides within] your tent.**
>
> *Apocalypse Explained* §659.18

This passage rather contradicts those above. But we do have to remember that this church probably lasted for thousands of years and was spread over many lands, so that generalizations may be misleading. Maybe this refers to a late period of that church's history. Alternatively we may assume that the worship carried on in these tents was of an intimate family nature, which Swedenborg would not categorize as the 'external worship' he excludes in *Arcana Caelestia* §4493.

MATERIAL CULTURE

Location

> For in that land [Canaan] there existed people of the Most Ancient Church. There were also those who had belonged to the Ancient Church, especially from that Ancient Church called the Hebrew Church
>
> *Arcana Caelestia* §4517

There are several passages similar to this occurring where Swedenborg is explaining the significance of 'Canaan'. They can be taken to indicate that the Most Ancient Church was therefore only located in Canaan. We do not, however, make a similar assumption that the Ancient Church was only located in Canaan, because some passages state that that church spread westward as far as Italy and eastwards as far as 'the Indies' (*The True*

Christian Religion §275). We have no similar passage describing the spread of the Most Ancient Church. Nevertheless *The True Christian Religion* passage begins:

> Religion existed from most ancient times, and the inhabitants of all parts of the world knew about God, and something about life after death.
>
> *The True Christian Religion* §275

This would seem to indicate that some form of the Most Ancient Church was widespread. Perhaps we should assume that the 'church specific' was at that time in the Middle East, but that the 'church universal' was indeed universal then.

Tents, Journeys

> We went across this plain and saw tents upon tents to the number of many thousand extending as far as the eye could see before us and to the sides in all directions. [. . .] These most ancient people lived, when they were in the world, in tents, so they continue to do so now.
>
> *Conjugial Love* §75.3

Swedenborg saw the above scene in the heavens of the Golden Age. I assume such large concentrations of tents and people would not have been usual on earth in Palaeolithic times due to problems of limited food supply.

> Among the ancients 'wandering about and dwelling in tents' was a common expression, [. . .] for the reason that the most ancient people not only wandered about with tents but also dwelt in tents and used to celebrate holy worship in them. Consequently 'wandering about and dwelling' also meant in the internal sense living.
>
> *Arcana Caelestia* §1102.1

> [. . .] those who belonged to the church in the most ancient times dwelt in tabernacles and tents, which they also took on their journeys.
>
> *Apocalypse Explained* §799.1

Chapter Three—The Most Ancient Church

[. . .] the most ancient people dwelt in tents and celebrated their most holy worship in them, and this also is why 'tents' in the Word means the holiness of worship [. . .] And since 'tents' meant the holiness within worship, 'dwelling' in a good sense also means living, or life. In a similar way it is because the most ancient people travelled around with their tents that 'travelling' in the internal sense of the Word means the established patterns and order of life.

Arcana Caelestia §1293

Fig. 3 **Palaeolithic Tents**. Ridge tent structures of branches covered with skins or leaves are commonly used by hunter-gatherers. Archaeologists have found the footprint of such shelters associated with Palaeolithic artefacts.

This idea that travelling is sacred reminds one of the importance Australian Aborigines attach to 'going walkabout' and to the journeys of their ancestors, which they still re-enact and record in art forms.[4]

Swedenborg makes several mentions of the most ancients' habit of living in tents and also of 'wandering'. He never offers any explanation as to why they did so, his only interest seeming to be the symbolism of tents and journeys.

'Wandering about and dwelling in tents' is, however, a very good description of the Palaeolithic lifestyle. Before the discovery of agriculture people had to gather or hunt for food and, more often than not, quickly exhausted local supplies of fruit etc. So they found it desirable to 'wander' from place to place looking for food and therefore needed portable dwellings such as tents; or to build temporary shelters which are usually very similar.

There used to be a supposition that all Palaeolithic people were 'cave men', as this is where their remains are best preserved away from wind and rain, yet many areas where they lived had no caves available. More recently archaeologists have been digging up Palaeolithic levels in open plains and finding small oval areas with stones around their margin, and perhaps post holes at their ends, which they identify as the remains of tents or shelters.

But little or nothing was known about the existence of hunter-gatherers in the eighteenth century. Swedenborg's reporting of their tents and wandering therefore tends to prove his claim to special mystic knowledge. He knew something of the Lapps, but seems not to have realized they had affinities with his most ancients. In his little book *On the Sacred Scripture* Swedenborg refers to Ovid's *Metamorphoses*, but makes no mention of the description it contains of the Golden Age, which is a surprisingly good portrayal of pre-agricultural Palaeolithic life:

> The earth itself, without compulsion, untouched by hoe, unfurrowed by any plough-share, produced all things spontaneously and men were content with foods that grew without cultivation. They gathered berries and wild strawberries, cherries and blackberries [. . .] or acorns fallen from Jupiter's spreading oak.[5]

(While quoting Ovid, note that in the next paragraph about the Silver Age he says 'Then corn [. . .] first began to be sown [. . .]' implying there was no agriculture in the Golden Age.)

I feel sure this was how the most ancients lived, a simple hunter/gatherer life, but I must in all honesty also quote the following lines from *Divine Providence*, although I feel they are partly misleading. If you read the whole passage I think you will agree that here Swedenborg is not actually reporting 'things heard and seen', as he terms it, but is using his own eighteenth-century imagination to illustrate the most ancients' healthy utilitarian attitude to material possessions. Or perhaps these most ancients (who are in heaven) could have been allowed to 'update' their lifestyles or maybe this is a transitional half-Ancient society. In any case, it seems unlikely that the most ancients would employ servants—at least as we know them?

Chapter Three—The Most Ancient Church

In the most ancient times when tribes and families had dwelling-places apart from one another there was no other love of riches than the desire to possess the necessaries of life, which they procured for themselves by means of their flocks and herds, and their lands, fields and gardens from which they derived their living. Among their necessaries of life were also beautiful houses, furnished with useful articles of every kind, and also clothing. Parents, children, men-servants and maid-servants, who formed the household, were engaged in the care and labour connected with all these things.

Divine Providence §215.4

Swedenborg's own mental image of the most ancients does seem to be of 'pastoralists', which perhaps was the oldest concept of social organization an early eighteenth-century education could offer one—if the significance of Ovid's information had not been digested. The idea of Stone Age man was only dimly perceived during Swedenborg's lifetime. The memories of readers well versed in Swedenborg may be nagged by the following familiar passage where, in the most ancients' heaven, Swedenborg did come across sheep. But note that they were not there to be 'herded', but for correspondential reasons.

[. . .] the angel said; 'Now we are on the mountain not far from the summit.' So we went on and a little beyond the cedars came upon a circular plain, where lambs of both sexes were feeding. These were forms intended to picture the state of innocence and peace among the mountain-dwellers.

Conjugial Love §75.3

Regarded in itself eating animal flesh is something profane, for in most ancient times people never ate the flesh of any beast or bird, but only different kinds of grain, especially wheaten bread, also the fruit of trees, vegetables, milk, and milk products such as butter. Slaughtering living creatures and eating their flesh was to them abominable, akin to the behaviour of wild animals. [. . .] But in the process of time when mankind began to be as savage as wild animals, indeed more savage, they first began to slaughter living creatures and eat their flesh.

Arcana Caelestia §1002

Swedenborg included this reference to the most ancients while commenting on Genesis 9, where the eating of flesh containing blood is prohibited. He is perhaps recording a passing thought rather than a considered observation. At one time it was generally considered that it was the need for hunting skills that had motivated the evolution of the superior human brain. However anthropology is now showing that in many tribes by far the greater part of the tribal food supply is 'gathered' from vegetable sources, and that 'hunting' only supplies an occasional feast. The pattern is different in Arctic climates, but these would not have been colonized in the early days of the Palaeolithic era.

Personally I regard the references to wheat and dairy products as only being well-intended guesses on Swedenborg's part. It is, however, possible that he might have in mind remnants of the most ancients living a 'Mesolithic' lifestyle, transitional between the Palaeolithic and Neolithic, where wild grasses were being harvested.

Social Life

They were divided into houses, families, and nations, and used to contract marriages within their own houses and families, in order that genera and species of perception might be established and be derived from parents.

Arcana Caelestia §483.2

I have been told by angels that those who lived in the most ancient times live today in the heavens, arranged by households, by families and by tribes, in much the same way as they had lived on earth, with hardly any missing from their households.

Conjugial Love §205

In the most ancient times status was such as existed in the relationship between parents and children. They were 'honours' of love, full of respect

Chapter Three—The Most Ancient Church

Fig. 4 **Palaeolithic Villages**. Aboriginal tribes in various parts of the world live in small extended family groups. This sketch is based on villages in the Congo jungle documented in Colin Turnbull's book *The Forest People*.

> and veneration, not because children received birth from their parents but because they received instruction and wisdom from them. [. . .] This was the only 'honour' in the most ancient times; for then tribes, families and households dwelt separately, and not under governments as at the present day. It was the head of the family in whom this honour was vested.
>
> *Divine Providence* §215.2

When discussing the lives of the biblical patriarchs and other subjects Swedenborg often makes similar comments on these matters. One advantage of these close family groups seems to be that special affections and interests were passed from generation to generation and nurtured by each group. One wonders if the passing on of 'secret' information at tribal initiation ceremonies, observed in more recent times, is not a less perfect echo of this practice.

One point he is making is that they did not live in villages or cities and were not ruled by kings but by family elders. This is more obvious in *Arcana Caelestia* §10160, where spirits who were similar to the most ancients (though from another planet), were 'annoyed' when Swedenborg asked if they had 'kings or governors', a practice they seemed to deem quite wrong. The following quotation compares most ancient society with later forms.

> [. . .] people lived divided up into nations, families, and households; and each household lived by itself. It did not enter anyone's head to encroach on another's inheritance and thereby to acquire wealth and control. Self-love and love of the world were far from them then. Each person rejoiced in his heart in his own well-being, and no less in that of another.
>
> But this scene was changed. In course of time it turned into the opposite, when people's minds were taken over by the desire to control others and possess their goods. For its own protection the human race was then gathered into kingdoms and empires.
>
> *Arcana Caelestia* §8118

This statement is also comparable to points Ovid makes about the Golden Age: 'Their towns were not yet surrounded by moats [. . .] they had no helmets or swords. The peoples of the world, untroubled by fear, enjoyed a leisurely and peaceful existence'.[6]

It is a point often noted by modern anthropologists too. If you live an itinerant life, the gathering of personal riches will become an inconvenience so you only keep the bare necessities. Nevertheless hunter-gatherers are actually far from poor; they are surrounded by the riches of nature, the gifts of God, innumerable substances and materials which they are expert at putting to good use.

Family life

> Genuine conjugial love is not possible except between pairs, that is, in the marriage of one man with one wife, but not with many wives; because conjugial love is mutual and reciprocal, and the life of one interchangeably in that of the other, so that they are as one. Such a union is given between pairs, but not between many, for many destroy that love. The men of the Most Ancient Church, who were celestial and in the perception of the

union of good and truth like angels, had one wife only; they said that they perceived with one wife celestial delights and happiness, and when marriage with several was merely mentioned, they were horrified.

De Conjugio §119

They said that at that time [when they were on earth] their greatest delight in life was in producing offspring, and thus that their greatest pleasures lay in loving their married partner for the sake of offspring. They called those pleasures most delightful, and the delights most pleasurable, adding that the perception of these delights and pleasures came from an influx from heaven because the Lord was going to be born.

Arcana Caelestia §1123

Marital and parental bonds were particularly strong among the members of the early church. Such is often the case with hunter-gatherer tribes today.

Men and women are equals—although with different functions—but in later ages women become more and more subordinate. In later ages archaeologists find the 'grave goods' placed in the graves of men are significantly more valuable than those in women's graves, but in the Palaeolithic Age they are of similar value.

Similarly in most tribes great delight is taken in children and they are very much a part of society, whereas in later ages children were often ignored and kept 'in their place' until adulthood.

PSYCHO-SPIRITUAL CHARACTER

Psychology

I have also been shown the situation in general with regard to the will part of the mind and the understanding part. The most ancient people who constituted the Lord's celestial Church [...] had a will which contained good and an understanding which contained truth derived from that good; and with them these two parts made one. The ancients however who formed the Lord's spiritual Church had a will that was completely destroyed, but an intact understanding within which, through regeneration, the Lord formed a new area of will, and through this a new area of understanding also.

Arcana Caelestia §4328

Will and understanding [with the most ancients] made one, and so one mind, and on that account they had from good a perception of truth. For the Lord was flowing in by an internal route into the good present in their will and from this into the good present in their understanding, that is, into their truth.

Arcana Caelestia §4454

The most ancients did not have—and initially did not need—a conscience. Their understandings were directly linked to, and automatically served, the desires of the will. They 'did whatever they liked', which we today know is a dangerous state of affairs. But they were in a state of kindly innocence and did not take advantage of that freedom. They were, however, guided in other ways which we will come to.

There are echoes of this attitude in 'primitive' people today. When an Aborigine labourer feels a need to recharge his spiritual batteries and 'go walkabout', he has no conscientious qualms about letting down his employer, but trots off there and then. If we are tempted to drink a whole bottle of spirits our consciences generally stop us, but tribesmen in many parts of the world are known for their low resistance to alcohol addiction.

Worrying as this may be to us, we have to recognize that the spontaneous 'freewill' situation is the most natural attitude and when attained should be a happier state of mind—the relaxed attitude to life that Europeans often envy in Africans and other nations.

Being celestial people, whatever they were thinking shone out of their face and eyes which altered correspondingly. They were quite incapable of assuming facial expressions that did not accord with what they were thinking. Pretence, and still more deception, was to them something absolutely outrageous.

Arcana Caelestia §1118 (see also §4326)

The separation of will and understanding in our minds means that we can think one thing and express another in our facial expression—though we found this more difficult in childhood. For the most ancients, however, it was impossible and anthropologists make similar observations about aborigines etc.

One anthropologist records a significant incident that occurred when trying to get Bushmen to re-enact a courtship ceremony for a documentary film. His cameraman, in Western tradition, automatically chose the best-looking girl and boy to act the parts, who were not man and wife. They initially refused to cooperate, but after much persuasion relented. Nevertheless their performance was completely lacking in feeling; they could not simulate an affection they did not feel.[7]

Perception and communication with the heavens

> The most ancients knew from perception whether a thing was good and consequently whether it was true. There was an influx from the Lord by way of heaven into the rational part of their minds, and from that influx when they thought about anything holy, they perceived instantly whether a thing was so or was not so. Later on such perception with mankind perished and people began to entertain heavenly ideas no more, but only worldly and bodily ones; and when this happened the place of such perception was taken by conscience (which is also a kind of perception) [...] But perception that goes with conscience does not originate in inflowing good, but in truth which from earliest childhood has been implanted in the rational part of the mind, in accordance with the holiness of people's worship, and after that has been confirmed; [...]
>
> *Arcana Caelestia* §2144

I have been taught from heaven that the most ancient peoples on our earth, who were celestial men, thought from correspondences themselves, the natural things of the world before their eyes serving them as the means of thinking in this way. Being of such character, they were in fellowship with angels and spoke with them. Thus, through them heaven was conjoined to the world. For this reason, that period was called the Golden Age, of which it is said by ancient writers that the inhabitants of heaven dwelt with men and associated with them as friends with friends.

Heaven and Hell §115

I have been told from heaven that the most ancient people, because their interiors were turned heavenwards, had direct revelation, and by this means there was at that time a conjunction of the Lord with the human race. After their times, however, there was no such direct revelation, but there was a indirect revelation by means of correspondences.

Heaven and Hell §306

These passages talk of a world almost entirely outside our experience, yet it may be familiar enough to some shamans, even if they communicate with spirits rather than angels. It also sounds reminiscent of the Aborigines' Dreamtime concepts.

We can only learn spiritual truth by reading sacred literature, but they were taught by the 'author' in person, so to speak (or by his 'students'). Even when not in direct contact with the spiritual world, they had only to read the correspondences in 'the natural things of the world before their eyes'. For most ancient peoples today, 'natural things' carry symbolic messages. They have few abstract words but can convey such thinking by involving the abundant metaphors available from nature.

(For Swedenborg 'correspondences' were more than symbols. Heat is not just a simile for love; heat is the physical manifestation on this plane of the spiritual quality love in heaven. Pleasant animals and plants manifest the loves and thoughts of the angels.)

In addition they had 'perception' (intuition and reception are also possible translations of the Latin word *perceptio*). Anthropologists say ancient peoples have intuition and even modern man attributes it to women or artists.

I have learned in addition that members of the Most Ancient Church experienced most delightful dreams, as well as visions, and that what these meant was instilled at the same time. This was the source of their representations involving paradise gardens and much else. To them therefore earthly and worldly objects of the external senses were as

nothing. They did not perceive any delight in those objects, only in the things which they meant and represented.

Arcana Caelestia §1122

Experiencing and interpreting dreams was not peculiar to the most ancients, but they apparently derived much more benefit and pleasure from them than did later ages. Swedenborg explains in other contexts that our dreams are 'supervised' by angels (see *Arcana Caelestia* §1977).

COMMUNICATION, SPEECH AND BREATHING

I was told by the angels that the earliest kind of speech of all peoples on each world was by facial expression; and it originated from two areas, the lips and the eyes. The reason why this was the earliest form of speech was that the face was designed to portray what a person thinks and wants. The face is therefore called the picture and indicator of the mind. Another reason is that in the most ancient or earliest times honesty demanded that what a person wanted should shine out from their face, and no one thought of doing anything else or wanted to do so. Thus too the affections of the mind and the thoughts arising from them could be vividly and fully displayed. This enabled many things to be presented simultaneously to the eye, as it were, in visible form. This kind of speech in consequence was as much better than verbal speech as sight is better than hearing: the difference between seeing the countryside and envisaging it by listening to a verbal description.

They also said that this kind of speech matched the speech of angels, with whom human beings were in the habit of communicating in those times. In fact, when the face speaks, or mind speaks through the face, angelic speech reaches its final, natural form in a person; but not when the mouth speaks in words. Anyone can grasp that the most ancient people could not have had verbal speech, since the words of language are not directly inherent in things, but need to be invented and applied to them; and this could only happen over a period of time.

Worlds in Space §54.2

Something as yet unknown to the world and perhaps hard to believe is that the member of the Most Ancient Church possessed internal breathing, but no external breathing except that which was soundless. Consequently people spoke not so much by means of vocal utterances, as they did in later times and as they do nowadays, but like angels, by means of ideas. They were able to express ideas by means of countless alterations in their facial expressions and in their looks, and especially by means of alterations of the lips where there are innumerable threads of muscular fibres which are all knotted up nowadays but which had freedom of movement in those times. They were in this way able to present, mean, and represent inside a minute things which nowadays take an hour by the use of articulated sounds or utterance. And they did so far more fully and more clearly to the comprehension and understanding of those present than can possibly be done with words or sentences. This is perhaps hard to believe but is nevertheless the truth.

Arcana Caelestia §607.2

It is 'hard to believe', but easier if you are familiar and happy with the concept of telepathy, a word which had not been coined in Swedenborg's time. If you will concentrate on the words in the second sentence 'people spoke not so much by means of vocal utterances [...] but like angels, by means of ideas', I believe you will grasp the most significant point of this paragraph.

The references to 'internal breathing' are very enigmatic and it is difficult to be sure of Swedenborg's meaning. It has to be realized that oxygen was only discovered about the time of his death, so the nature of respiration was not properly understood when he was writing. Aristotle's theory that the heart was a sort of furnace for which the lungs acted as bellows was still unthinkingly accepted. Swedenborg understood the matter better, as is clear from a passage in his *The Divine Wisdom* §121 saying that: 'The lungs [...] not only purge the blood of its impurities [...] but also provide nutrient for it out of the air'.

Nevertheless he seemed to consider that the main function of the lungs was to facilitate speech. In *Arcana Caelestia* §3893 he comments on angelic choirs that: 'belonged to the province of the lungs and their functions; for singing belongs to these, because this is the office of the lungs'. In *Arcana Caelestia* §4791 he also erroneously suggests that the folds of the lungs are to articulate words and musical tone.

Hence it is reasonable to assume that when Swedenborg talks of 'breathing' he has in mind speech and not respiration in the sense of absorbing oxygen. It is also clear from the first of the two passages above that he uses the word speech to cover other kinds of communication. So by 'internal breathing' I assume he means something like 'internal communication', which I would suggest is what we would term 'telepathy'. Several anthropologists have noted that telepathy is quite common among ancient peoples, although it certainly isn't their routine way of communicating.

Nevertheless there is probably more to Swedenborg's concept of internal breathing, a subject which he discussed frequently and at length in the *Arcana Caelestia* and *Worlds in Space*. And yet there is no mention of it in his later works; and this in spite of his reputation for repeating himself. The fullest description of the subject is probably that in *Arcana Caelestia* §§1118-20.

One has also to reflect that 'breath' and 'spirit' are very closely associated. Even if you don't know about oxygen it is obvious that breathing is essential to life. A study of Swedenborg's use of the words in *The Swedenborg Concordance* or the NewSearch computer program will lead you in all sorts of directions.

The references to innumerable muscular fibres in the face puts me in mind of photographs of the wrinkled faces of Bushmen, Aborigines and Eskimos. Are their wrinkles just caused by weather or old age, or did they not so long ago use facial muscles to communicate by facial expression? Scientists are also now suggesting that human communication used facial expression before oral speech was developed.[8]

Writing

[In heaven] I was allowed into a library where there was a large number of books. Those who were there [. . .] told me that in it were books from the ancients, written by means of correspondences. The inner parts of other libraries contained books written by those who belonged to the Ancient Churches, and in parts further in than these there were books for the most ancients, from whom the group called Enoch gathered together correspondences which were of use in later times to people within the Churches that existed in those later times.

The Spiritual Diary §5999

It is well known that in Egypt there were hieroglyphics [. . .] They were nothing else than correspondences of natural and spiritual things, which the Egyptians studied more than any other people in Asia of their time, and according to which the oldest writers of Greece composed their fables. The most ancient style of writing was no other.

White Horse Appendix

The Word was able on our planet to be set down in writing. This is so because the art of writing has existed here since most ancient times, first on tablets, then on parchment, after that on paper, and finally as printed type.

Arcana Caelestia §9353

Firstly one should question whether Swedenborg is here using 'most ancient' in a particular sense (applying to his Most Ancient Church) or just in a general sense.

Taught as we are that the art of writing was first developed in the Middle Eastern civilizations about 3000 BC, one is tempted to reject Swedenborg's many references to the most ancients' writing. He did, however, use the term loosely e.g. 'the Word was written on their hearts'. It may also have been written in their memories, as were the Norse Sagas. A whole 'book' can be held in the memory. Islamic mullahs are still expected to commit the entire Koran to memory, as it must be recited, and not read, in mosques. It is also worth noting that Swedenborg says the ancients received knowledge from the most ancients 'orally' (*Arcana Caelestia* §1241). But was this because the most ancients had no writing, or because the ancients could not read the most ancients' symbols?

But the above passages are not talking about alphabetic letters but hieroglyphs and 'signs'. In *Heaven and Hell* §260 Swedenborg talks about the elaborate detail of Hebrew characters and says: 'I have been told that the most ancient people on this earth, before letters were invented, also had such writing'. Had the term been available he might well have called the symbols pictograms, which are turning up earlier and earlier as archaeologists realize that many decorations and ornaments on pottery and other objects are also intended to convey meaning.

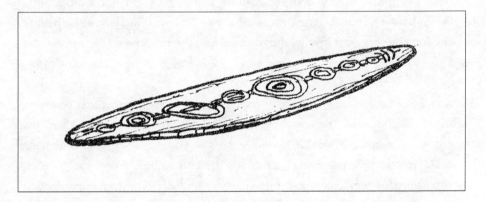

Fig. 5 **Aborigine Turinga**. A wooden tablet with symbols to identify locations along the route of a journey. An example of how ideas were communicated long before the invention of writng as we know it

The reference to 'wooden tablets' puts one in mind of the Aborigines' 'turinga'; long wooden plates which on the surface are route maps, but depict sacred journeys of the Dreamtime ancestors which seem to have deeper symbolism. Sadly wooden tablets do not last long, so we are most unlikely to dig any up from prehistoric times.

THE PROGRESS OF THE CHURCH

Swedenborg interprets the early chapters of Genesis as being an allegorical history of the Most Ancient or 'Adamic' age. He calls it the 'internal sense'. The following are very brief summaries and readers may need to check the texts of Genesis and *Arcana Caelestia* to fully understand the matter.

[The internal sense of Genesis Chapter 3. 'Garden of Eden'.]

The subject is the third state of the Most Ancient Church, which set their heart on their proprium [selfhood], even to the point of loving it.

Because at this time, by reason of their self-love or very own love, they were beginning not to believe anything which they did not apprehend through their physical senses; the sensory part is represented by the serpent; self-love or very own love by the woman; and the rational by the man.

Arcana Caelestia §§190-1

May I emphasize that Adam and Eve do not represent the sexes, but peoples' hearts and selfhoods. Swedenborg's concept of the proprium (a Latin term he uses to mean that which one takes to oneself) is akin to self-awareness, even to the 'ego'. It might seem that it would be better if we were mere puppets, like the animals. But as God says in Genesis 'It is not good for man to be alone'. He creates us essentially as 'loving hearts' designed to enjoy the experience of sharing love with others. But, through the sense of self, he allows us the freedom to keep that love for ourselves, if we so wish, although we will get no real pleasure from doing so.

[The internal sense of Genesis Chapter 4. 'Cain and Abel'.]

Since the subject in this chapter is the degeneration of the Most Ancient Church—that is, the falsification of doctrine—and consequently the heresies and sects which the names of Cain and his descendants cover, it must be realized that nobody can begin to understand how doctrine was falsified, that is, understand the nature of the heresies and sects of that Church, unless he has a proper knowledge of the nature of the true Church. [...] The Most Ancient Church was celestial, and acknowledged no other faith than faith that originated in love to the Lord and towards the neighbour. It was through that love from the Lord that they possessed faith. Consequently they were not even willing to mention faith for fear of separating it from love.

People who falsified doctrine in this way, or who separated faith from love [. . .] were at that time called 'Cain'; and such a thing with them was a gross error.

Arcana Caelestia §337

[From chapter 4 of Genesis] it is evident that during the most ancient period there were several doctrinal systems separated from the Church, and heresies too, each one of them having a name of its own.

Arcana Caelestia §442

[The internal sense of Genesis Chapter 4. 'The Generations of Adam'.]
    The names which follow—Seth, Enosh, Kenan, Mahalalel, Jared, Enoch, Methuselah, Lamech, and Noah—mean just so many Churches, the first and chief one of which was called Man [Adam]. The chief characteristic of these Churches was perception, and therefore the differences between the Churches of that period were primarily differences in perception.

Arcana Caelestia §483

The symbolic sense within the first two chapters of Genesis deals with the foundation of the Most Ancient Church but the next four chapters chart its gradual decline. As *Arcana Caelestia* §442 notes, the story is complicated by the introduction of 'heresies', such as Irad, Methusael, etc., and revived but imperfect churches, such as Jabal, Jubal and Tubal-cain, whose history runs parallel to the mainstream symbolized by Seth. In the symbolic sense the chapters are not necessarily a continuous sequence, however, and some can stand on their own. The Garden of Eden story tells how some began to turn from love to self; it is also interpreted in *Coronis* §§25-31 as covering the whole history of the Church picturing its 'morning-noon-evening-night' stages.

    The story of Cain and Abel symbolizes how some allowed faith to destroy charity. Their Neolithic occupations of farming and herding may seem to undermine the placing of the Most Ancient Church in the Palaeolithic Age, but it has to be remembered that the Old Testament was finally written in the Iron Age and the literal fabric of Genesis was designed or updated to suit the times. On this literal level the changes from Adam's lifestyle to those of his sons could also be a myth about the changes and traumas of the Neolithic revolution.

Seth and Enosh represent continuations of the Adamic most ancient frame of mind, if less perfect ones. (Intriguingly, just before the establishment of Islam, there were groups in Arabia following the 'ancient religion of Seth and Enoch'.)⁹ From Enosh on, however, it is downhill, although Enoch has a special role:

> **I was also taught that Enoch, who is mentioned in Genesis 5:21-24, together with his colleagues collected these correspondences by listening to their talk, and transmitting this science to posterity. As a result the science of correspondences was not merely known but held in high esteem in many Asiatic kingdoms, especially in the land of Canaan, Egypt, Assyria, Chaldaea, Syria, Arabia, Tyre, Sidon and Nineveh. From there it was transmitted into myths, as is evident in the earliest Greek authors.**
>
> *The True Christian Religion* §202 (see also *Arcana Caelestia* §609)

Swedenborg here talks about Enoch as if he were a person, although he has told us the patriarchs symbolized churches and elsewhere will mention 'the group called Enoch' (*The Spiritual Diary* §5999). The activity of this group is a picture we will find echoed in the history of all the 'four' churches. All are launched with revelation, but before the state of moral decay proceeds too far the teachings are carefully collected, by well-chosen groups of scholars, into a suitable form for the use of the latter phases of a church and, especially, the succeeding church. Both the Old and New Testaments seem to have gone through such a process.

Notice that Enoch collected the correspondences 'from listening to the talk' of men of the Most Ancient Church. There is no mention of writing.

> **[...] Lamech means a Church in which the perception of truth and good was so general and vague as to be almost none at all, and so it was a vastated Church [...] And the one who begot him even bore a similar name, which was Methusael. Consequently things that were almost the same were meant by these names; Methusael and Methuselah both mean**

something that is about to die, while Lamech means that which has been destroyed.

Arcana Caelestia §527

That 'a flood' means a deluge of evil and falsity is clear from what has been stated already about the descendants of the Most Ancient Church being possessed with filthy desires and immersing doctrinal matters concerning faith in them. This immersing led to false persuasions within them which annihilated all truth and good and simultaneously closed off the road for remnants [of truth] and so made it impossible for them to do their work. It was inevitable therefore that these men would destroy themselves. When the road for remnants has been closed off a person is no longer human, for he can no longer be protected by angels but is wholly and completely possessed by evil spirits who long and desire to do nothing else but annihilate man. It was this that led to the death of the people who existed before the Flood, a death described by 'a flood' or utter deluge. Indeed the influx of delusions and desires from evil spirits is not unlike a flood. Consequently in various places in the Word that influx is called a flood or a deluge.

Arcana Caelestia §660

So the minds of the people of this church, which Swedenborg at first described in such glowing terms, fell into the depths of evil and falsity. One feels very sorry for them, particularly as unlike us, they had no written Word to guide them. They originally, however, had a direct line to heaven which they gradually allowed to fall into disuse. As it was allowed to decay, the knowledge of how to operate it was forgotten too and will never be fully recovered—even if a 'mature innocence' such as some old people possess becomes more common.

The Genesis story reads as if 'all mankind'—apart from Noah's family or church—were destroyed. Discussing the 'flood' Swedenborg seems to go along with this, but elsewhere he does in fact claim that the Most Ancient Church kept going in some places.

> Remnants of the Most Ancient Church which was celestial still existed in the land of Canaan, especially among those called Hittites and Hivites. The reason why such remnants did not exist anywhere else was that the Most Ancient Church called 'Man' or 'Adam' existed in the land of Canaan, where the 'garden of Eden', by which was signified the intelligence and wisdom of the members of that church, and by the trees in it their perception, was therefore situated.
>
> *Arcana Caelestia* §4447.2

Swedenborg is here commenting on the story of Dinah the daughter of Jacob in Genesis 34. So he says that a remnant of the Most Ancient Church was alive at the time of the foundation of the Jewish Church. According to my calculations this would be about 1500 BC, more than 6000 years after the nominal end of the Most Ancient Church at the beginning of the Neolithic Revolution. (Incidentally the biblical Hittites do not seem to correspond with the Anatolian Hittites known to history.)

I find it discouraging that he says 'these remnants did not exist anywhere else'. I would suggest that Swedenborg in the eighteenth century, was under that impression, because he knew nothing of the hunter-gatherer cultures we know about today. Indeed little was really known in the early eighteenth century of the world beyond the Mediterranean area, apart from coastal areas. Nor was it thought that lands outside 'Christendom' would be worthy of scholarly study.

Alternatively, when Swedenborg talks of remnants of the Most Ancient Church he may be talking only of the direct and purest strain of that Church (the church specific), whereas the Bushmen or Australian Aborigines etc., although sharing the same culture and psychology, could be spiritually of a less enlightened strain. He might think of them as 'gentiles' (the universal church). The rather casual mention Swedenborg makes in the following passage to 'other' churches leaves all sorts of possibilities open.

> This new Church called Noah [...] was of an entirely different disposition from the Most Ancient Church. In addition to this Church others also existed at that time, such as the one called Enosh dealt with already at

[Genesis] Chapter 4:25, 26, and others again of which no such mention or description has come down to us. Only the Church of Noah is described here because it was altogether different in disposition from the Most Ancient Church.

Arcana Caelestia §640

We began by noting that the most ancients were motivated by love. Sadly a confirmation of this is perhaps the fact that many people following 'animist' religions today seem to be motivated by fear, the opposite of love, and spend much time propitiating feared evil spirits.

*

MARRIAGE LOVE IN THE GOLDEN AGE
From Swedenborg's *Conjugial Love* §75

I was once meditating about conjugial love, when my mind was seized with a desire to know what this love had been like in the case of those who lived in the Golden Age, and also in the following ages, which were named after silver, copper and iron. Knowing that all who lived good lives in those ages are in the heavens, I prayed to the Lord to allow me to talk with them and be taught by them.

At once I found an angel beside me, who said: "I have been sent by the Lord to be your guide and companion. First I shall guide and accompany you to those who lived in the first era or age, known as golden. The route to them", he added, "is steep, leading through a dark forest, which no one can penetrate unless supplied with a guide by the Lord".

[2] I was in the spirit, so I prepared myself for travelling, and we set our faces towards the east. As we went I saw a mountain, the top of which was higher than the level of the clouds. We crossed a great desert and reached a forest thickly filled with trees of various kinds, so dense they

made it dark, as the angel had said beforehand. But the forest was cut by numerous narrow paths, and the angel told me that all of these were a maze to lead people astray, and unless the Lord opened his eyes to see the olive-trees wreathed in grape-vines, and so to follow the path from one olive to the next, a traveller would stray into Tartarus, which is the region surrounding this at the sides. The forest is like this to guard the approach. For none but the primeval people live on this mountain.

[3] After we entered the forest, our eyes were opened and we saw here and there olive-trees entwined with vines, from which hung bunches of dark blue grapes. The olives were arranged in continuous curves, so as we spied them we went round and round. At length we saw a group of tall cedars with some eagles on their branches. On seeing them the angel said; "Now we are on the mountain not far from the summit". So we went on and a little beyond the cedars came upon a circular plain, where lambs of both sexes were feeding. These were forms intended to picture the state of innocence and peace among the mountain-dwellers.

We went across this plain and saw tents upon tents to the number of many thousand extending as far as the eye could see before us and to the sides in all directions. "Now", said the angel, "we are in the camp where is the Army of the Lord Jehovih—that is what they call themselves and where they live. These most ancient people lived, when they were in the world, in tents, so they continue to do so now. But let us turn aside to the south, where the wiser among them are, so that we can find someone to talk with".

[4] As we went I saw at a distance three boys and three girls sitting at the door of a tent. But as we came closer, they turned out to be like men and women of middling height. "All the inhabitants of this mountain", said the angel, "look from a distance like children, because they are in a state of innocence, and childhood is how innocence appears".

When these men saw us, they hurried up to us and said: "Where do you come from, and how have you come here? Your faces are not those of the people of our mountain".

Chapter Three—The Most Ancient Church

The angel replied telling them how we had been given permission to come through the forest, and why we had come. On hearing this one of the three men invited us in and took us into his tent. The man was dressed in a cloak of blue colour and a tunic of pure white wool. His wife was dressed in a purple robe with underneath it a blouse of fine embroidered linen.

[5] Since I was thinking that I wanted to know about marriage among the most ancient people, I looked in turn from husband to wife and back again, and observed that their faces showed how they were almost of one soul. So I said: "You two are one". The man replied: "We are one. Her life is in me and mine is in her, so we are two bodies, but one soul. The union between us is like that of the two cavities in the chest, called the heart and lungs. She is my heart and I am her lungs. But since by heart we understand here love and by lungs wisdom, she is the love of my wisdom, and I am the wisdom of her love. Her love therefore forms the outer covering of my wisdom and my wisdom is inwardly inside her love. As a result, as you said, the unity of our souls is to be seen in the look of our faces".

[6] Then I asked, "If your union is such, are you able to look at any woman other than your own?" "Yes", he replied, "I can, but because my wife is united with my soul, we two look together, and so not the slightest spark of lust can enter in. For when I look at other people's wives, I see them through my wife, whom alone I love. Since she is capable of perceiving all my feelings, as an intermediary she directs my thoughts, taking away anything discordant, and at the same time striking into me a feeling of coldness and horror at anything unchaste. It is therefore as impossible for us here to look lustfully on any of our companions' wives as it is to look upon the light of our heaven from the shades of Tartarus. So we do not either have any idea in our thinking, much less a word in our language, for the enticements of lustful love". He could not use the word fornication, because the chastity of their heaven prevented it. My angel guide said: "Now you can hear how the angels of this heaven speak, a language of wisdom, since it is derived from causes".

[7] After this I looked around and saw that their tent was as if gilded. So I asked, "Why is this?" He answered that it was "the result of the flaming light, which glitters like gold, flooding and striking the curtains of our tent, while we are talking about conjugial love. For then the heat of our sun, which in its essence is love, bares itself and tinges the light, which in its essence is wisdom, with its own, gold colour. This happens because conjugial love in origin is the play of wisdom and love. For man was born to be wisdom, woman to be the love of her man's wisdom. This is the source of the delights of that play in conjugial love, and thus between ourselves and our wives. We have witnessed here over thousands of years how these delights are surpassing and excellent in quantity, degree and strength in proportion to our worship of the Lord Jehovih, who is the source from which that heavenly union, the heavenly marriage of love and wisdom, flows in".

[8] After this speech I saw a great light above a hill in the middle of the tents. "What is that light coming from?" I asked. "It is", he said, "from the sanctuary of our tent of worship". I asked if one might approach it. "Yes", he said. So I went near and saw a tent which both within and without exactly matched the description of the tabernacle constructed in the desert for the Children of Israel, the plan of which was shown to Moses on Mount Sinai (Exod. 25:40; 26:30). "What", I asked, "is there in the sanctuary to give so much light?" "There is a tablet", he answered, "bearing the inscription 'The Covenant between Jehovah and the heavens'". He said no more.

[9] As we were then preparing to leave, I asked: "Did any of you, when you were in the world, live with more than one wife?" He answered that he knew of none. "For", he said, "we could not think of several. Those who had thought so told us that the heavenly blessedness of their souls at once fled from the inmost to the outermost parts of the body, even to the finger-nails, and at the same time also their virility departed. When this was noticed, they were thrown out of our country".

Chapter Three—The Most Ancient Church

After saying this, the man hastened back to his tent and came back with a pomegranate containing a mass of golden seeds. He presented it to me, and I brought it away as a token that we had visited those who lived in the golden age. Then after wishing each other peace, we departed and returned home.

Chapter Four—
The Ancient Churches

Alternative concepts:

The Silver Age;

The Neolithic Age;

Noah; The Ark;

Summer; Noon; Childhood;

A Spiritual Church.

INTRODUCTORY

The story of the Churches after the Flood is as follows: There were three Churches which receive specific mention in the Word—the first Ancient Church which took its name from Noah, the second Ancient Church which took its name from Eber [Heber], and the third Ancient Church named from Jacob, and subsequently from Judah and Israel.

Arcana Caelestia §1327

Swedenborg uses the term 'ancient' in both the general sense, when talking about 'old things' and specifically to cover things relating to the people of the 'Ancient Church'. Similarly when talking about the Ancient Church he may mean the First Ancient Church only, both the First and Second, or all three. We often have to judge from the context how widely or narrowly one can apply each reference. Although this chapter is primarily about the First Ancient Church much of it pertains to the other churches too.

The evidence for the consecutive stages of the Ancient Church—its rise or morning, its advancement into light or daytime, its destruction or evening and its consummation or night—is too small to allow us to go on and describe them in the same way as the states of the Most Ancient

Church were described above, because the states of the Ancient Church cannot be gathered in like manner from our Word. For the descendants of Noah receive only brief mention there, in only one or two pages [of Genesis]. Furthermore that Church was widespread, existing in a large number of countries; and in each one the form it took varied from that taken in the others; consequently it underwent and passed through the aforesaid states in differing ways.

Coronis §41

Regarded in itself, good is a single whole, but it is made various by means of truths.

Arcana Caelestia §4149.2

Compared with his more straightforward presentation of the Most Ancient Church, Swedenborg's description of the Ancient Church had to be more complex and unfortunately less complete. The principle stated in *Arcana Caelestia* §4149.2, that good promotes unity while truth inspires variety, is a common theme in Swedenborg. So the Most Ancient Church, a Celestial Church, although spread around the world, was to a large extent of a consistent nature. But the Ancient Church, a Spiritual Church (at least in its first stage), varied geographically according to the doctrines it held most important, so it can be misleading to generalize about this later church the way one can about the Most Ancient.

The Ancient Church did not differ in the slightest from the Christian Church as to its internal features, only as to its external. Worship of the Lord that stems from charity cannot possibly be different, no matter how much externals may vary.

Arcana Caelestia §1083.3

The Most Ancient Church was unusual in many ways and so in the last chapter its many special characteristics had to be noted, but the Ancient Churches were basically similar to our own Christian age, so Swedenborg has less need to explain details.

GENERAL

[. . .] this Church was quite different in disposition from the Most Ancient Church; that is to say, it is a spiritual Church, whose nature is such that an individual is born again by means of doctrinal matters concerning faith. Once these have been implanted, conscience is instilled into him to prevent his doing things contrary to the truth and good of faith. In this way charity is conferred on him which then governs his conscience, from which he accordingly starts to act.

Arcana Caelestia §765

[. . .] this Noachian, or Ancient Church, was disseminated throughout Asia. It spread in particular into Syria, Mesopotamia, Assyria, Chaldea, the land of Canaan, and its neighbouring lands—Philistia, Egypt, Tyre, Sidon, Nineveh, and also into Arabia and Ethiopia, and in course of time into Great Tartary, and from there down to as far as the Black Sea, and from there into parts of Africa.

Coronis §39

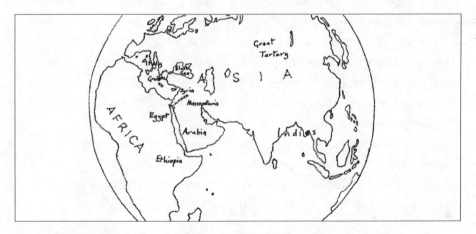

Fig. 6 **The extent of the Ancient Church**. It seems to cover all of the sub-tropical lands known to Swedenborg. In his *Doctrine of the Sacred Scripture* §117, Swedenborg suggests the Ancient Word was also spread to the Indies, which term was used to cover an enormous undefined area.

The Five Ages

The people of the Ancient Church were psychologically similar to us, guided by conscience which could restrain emotional excesses. The Church seems to have developed in the Middle East in the areas where herding and agriculture first developed and spread over much of the 'ancient world'.

> I was told that Enoch, who is mentioned in Genesis [5:21-4], together with his companions made a collection of correspondences from the angels' lips, and transmitted the knowledge of them to their descendants. As a result the knowledge of correspondences was not only widespread, but prized in many kingdoms of Asia, especially in Egypt, Assyria and Babylon, Syria, Mesopotamia, Arabia, and also Canaan. From there it spread to Greece, but there it was converted into myths.
>
> *On the Sacred Scripture* §18

Ancient peoples [...] possessed a knowledge of correspondences, which is also that of representations. This was to them the highest form of knowledge, and it was particularly developed by the Egyptians, and formed the basis of their hieroglyphs. It was this knowledge which enabled them to know the meaning of every kind of animal, every kind of tree, the meaning of mountains, hills, rivers and springs, of the sun, the moon and the stars. This knowledge was the means by which they knew about spiritual matters. For the things they represented, which are the kind of things that make up the spiritual wisdom possessed by angels in heaven, were the origins of these objects.

[...] Moreover, they made carved images of horses, cattle, calves, lambs, even birds, fishes and snakes. They placed these in their homes and elsewhere, arranged in sequence to match the spiritual ideas of the church to which they corresponded, that is, what they represented.

Conjugial Love §342

Nobody who keeps merely to the sense of the letter is able to see this [the spiritual sense of the Noah's Ark story], the chief reason being here that all those details are linked together as a tale of history, and give the idea of historical events. But the style belonging to that period—a style that gave them the greatest pleasure—was such that everything was embodied in allegory and woven together as a historical tale. And the better everything held together as an undivided tale the more it appealed to those people. For in those early times people were not so much inclined towards the things known today but to profounder thoughts whose offspring were the kind of things mentioned here. This was what constituted the wisdom of men of old.

Arcana Caelestia §605

It would seem that the concept of correspondence or symbolism was second nature to these ancient people. This can be seen in their myths and fables—even in what appears to be their histories. It is similarly apparent in their art and architecture, both in their choice of subjects and in the decoration they applied to them. It was also apparent in many of their customs which we now label as superstitions.

This use of symbolism was, as Swedenborg says in the above quotation, 'the means by which they knew about spiritual matters' and also the means by which they expressed their awareness and deep respect for spiritual matters, allowing it to affect most aspects of their lives.

CONCEPT OF GOD

The God whom people worshipped in the Ancient Church was the Lord [. . .] and it was well known to those people that the Lord was the One who was represented in each particular religious observance of their Church. A large number of them also knew that the Lord was going to come into the world, when He would make the Human within Himself Divine. Nor did the people of that Church take Jehovah to mean anyone else, for whenever He appeared to them He did so as a Divine Man, and was called Jehovah, as He also appeared at a later time to Abraham, (Gen.

18:2) He was acknowledged as God overall, and as the one and only God whom they were to adore.

Arcana Caelestia §6846

[…] in ancient times people gave the Supreme Deity, or the Lord, various illustrious names. They used these in accordance with His attributes and in accordance with the kinds of good derived from Him, as well as in accordance with the kinds of truth, which are manifold, as everyone knows. By all those descriptive names members of the Ancient Church meant none but the one God, namely the Lord, whom they called Jehovah. But after the Church fell away from goodness and truth, and at the same time from such wisdom, they started to worship as many gods as there were descriptive names of the one God—so much so that each nation, and at length each family, acknowledged one of them as its own god. This was how so many gods came into being.

Arcana Caelestia §3667

Not so long ago this idea of an original universal god would have been considered improbable, but it is now more commonly realized that God was known by different names in different nations and at different times. The possibility that these names could all be traced back to one original conception of the Divine can be neither proved or disproved, but is a reasonable working hypothesis.

The ancients, when they represented God in their pictures, represented Him as Man, surrounded about the head with a radiant circle, as if the rays of the sun were round about it. So is the Lord represented by those of the present day; and this from the common idea which all have from heaven, that the Divine is like the sun, or that God is encompassed with a sun.

Athanasian Creed §153

One is reminded of examples of 'sun worship' all over the world, particularly where the

Fig. 7 Ahura Mazda. The Zoroastrian God was originally represented by the 'sun disc' but in time was given a human head, and wings to help him fly across the sky. Many Egyptian gods wear sun discs on their heads.

sun is obviously primarily a symbol, as in the case of the Zoroastrian concept of God, Ahura Mazda.

THE NOAH STORY

The subject now [in Genesis Chapter 6] is the formation of a new Church which is called Noah. The formation of it is described by the ark into which living creatures of every kind were admitted. But before that new Church could come into existence, the member of the Church, as is normal, had inevitably to undergo many temptations, which are described by this ark's being lifted up, carried along, and coming to a stop, on the waters of the flood.

Arcana Caelestia §605

And of every living creature of all flesh, you shall cause pairs of all to enter the ark, to keep them alive with you; male and female they shall be. Gen. 6:19.

'[. . .] you shall cause pairs of all to enter the ark to keep them alive', means the regeneration of these [things of the understanding and the will]. This becomes clear from what has been stated in the previous verse, to the effect that truths cannot be regenerated except by means of forms of good and of delight. Nor therefore can things of faith be regenerated except through those of charity. Hence the statement here about pairs of all having to enter, clearly meaning that both truths, which belong to the understanding, and forms of good, which belong to the will, were to do so.

And take for yourself of all food that is eaten, and gather it to yourself, and it will be food for you and them. Gen. 6:21.

'He was to gather them for himself' means truths [. . .] for 'gathering' has reference to the things that are in a person's memory, where they have been gathered together. It embodies in addition the point that the former and the latter—forms of good and truth—need to be gathered together in man before regeneration takes place. Indeed unless these have been gathered together to serve as means through which the Lord may do His work, a person cannot possibly be regenerated, as has been stated. From this it follows then that 'it was to be food for him and them' means both forms of goodness as well as truths.

selected from *Arcana Caelestia* §§669-79

Of the clean beast, and of the beast that is not clean, and of the bird, and of everything that creeps over the ground. Two and two they went to Noah into the ark, male and female, as God had commanded Noah. Gen. 7:8-9.

'The clean beast' means, as previously, affections for good. 'The beast that is not clean' means evil desires. 'Bird' in general means thoughts. 'Everything that creeps over the ground' means the sensory part and every associated delight. 'Two and two' means complementary things. 'They went into the ark' means that they were protected. 'Male and female', as previously, means truth and good.

Arcana Caelestia §743

Swedenborg spends many pages explaining the symbolism of the Flood story which pictures the establishment of the Ancient Church on earth or in our minds. From the brief passages above I hope it can be seen that the 'Spiritual' people of the Ancient dispensation were to gather truths into their memories for safe keeping so that they could apply them when required at a later date. However, it is noted that the memory will also gather unclean thoughts, which are in fact desirable, as later we need to prove the strength of our willpower by rejecting them.

I think it is worth noting that the Ark story is a mirror of the typical policy of the Neolithic people who, unlike Palaeolithic tribes, were good at storing food away for a rainy day. Neolithic dwellings usually have adjacent store buildings and/or storage pits.

> *And Noah became a man of the soil and planted a vineyard.* Gen. 9:20.
>
> That 'Noah became a man of the soil' means in general a person who has been instructed from matters of doctrine concerning faith is clear from the meaning of 'the soil', as the member of the Church, or what amounts to the same, the Church. [. . .] The Church is called 'the soil' from the fact that it receives the seeds of faith. [. . .] 'Noah became a man of the soil' therefore means a person who has been instructed from matters of doctrine concerning faith.
>
> That 'he planted a vineyard' means a Church resulting from this, 'vineyard' being the spiritual Church [. . .] The Ancient Church, being spiritual, is described as 'a vineyard' on account of its fruit, namely grapes, which represent and mean charitable works.
>
> *Arcana Caelestia* §§1067-9

Swedenborg goes on to note numerous passages in the Bible where vineyards or vines are used to symbolize the church such as in Isaiah 5, Amos 9, Matthew 20 and John 15.

The information that Noah 'became a man of the soil' would also neatly place the Ancient Church after the agricultural revolution at the beginning of the Neolithic Age.

RELIGION—WORSHIP

> [. . .] those who belonged to the Most Ancient Church were internal people and had no external forms of worship, while those who belonged to the

Ancient Church were external people and did have them. For the former saw external things in the light of internal ones, [...] whereas the latter saw internal things in the light of external ones.

Arcana Caelestia §4493.3

[...] holy worship in the Ancient Church was offered on mountains and in groves. It was offered on mountains because 'mountains' meant the celestial things of worship, and in groves because 'groves' meant the spiritual things of it. As long as the Ancient Church retained its simplicity their worship on mountains and in groves was holy, the reason being that celestial things, which are those of love and charity, were represented by places that were high and lofty, such as mountains and hills, while spiritual things, which derive from celestial, were represented by places with fruits and foliage, such as gardens and groves.

Arcana Caelestia §2722.1

The reason why pillars were signs representative of worship was that among the ancients it was customary to set up pillars, anoint them with oil, and in so doing make them holy objects. The ancients performed their worship chiefly on mountains, on hills, and in groves, where they set the pillars up. The reason why they set them up on mountains was that mountains served to mean the heaven where celestial love, which is love to the Lord, reigns; the reason why they set them up on hills was that hills served to mean the heaven where spiritual love, which is love towards the neighbour, reigns; and the reason why they set them up in groves was that groves served to mean heavenly wisdom and intelligence. [...] The pillars which were set up in those places served as signs of Divine Truth; for the pillars were pieces of stone, and 'stone' means truth.

Arcana Caelestia §10643.1

Swedenborg may have originally gathered something of these ideas from the Old Testament, as well as from heavenly sources, but they are also fully in agreement with what we know of the Neolithic practices of worship. That there is a symbolic reason for

Chapter Four—The Ancient Churches

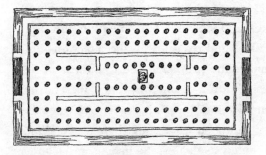 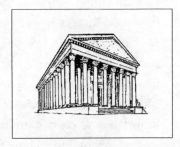

Figs. 8a and 8b Greek and Roman Temples. Classical temples, both inside and out, were surrounded by rows of columns giving the feeling of a 'grove' of trees, as is apparent in the above plan of the Temple of Artemis at Ephesus. The capitals of the Corinthian columns popular with the Romans were decorated with acanthus leaves, thus creating a formalized tree. The podium of steps the temples were raised on could well be formalized sacred mountains.

choosing hilltops is obvious, and stones and groves presumably had spiritual meanings for ancient races too. It is assumed that the columns surrounding Greek and Roman temples symbolized groves; Corinthian columns being formalized trees.

> Let me touch briefly on the way in which the representative Church was turned into an idolatrous one. Everything spiritual that constitutes heaven was displayed to them [. . .] by means of the images of things that existed within the natural order. Such things within the animal, vegetable and mineral kingdoms were drawn on to represent the realities that belong to the spiritual kingdom. They placed such images in their shrines, in the inner recesses of their houses, and in their market places and streets; and they arranged these images there in accord with their spiritual meanings.
>
> *Coronis* §43
>
> The ancient people who possessed the science of correspondences made themselves images to correspond to heavenly ideas; and they took pleasure in them because they stood for such things as concern heaven and the church. They placed these images therefore not only in their temples, but also in their houses, not so as to worship them, but to call to mind the

heavenly ideas they stood for. Hence it was that in Egypt and elsewhere they used images of calves, oxen and snakes, not to mention children, old men and young women. Calves and oxen meant the affections and powers of the natural man, snakes the prudence and craftiness of the man who relies upon his senses. Children meant innocence and charity, old men wisdom, young women affections for truth, and so on. Once the knowledge of correspondences had been wiped out, their descendants started to worship as holy, and finally as deities, the images and statues their ancestors had erected, because they were in or near temples.

The True Christian Religion §205

Here we have moved from the rural Neolithic world to the more urban Bronze Age; to worship practised in temples, furnished with the more sophisticated works of art we are familiar with from civilizations such as Mesopotamia, Egypt, and Greece. These were designed to express deeper meanings as well as to please the eye. The gods tended to be always dressed the same way and always carry the same implement symbolic of their role.

THE ANCIENT WORD

Angels of the third heaven have told me that the ancients had a Word among them, written, [. . .] solely in terms of things that correspond, but which has since been lost. They also said that this Word is still preserved among them, and is used by the ancients in that heaven, for whom this was the Word when they lived in the world.

These ancients among whom this Word is still used in heaven came partly from the land of Canaan and its borders, also from certain kingdoms in Asia, such as Syria, Mesopotamia, Arabia, Chaldea and Assyria, and from Egypt, Sidon and Tyre. The inhabitants of all those kingdoms possessed a representational worship and therefore had a knowledge of correspondences. They acquired the wisdom of that age from that knowledge, since by it they had communication with the heavens and an interior perception.

[...] I further have been told that the first seven chapters of Genesis appear in the same Ancient Word so completely that not the least word is missing.

The religious beliefs and practices of many nations were derived and transmitted from that Word. For instance, they were transmitted from the land of Canaan and from various places in Asia to Greece, and from Greece to Italy, and through Ethiopia and Egypt into several countries in Africa. But in Greece the people used correspondences to create fables, and they turned the attributes of God into so many deities, [...]

On the Sacred Scripture §§36-8

So the Ancient Word was originally like the early chapters of Genesis, but in time was metamorphosed into myths and folklore such as Aesop's Fables. Had Swedenborg known of the mythology of the Middle East and India he might well have identified it as being derived from this Ancient Word. He illustrates the Greek use of correspondences in the following passage:

[...] the knowledge of correspondences [...] spread to Greece; there it was converted into myths.

This can be established merely by considering Olympus, Helicon and Pindus near Athens, and also from the winged horse named Pegasus using its hoof to make a spring burst forth, by which the nine maidens made their dwelling. For a mountain, such as Helicon, by correspondence means the higher heaven, the hill beneath the mountain of Pindus the heaven below that, the winged horse Pegasus means the intellect enlightened by the spiritual, a spring intelligence and learning, the nine maidens the knowledge of truth and sciences. The rest of the stories known as myths written by the earliest peoples in Greece are similar; these have been collected and described by Ovid in his *Metamorphoses*.

On the Sacred Scripture §18

Helicon and Pindus are not as close to one another as Swedenborg seems to suggest, but as there would have been no maps of Greece showing classical locations, before the Neo-classical revival, he can be forgiven. The 'nine maidens' are the Muses, the patronesses of the arts and sciences, who indeed symbolize the knowledge Swedenborg specifies.

The [Ancient] Word which they [the ancients] had was a written Word, consisting of Historical Sections and Prophetical Parts, like the Old Testament Word. [. . .] The historical sections were called *The Wars of Jehovah*, and the prophetical parts the *Prophecies*, as is clear in Moses, Num. 21, where they are quoted. The historical sections of their Word were written in the prophetical style and were for the most part made-up historical narratives, like those in Chapters 1-11 of Genesis, as is evident from the quotations of those historical narratives in Moses, where the following words occur [when the route of the Israelites' journey through the wilderness is described],

Therefore it is said in The Book of The Wars of Jehovah: Waheb in Suphah, and the streams of Arnon, and the descent of the streams which runs down to the dwelling at Ar and leans to the border of Moab. Num. 21:14-15.

The prophetical parts of their Word were written in a style similar to the prophetical parts of the Old Testament, as is also evident from the quotation of these in Moses, where the following words occur,

Therefore the prophetic poets say,
Come to Heshbon, let the city of Sihon be established.
For fire went out of Heshbon, flame out of the city of Sihon.
It consumed Ar of Moab, the lords of the high places of Arnon.
Woe to you, O Moab!
You have perished, O people of Chemosh!
He gave his sons as fugitives, and his daughters into captivity, to Sihon, king of the Amorites.
But we shot at them; Heshbon has perished even to Dibon; and we

have laid waste even to Nophah, which reaches even to Medebah. Num. 21:27-30.

These prophecies embody heavenly arcana in the same way as the prophetical parts of the Old Testament. This is quite evident not only from the fact that Moses copied them and applied them to the state of affairs prevailing in his own day, but also from the fact that almost the same words occur in Jeremiah 48:45,46

Arcana Caelestia §2897

OTHER KNOWN BOOKS OF THE ANCIENT WORD

Up to the present time it has remained unknown what correspondence is. Yet in the most ancient times it was very well known; for those who lived at that period regarded the knowledge of correspondences as the outstanding science, and it was so universally known that all their documents and books were written by means of correspondences. The book of Job, which is a book of the Ancient Church, is full of correspondences. The hieroglyphic writings of the Egyptians, as well as the myths of the most ancient peoples, were nothing else.

The True Christian Religion §201

As regards the book [...] called the Song of Songs, [...] it is written in the ancient style, and is full both of things with spiritual meanings that were gathered together from the books of the Ancient Church, and also of many things which in the Ancient Church meant celestial and spiritual love, especially conjugial love. The fact that it is a book of this nature is also evident from the consideration that, unlike the books known as Moses and the Prophets, the sense of the letter presents many things which are quite improper. But because the kind of things that have heavenly and conjugial love as their real meaning are massed together there, this book is therefore seen to have some mystical meaning.

Arcana Caelestia §3942

Egyptian hieroglyphs were not deciphered until 1823, but had he lived later, Swedenborg would have been interested to know that the Book of Proverbs, possibly contemporary with the Song of Songs, bears remarkable similarities to the Egyptian *Instruction of Amenemopet* (*c*.1250 BC), much of which is drawn from an earlier collection of sayings from prehistoric times compiled by Ptahhotep (*c*.2400 BC).[1]

> **I am allowed to report this new piece of information about the ancient Word, which was in Asia before the Israelite Word existed. It is still preserved there among the peoples who live in Great Tartary. I have spoken with spirits and angels in the spiritual world who came from there. They said that they possess the Word, and have done so from ancient times; and they conduct their Divine worship in accordance with that Word. It is composed purely of correspondences. They said that it also contains the book of Jashar mentioned in Joshua (10:12, 13), and in the Second Book of Samuel (1:17, 18); they also have the books called The Wars of Jehovah and The Utterances, which are mentioned by Moses (Num. 21:14, 15 and 27-30). When I read in their presence the words which Moses took from this source, they looked to see whether they were there, and they found them. This made it clear to me that they still have the ancient Word. During our conversation they mentioned that they worship Jehovah, some of them as an invisible God, and some as visible.**
>
> *The True Christian Religion* §279.3

Great Tartary was the name given in the eighteenth century to what became Asian Russia and northern China; a very extensive area. However, from other references Swedenborg makes to this subject it would appear he was speaking to spirits from Mongolia or Manchuria. Research by Swedenborgians into early religion in this area has identified some traits comparable to those of the Ancient Church. Interestingly the Mongul/Manchu script seems to be derived from the ancient Sogdian script which was based on the Aramaic script.[2]

Chapter Four—The Ancient Churches

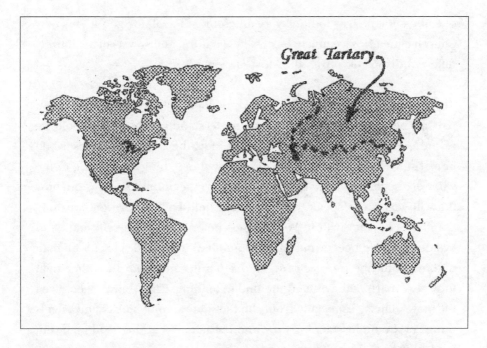

Fig. 9 Great Tartary. This was the name given in the 18th century to what later became Asian Russia, when the Russian Empire expanded to the east. The name Great Tartary appears on maps of Swedenborg's time.

PSYCHO-SPIRITUAL CHARACTER

You will recall that the people of the Most Ancient Church were infant-like, their minds dominated by the heart and will, which were served by compliant subservient understandings. This was fine as long as their wills were loving, but when hatred and evil took over their wills it became a fatal weakness.

> When the Lord foresaw that mankind would perish [. . .] He made provision for the will part to be separated from the understanding part. Man was to be formed, not as he had been formed previously by a will for good, but by having charity conferred on him through the understanding

of truth; such charity looking very much like the will for good. This new Church called Noah came to be of such a nature, and so was of an entirely different disposition from the Most Ancient Church.

Arcana Caelestia §640

The member of the [Ancient] Church needed to be reformed as to that part of the man which is called the understanding before he could be reformed as to the other part referred to as the will. So it is described here [in the description of the Ark] how those things belonging to the will were separated from those belonging to the understanding, and how the will was, so to speak, protected and held back to prevent anything coming in contact with it. For if things belonging to the will, that is, to evil desires, had been aroused, he would have perished. [. . .] With man nothing could be more distinct and separate one from the other than those two parts, the will and the understanding. This I have been given to know plainly, especially from the fact that among spirits and angels things of the understanding flow into the left side of the head or brain, while things of the will flow into the right.

Arcana Caelestia §641

This change to our psychology not only placed a rein on our evil tendencies, but also meant that we were now open to guidance, from the teachings of the Ancient Word and other good influences, which were developing our consciences.

DEATH AND HEAVEN

In the internal sense of the Word 'a grave' means life, which is heaven, and in the contrary sense death, which is hell. The reason it means life or heaven is that angels, who possess the internal sense of the Word, have no other concept of a grave, because they have no other concept of death. Consequently instead of a grave they perceive nothing else than the continuation of life, and so resurrection.

[...] As 'burial' meant resurrection in general and every individual resurrection, the ancients were therefore particularly concerned about their burials and about the places where they were to be buried— Abraham, for example, was to be buried in Hebron in the land of Canaan [...] Joseph's bones were to be carried up out of Egypt into the land of Canaan, [...] David and subsequent kings were to be buried in Zion, [...] the reason being that the land of Canaan and also Zion represented and meant the Lord's kingdom, while burial meant resurrection.

Arcana Caelestia §2916

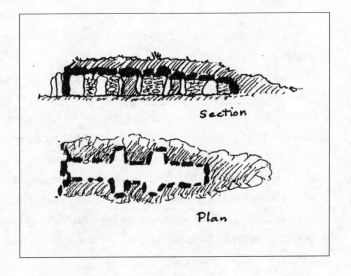

Fig. 10 A Neolithic Long Barrow. The elaborate nature of these structures, which were shared by the families of a small tribe, is typical of the large graves/caves, barrows and other funerary structures of these times. In the succeeding Bronze Age the graves of chiefs and kings were to become ever more elaborate and indicative of an obsession about the afterlife, as in the case of the Pyramids and the tombs of the Chinese Emperors.

This passage reflects the particular interest shown during the Neolithic and Bronze Ages in the methods and manner of burial. As a result we find elaborate tombs and burials, such as pyramids or barrows, all over the world. Europeans may imagine our barrows are one of the more numerous examples, but in the Persian Gulf on the smallish island of Bahrain, there are 250,000 burial mounds. It is thought that like Canaan, Bahrain was probably a site symbolic of heaven, a mythical 'isle of the dead'.[3] Archaeology can provide many similar examples.

The ancients also knew that when a person is withdrawn from perceiving things with his physical senses he is drawn up or raised to the light belonging to his spirit, that is, the light of heaven. So it was also that learned ancients knew that when their body had decayed they would be living a more internal life, which they called their spirit. And since they regarded this life to be the truly human life they also knew that they would be living within a human form. Such was the idea they had regarding a person's soul. And since that life partook of Divine life they perceived that their soul was immortal; for they knew that that part of a person which was a partaker of Divine life and for this reason linked to it could never die.

Arcana Caelestia §10099.3

It is common, and it is proper to mankind, to speak with spirits and angels.

Mankind was created to be able to speak with spirits and angels, so that earth and heaven may thus be joined together. In the Most Ancient Church this was so, in the Ancient, and in the primitive church [Christian] likewise they perceived the Holy Spirit. Such are the inhabitants of other planets. For the human being is a human because of being a spirit, with the only distinction that the spirit of a person on earth is clothed about with a body for the purpose of functioning on earth.

That earth and heaven are now separated on this planet is due to the fact that humanity here has passed in the course of time to outer qualities, away from inner ones.

The Spiritual Diary §1587

Although Swedenborg warned against 'contacting spirits' in his own day, he seems to regard it as normal in spiritually healthy societies. We are in fact in constant contact with spirits, but neither we nor they are conscious of it. In decaying primitive societies it is still common to contact 'the ancestors' and in Bronze Age cultures consulting oracles was routine.

Chapter Four—The Ancient Churches

SECULAR CULTURE

'We came,' they [people of the Silver Age] replied, 'from the peoples of Asia. Our age was devoted to the study of truths, the means by which we acquired intelligence—this was the kind of thing that appealed to our souls and minds. But the thing that appealed to our bodily senses was devising forms to represent truths. Our knowledge of correspondences made a link between our bodily sensations and the perceptions of our minds, so giving us intelligence.'

Conjugial Love §76.4

This would seem to support the idea of 'expression work' used in schools, where pupils draw or construct items representing the ideas contained in a lesson. The arts and crafts of the ancient world do seem to delight in expressive ornamentation.

I was admitted into a Library [in heaven] where was a great number of books. [. . .] They said that there were there books of the Ancients, written by correspondences. In the interior of other libraries were books written by those who were of the Ancient Churches. Still further in the interior, books for the Most Ancients, where the communion called Enoch had collected the correspondences which were afterwards of service to those who were in succeeding Churches; which are to be styled the Ancient Churches. There was a vast number who studied the books; and some of them become learned, many intelligent and others wise. There appeared places, or repositories, more and more bright, for interior Libraries—but to me and to them, in a dimmer light, because we were incapable of penetrating those depths of wisdom which are there; and, besides, those who are in exteriors are not allowed to enter into the interior parts for various reasons. The places in these libraries were divided into many [repositories], according to the faculties of those who studied.

The Spiritual Diary §5999

Swedenborg does not say in which part of the heavens this library was or whether he actually knew of libraries in the 'Ancient church', nor does he define what form these 'books' took (tablets, rolls, etc.). However, he does definitely mention 'books of the Ancients', which in due course became numerous enough to require libraries, such as that at Alexandria. Libraries of hand-copied documents were certainly common in the classical world, there were even 'bookshops' in Athens.

> [. . .] in the rituals of the Ancient Church [. . .] 'eating' meant making one's own and being joined to him at whose house they had eaten, that is, shared his bread. 'Food' meant in general those things which are the signs of love and charity, that is, the very things that constitute celestial and spiritual food—'bread' in that case meant things that are the sign of love to the Lord, and 'wine' those that are the sign of charity towards the neighbour. When these things had been made their own, those persons were joined together. They accordingly talked to one another from affection and shared one another's company.
>
> *Arcana Caelestia* §3596

Swedenborg frequently uses the phrase 'making one's own' in connection with food and especially with the bread and wine of the Holy Supper. It implies a full and sincere personal acceptance of the affections or ideas involved. One assumes there was, perhaps, a correspondential 'language of food', not unlike the 'language of flowers', and that in choosing to offer certain foods or wine, the host was 'opening up certain lines of conversation'. In selecting this or that food, the guest could show where common interests lay.

THE EXTENT OF THE CHURCH

> The Noachian, or Ancient Church, was diffused throughout Asia, especially into Syria, Mesopotamia, Assyria, Chaldea, the land of Canaan, and the lands adjacent, Philistia, Egypt, Tyre, Sidon, Nineveh, and also into Arabia and Ethiopia, and in course of time into Great Tartary, and thence downwards as

far as to the Black Sea, and thence into parts of Africa. It is a well known fact that nations everywhere in the world have possessed some kind of religion and therefore worship. But no kind of religion can exist except through some type of revelation and the transmission of this from one nation to another.

Coronis §39

For the Lord's Church had existed since most ancient times in the land of Canaan [. . .] From there such things as belonged to the worship of God spread to the nations round about and also to the neighbouring Greeks, and from the Greeks to the Italians or Romans.

Arcana Caelestia §8944.2

Swedenborg made several lists like those above, that in the *Coronis* being the most extensive, though it does not mention Greece and Rome, as the above *Arcana* passage does. Other slightly varying lists can be found in *Arcana Caelestia* §§1238, 2385 and 10177.10, *Apocalypse Explained* §391.32, and *Heaven and Hell* §327.

Very similar lists describing the distribution of the 'Ancient Word' can be found in *The True Christian Religion* §§275, 851, and *Doctrine of the Sacred Scripture* §102. *Doctrine of the Sacred Scripture* §117 also mentions 'the Indies'.

In that Swedenborg seems to list every non-European country he is aware of, it could be supposed that the Ancient Church also influenced other lands he was not aware of, where Neolithic or Bronze Age culture flourished, such as South-East Asia and America.

PROGRESS AND DECLINE OF FIRST ANCIENT CHURCH

All the spiritual things which are of heaven and the Church were presented before them in visible and tangible images [. . .] taken from the subjects of the three kingdoms of nature, animal, vegetable and mineral, by which were represented such things as are of the heavenly kingdom. They placed these typical images in their sanctuaries, in the inner chambers of their houses, and in the market-places and streets, arranging them according to their signification.

Fig. 11 Canaanite Gods. Statuettes of gods, goddesses and animals such as this bull, who symbolized Baal, often turn up in Middle Eastern archaeological excavations.

But after the knowledge of correspondences was wiped out and any awareness of the significance of such correspondences was consequently lost, people in a later age began to regard and accept these objects, however so many, as being actually divine and sacred. To some of them they bowed the knee, some they brushed with their kisses, some they adorned and decorated with torques, pomanders, and anklets, just as children do with their dolls or Papists do with their statues. They made household gods out of some, guardian-demigods out of others and oracles out of yet others. Some however, in miniature form, they carried around in their hands, some they held to their bosom, caressed, and whispered petitions to them, and so on. So it was that heavenly tokens were converted into hellish ones, and the Divine things of heaven and the Church into idols.

Coronis §43

The Ancient Church [...] was widespread in much of the Asiatic world and in many kingdoms there. And although differences existed among them so far as teachings about matters of faith were concerned, there was nevertheless one Church because all people everywhere made charity the essential element of the Church. People at that time who separated faith from charity and made faith the essential element of the Church were called Ham. But in process of time this Church turned aside to idolatrous practices, and in Egypt, Babylon, and other places to magical ones; for they began to worship external things devoid of anything internal. So because they departed from charity, heaven departed from them, and in its place spirits from hell came and led them.

Arcana Caelestia §4680.2

[. . .] in the course of time, as usually happens to Churches, that Church also started to decline, chiefly because many people started to divert worship to themselves so as to set themselves above others, as is clear

Fig. 12 A reconstruction of the Ziggurat of Ur. Sumerian and Akkadian Ziggurats were undoubtedly the basis for the Tower of Babel story. Equally interesting is the assumption that they are 'substitute mountains' for a highland people used to worshipping on mountains who, when they migrated into the flat Mesopotamian plain, felt a need to create 'high places'.

from verse 4 [of Genesis 11, concerning the Tower of Babel story]—'they said, Let us build ourselves a city and a tower, and its head in heaven, and let us make a name for ourselves'. In the Church such people were inevitably like some fermenting agent, or like firebrands that start a fire. When the danger of profaning what is holy was consequently near at hand, [. . .] the state of this Church was, in the Lord's Providence, altered. That is to say, its internal worship perished but its external worship remained, which here is meant by the statement that 'Jehovah confounded the lip of the whole earth'. From this it is also clear that the kind of worship called Babel was not prevalent in the first Ancient Church but in those that followed when people started to be worshipped in place of gods, especially after they had died. This was the origin of so many pagan deities.

Arcana Caelestia §1327.2

The Babel story seems to take us into the Bronze Age—and towards the mood of what Swedenborg calls the Second Ancient Church.

The reference to the Tower of Babel story, which we assume to have been set in the Sumerian and Akkadian civilization, offers a helpful historical point of reference. The Sumerians did come from the east; they were the first to build ziggurats; and their language was 'confused' when the Akkadians imposed their quite different language upon them, although Sumerian was kept for religious purposes.[4] Ziggurats are, of course, artificial mountains in the middle of the flat plain, for people who are used to worshipping on mountain tops, as we noted earlier.

The 'worship of people in place of gods, especially after they had died' certainly fits Egyptian and Roman practices, and the Mesopotamian king/priests regarded themselves as the appointed agents of their gods.

Unlike the Most Ancient Church, the Ancient Church does not come to a dramatic destructive close, as represented by the Flood story. Like the people of the Tower of Babel and the Jews of later times it was dispersed. It lost its integrity, but providence was probably able to make some use of its 'Babel' of confused ideas. In its heartland, however, the Church's traditions are preserved, if in a less perfect form by a 'remnant', which Swedenborg calls the Second Ancient Church, the subject of the next chapter.

*

MARRIAGE LOVE IN THE SILVER AGE
From Swedenborg's *Conjugial Love* §76

The next day the same angel as on the previous day came to me and said: "Would you like me to take and accompany you to the people who lived in the era or age of silver, so that we can hear from them about marriage in their time?" He said that these too were not to be approached except under the Lord's guidance. I was in the spirit, as previously, and I went with my guide, first to a hill on the border between east and south. When we were on the slopes of that hill, he showed me a great expanse of territory. We saw far off a towering mountain, between which and the hill on which we stood there was a valley, and beyond it a plain with a slope rising gently from it.

We came down from the hill to cross the valley, and saw in places on either side pieces of wood and stone carved to resemble human beings and various animals, birds and fishes. "What are they?" I asked the angel. "Are they not idols?" "Far from it", he answered. "They are shapes designed to depict various moral virtues and spiritual truths. The peoples of that age knew about correspondences; and since every person, animal, bird and fish corresponds to some quality, each carving depicts some aspect of a virtue or truth, and a number of them taken together depict the whole virtue or truth in its general full form. These carvings are what in Egypt are called hieroglyphics".

[2] We crossed the valley and on entering the plain saw horses and chariots. The horses had various kinds of metal disks on their harness and halters; the chariots were of different types, some carved to represent eagles, some whales, some stags with antlers, some unicorns. Also finally we saw some waggons with stables at either side of them. But when we came near the horses and chariots both disappeared, and we saw in their place people walking in twos, conversing and reasoning. The angel told me: "The kinds of horses, chariots and stables which can be seen at a distance are appearances of the rational intelligence of the people of that age. For a horse stands by correspondence for the understanding of truth, a chariot for its teaching, and stables for lessons. You know that in this world everything has an appearance in keeping with its correspondence".

[3] Passing these by we climbed a long ascent and at length we saw the city, which we entered. As we walked through, we looked at their houses from the streets and squares. They were all palaces built of marble. In front they had steps of alabaster, and at the sides of the steps columns of jasper. We also saw temples of precious stones, sapphire and azure coloured. "Their houses", said the angel, "are built of stones, because stones stand for natural truths, precious stones for spiritual truths. All the people who lived in the silver age were made intelligent by spiritual truths, and thus by natural truths. The meaning of silver is similar".

[4] As we toured the city, we saw here and there people in pairs, and since they were husbands and wives, we waited to be invited in somewhere. While we had this in mind, as we went past we were called back by two people and invited to their home. We went up and inside it. The angel spoke with them for me, explaining the reasons for my visit to this heaven. "It is", he told them, "so that he can learn about marriage among the people of antiquity, of whom you here are representatives".

"We came", they replied, "from the peoples of Asia. Our age was devoted to the study of truths, the means by which we acquired intelligence—this was the kind of thing that appealed to our souls and minds. But the thing that appealed to our bodily senses was devising forms to represent truths. Our knowledge of correspondences made a link between our bodily sensations and the perceptions of our minds, so giving us intelligence".

[5] After hearing this the angel begged them to tell us something about marriage among them. "There is", said the husband, "a correspondence between the spiritual marriage, that is, of truth with good, and the natural marriage, that is, of a man with one wife. Being students of correspondences, we saw that the church with its kinds of truth and good could not possibly exist except among those who live in truly conjugial love with one wife. For the marriage of good and truth makes the church in the individual. All of us, therefore, who are here now, assert that the husband is truth and the wife the truth's own good. Good cannot love any

Chapter Four—The Ancient Churches

truth but its own, nor can truth return that love to any but its own good. In other circumstances the inner marriage which makes the church would be lost, and the marriage would become merely outward; and it is not the church, but idolatry, to which this corresponds. We therefore call marriage with one wife a sacrament; but if it happened in our community with more than one, we should call that a sacrilege".

[6] Following this speech we were taken into an ante-chamber, where there were many devices on the walls and small pictures which looked as if cast in silver. "What are these?" I asked.

"They are", they said, "paintings and forms which depict for us many qualities, attributes and pleasures belonging to conjugial love. One group depicts the unity of souls, another the linking of minds, another the harmony of hearts, another the delights which arise from these".

As we gazed, we saw a kind of rainbow on the wall composed of three colours, purple, blue and white. We noted how the purple colour passed through the blue and turned the white dark blue; and this colour then flowed back through the blue into the purple, enhancing it so as to resemble a flaming ray.

[7] "You understand that?" the husband said to me. "Tell me", I replied. "The purple colour", he said, "because of its correspondence stands for the wife's conjugial love; the white colour stands for the husband's intelligence. The blue stands for the beginnings of conjugial love as perceived in the husband by the wife, and the dark blue, which tinged the white, stands for the conjugial love then present in the husband. This colour, flowing back through the blue into the purple and enhancing it so as to resemble a flaming ray, means the husband's conjugial love flowing back to the wife. We see such things depicted on our walls, when we think about conjugial love, its natural, successive and simultaneous union, and fix our gaze upon the rainbows depicted there".

To this I said, "These matters are more than mysterious to us today, since they are a way of picturing the secrets of the conjugial love of one man with one wife". "Yes, that is so", he replied, "but they are no secrets to us here, so not mysteries either".

[8] When he had said this, a chariot was seen a long way off, pulled by white ponies. On seeing it the angel said, "That chariot is a sign for us to leave". Then when we came down the steps, our host gave us a bunch of white grapes with vine-leaves attached; these leaves suddenly turned silver. We took them away as a token of our conversation with the peoples of the silver age.

Chapter Five—
The Second Ancient Church

Alternative concepts:

The Bronze or Copper Age;

Heber;

Autumn; Afternoon; Youth;

A Natural-Spiritual Church.

As mentioned in the last chapter, most of what Swedenborg says about the Ancient Church applies to both the First and Second Ancient Churches, so that much of what is said in the last chapter applies to the second church too. In this chapter are gathered passages applicable particularly to the Second Ancient Church.

INTRODUCTORY

> Once this [first Ancient] Church had been laid in ruins a new Church originating in Heber came into being, which was called the Hebrew Church. This existed in Syria and Mesopotamia, and also among other nations in the land of Canaan. But it differed from the Ancient Church in that it made sacrifices the essential requirement of external worship. It did, it is true, acknowledge charity as the inner substance of worship, but not so much with the heart as the Ancient Church had done.
>
> *Arcana Caelestia* §4680.3

> The first Ancient Church meant by Noah and his sons was not confined to a few people but was spread throughout many kingdoms [. . .] Subsequently however, a certain type of external worship started in Syria which spread

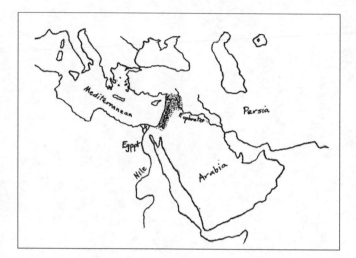

Fig. 13 Limited Extent of the Second Ancient Church.

far and wide from there and through many countries, particularly Canaan. It was a different form of worship from the worship of the Ancient Church. Because something of a Church arose in this way, that was separate from the Ancient Church, a new Church so to speak rose up from it which may therefore be called the second Ancient Church. Heber (or Eber) was its first founder, and therefore this Church took its name from Heber. As stated already, everybody at that time was distinguished into separate houses, families, and nations. One nation recognized one father from whom it also took its name, as is clear throughout the Word, the nation which recognized Heber as its father thus being called the Hebrew nation.

Arcana Caelestia §1238.2

Whereas the Adamic and Noachian Churches were spread over three continents, the Church of Heber seems to have been limited to a relatively small area, what we today sometimes call the Levant and was in biblical times called Canaan. Nevertheless it probably contained a fair proportion of the more developed population of the world at the time. Today it is the area covered by Syria, Lebanon, Israel and Jordan, an area coincident with what historians call the fertile crescent. Its inhabitants were the Canaanites who seem always

Fig. 14 The Phoenician Alphabet.

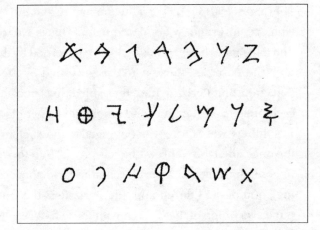

to have lived there and still continue to do so, even if large sections of the population have been forcibly moved from time to time.[1]

It should be noted, however, that the terms Canaan and Canaanite vary in their meaning, both in the Bible and hence in Swedenborg's expositions of the Bible. Canaan can mean the whole area between the Nile and the Euphrates, or it may just mean something like southern Syria and northern Israel. The Canaanites of the Bible lived in this smaller area, but had a wider influence in the earlier time we are now discussing.

Unlike its neighbours Mesopotamia and Egypt, Canaan perhaps lacked geographical unity, and although one race, the Canaanites were never one nation in the political sense. Nevertheless the Canaanite culture was comparable to those of Egypt and Mesopotamia. Many considerable independent city states, such as Ebla and Ugarit, grew up with highly developed commerce and culture. They invented the alphabet and some of their number—whom we now call the Phoenicians—spread their culture throughout the Mediterranean. Hebrew was a Canaanite dialect.

The Church of Heber is perhaps the first clear example of what Swedenborgians call the 'specific church'. It exhibited two necessary characteristics of such churches; the ability to nurture or record the Word, and then to spread it among other nations of the 'universal church'. Ugarit had trade links all over the eastern Mediterranean and Middle East and its scribes recorded ten different languages in five different scripts.[2]

[In Genesis 34:30, 31] 'To the Canaanite and the Perizzite' means those who are governed by good and truth. This is clear from the meaning of 'the Canaanite' here as those who are governed by the good of the Church, and 'the Perizzite' those who are governed by the truth of the Church. Canaanite and Perizzite have these meanings because the Ancient Church continued to exist in that land among those people [. . .] For in that land [. . .] there were those who belonged to the Ancient Church, in particular the one called the Hebrew Church [. . .] Therefore so long as the Church or something like the Church remained with them 'the Canaanites' meant the good of the Church and 'the Perizzites' the truth of the Church. But once everything of the Church with these had reached its end 'Canaanite' means evil and 'Perizzite' falsity.

Arcana Caelestia §4517

For a while in Genesis the Canaanites have a good symbolism and suggest that a healthy and spiritual church prospered there. Measured in terms of biblical verses not for long, but probably for many centuries in historical terms. By the time we get into the period of the Exodus, however, they are regarded as decadent, even if a certain amount of intermarriage with Israelites does go on.

WORSHIP

In the Hebrew Church [. . .] all worship was linked to sacrifices. This may be recognized from the fact that sacrifices were offered daily, and many at every feast. They were also offered when people were to be admitted into priestly functions or were to undergo purification; and there were sin-offerings and guilt-offerings, as well as those made as a consequence of vows, and those that were free-will offerings.

Arcana Caelestia §6905

The altar was [. . .] fundamental to the worship in the Ancient Church that was called the Hebrew Church, and therefore every single thing that

Chapter Five—The Second Ancient Church

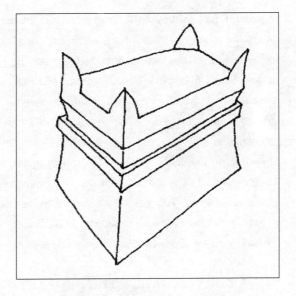

Fig. 15 A Canaanite Altar. They were made of metal or wood covered in metal. The 'horns' on the corners prevented carcasses from falling off.

went into the construction of the altar was representative, such as its dimensions—its height, breadth, and length—its stones, its network of bronze, its horns; and so was the fire which was kept burning on it perpetually; and above all the sacrifices and burnt offerings. What they represented were the truths and goods which are the Lord's and which come from the Lord. These were the internal things of worship which, because they were represented in that external object, were alike and took the same form as the truths and goods of the Most Ancient Church. Its dimensions—its height, breadth, and length—meant in general the good, the truth, and the holiness from these. 'Its stones' meant in particular those truths that are more basic. 'The bronze' from which the network around the altar was made meant natural good. 'The horns' meant the power of truth that springs from good. 'The fire' on the altar meant love. 'The sacrifices and burnt offerings' meant celestial and spiritual things, according to their various kinds. From all this it becomes clear that internal things were to be contained within external ones [. . .]

Arcana Caelestia §4489.2

In general the qualities of the Second Ancient Church are similar to those of the First, and to the religions (Swedenborg would call them churches) which were only decaying remnants of the former Ancient Church. The members of the Second Church, however, seem to be fairly obsessive traditionalists, not unlike the Jews who will claim descent from them. They carefully retain the religious practices of the Ancient Church which express spiritual correspondences, although they may not fully understand the symbols.

The picture Swedenborg draws of their worship is typical of many Bronze Age cultures. The prevalence of sacrifices, indicating a materialistic approach to God, elaborate rituals and sacred structures were common in the Middle East, the Mediterranean and elsewhere. He also mentions priests, who would become necessary, in this age of increasing specialization, to supervise ceremonies and religion.

THE ANCIENT WORD IN THE BRONZE AGE

> Next day my angel guide and companion came again, and said: 'Get ready, so that we can visit the inhabitants of heaven in the west, who are some of the people who lived in the third or copper age'.
>
> [...] There are sacred buildings made of olive-wood, and in their centre is a sanctuary containing in a chest the Word which was given to the inhabitants of Asia before the Israelite Word. Its historical books are called *The Wars of Jehovah*, its prophetic books *The Utterances*. Both of these are mentioned by Moses (Numb. 21:14, 15, 27-30).
>
> [...] Then the angel took me to one of the buildings, and we saw the sanctuary in the middle, all in the whitest light. 'The light,' said the angel, 'comes from the ancient Asiatic Word; for all Divine Truth shines in the heavens.'
>
> [...] After this he said, 'Come with me to our treasure house.' So we followed him, and he showed us the scriptures of the most ancient people; they were on boards of wood and stone, and later on books of smoothed tablets. The second age wrote its scriptures on skins; and he

> brought a skin on which the rules of the earliest people had been copied from stone tablets, and among them was that about marriage.
>
> *Conjugial Love* §77

It seems clear from this passage that there was some continuity between the Sacred Scriptures of the Canaanites and the Old Testament. If, as Swedenborg reports, they were recorded on parchment their chances of survival would be slim, as being organic it may decompose and is easily digested by insects. The earliest record of surviving parchment was at Pergamum in 196 BC, but there is good reason to think it may have been used earlier. Papyrus, which was utilized in a similar way, was widely used before it and examples are recorded in Egypt from as early as 2650 BC.[3]

> It was related to me by angels of heaven that there was a Word among the Ancients written by pure correspondences, but that it was lost; and I was told that it is still preserved among them, and is in use among the Ancients in their heaven who had that Word when they were in the world. Those Ancients, among whom that Word is still in use in heaven, were in part from the land of Canaan and from its neighbouring countries, as Syria, Mesopotamia, Arabia, Chaldea, Assyria, Egypt, Sidon, Tyre and Nineveh. The inhabitants of all these kingdoms were in representative worship, and consequently were versed in the science of correspondences. The wisdom of that time was derived from that science, and by its means they had interior perception and communication with the heavens. Those who had an interior knowledge of the correspondences of that Word were called wise and intelligent, but in later times, diviners and magi.
>
> But because that Word was full of such correspondences as remotely signified celestial and spiritual things and consequently began to be falsified by many, therefore of the Lord's Divine Providence it gradually disappeared in course of time, and at length was lost; and another Word was given, written by correspondences not so remote; and this was given through the Prophets among the Children of Israel. In this Word, however, there

were retained many names of places in the land of Canaan and in parts of Asia round about; and in this Word they signify the same things as in the Ancient Word. It was for this reason that Abram was commanded to go to that land, and that his posterity from Jacob were introduced into it.

Doctrine of the Sacred Scripture §102

DECLINE

That 'Terah' means idolatrous worship becomes clear from the derivatives mentioned from verse 20 [of Genesis Chapter 11] down to this point. This second Ancient Church declined from a kind of internal worship, becoming adulterated as it did so until in the end it became idolatrous, as Churches usually do. They pass from internal things to external, ending up with mere externals when internal things have been erased. The fact that the same happened to this Church, even to the extent that a large part of them did not acknowledge Jehovah as God but worshipped other gods, is clear in Joshua,

Joshua said to all the people, Thus said Jehovah, the God of Israel, Your fathers dwelt of old beyond the River, Terah, the father of Abraham and the father of Nahor, and they served other gods. Josh. 24:2.

[. . .] From this it is quite evident that Terah, Abram, and Nahor were idolaters.

Arcana Caelestia §1356

The third and fourth states of that church, which were its devastation and consummation, are described here and there in the Word, in both its historical and its prophetical parts. The consummation of the nations round about the Jordan, or round about the land of Canaan, is described by the destruction of Sodom, Gomorrah, Admah, and Zeboiim (Genesis 14 and 19); the consummation of the church of the nations within the

Jordan, or in the land of Canaan, is described in Joshua and in the book of Judges by the expulsion of some and the extermination of others. The consummation of that Church in Egypt is described by the drowning of Pharaoh and the Egyptians in the Red Sea (Exodus 14).

Coronis §41.3

The decline of the Second Ancient Church is pictured in several chapters of Genesis, leading to the destruction of Sodom and Gomorrah and later the campaigns of Joshua. At the same time, however, God is laying the foundations of a new church through Abraham, although he worships idols. Abraham shows himself to be willing to separate from his decadent heritage and follow Jehovah. Through his descendants Isaac, Jacob and Joseph, he becomes the foundation of a new church, based not on voluntary acceptance of the truth, but on blind obedience to rules and law. The law was symbolized especially by Moses. This is the Israelite Church which is the subject of our next chapter.

*

MARRIAGE LOVE IN THE BRONZE AGE
From Swedenborg's *Conjugial Love* §77

Next day my angel guide and companion came again, and said: "Get ready, so that we can visit the inhabitants of heaven in the west, who are some of the people who lived in the third or copper age. Their homes extend from the south through the west towards, but not into, the north".

When I was ready, I accompanied him, and we entered their heaven on its southern side. There we found a magnificent wood composed of palms and laurels. We passed through this, and then exactly on the border of the west we saw some giants twice as tall as the average human. They asked us: "Who let you in through the wood?" "The God of heaven", said the angel. "We", they answered, "are the guardians of the approach to the ancient western heaven; but you may go in".

[2] We passed through and from a view-point we saw a mountain soaring to the clouds. Between the view-point where we were and the mountain we saw one village after another, with gardens, woodland and fields between them. After passing through the villages we reached the mountain and climbed it. Its summit turned out to be not a peak, but a plain, on which was a large and spacious city. All its houses were of the wood of resinous trees, and their roofs of planks.

"Why", I asked, "are the houses here made of wood?" "Because", the angel answered, "wood stands for natural good, which was the good of the people of the earth's third age. Copper also stands for natural good, so the early people called this the copper age. There are also sacred buildings here made of olive-wood, and in their centre is a sanctuary containing in a chest the Word which was given to the inhabitants of Asia before the Israelite Word. Its historical books are called The Wars of Jehovah, its prophetic books The Utterances. Both of these are mentioned by Moses (Numb. 21:14, 15, 27-30). This Word is now lost in the kingdoms of Asia and is only preserved in Great Tartary".

Then the angel took me to one of the buildings, and we saw the sanctuary in the middle, all in the whitest light. "The light", said the angel, "comes from the ancient Asiatic Word; for all Divine truth shines in the heavens".

[3] On leaving the building we heard that the presence of two strangers had been reported in the city, and they were to be questioned about their origin and what business they had there. An officer hurried up to us from the assembly and summoned us to court. Asked where we came from, and what our business was there, we replied, "We have passed through the palm-tree forest and also the homes of the giants, who are the guardians of your heaven, and after that the region of villages. You can tell from that that it is not we ourselves, but the God of heaven, who has brought us here. Our business here is to learn about your marriages, whether you are monogamous or polygamous". "What does polygamous mean?" they answered. "Is it not the same as promiscuous?"

[4] Then this court of law delegated an intelligent man to take us home and teach us about this subject. When he reached home, he asked his wife to join him, and then spoke as follows. "The earliest or most ancient people, who enjoyed truly conjugial love, so that they excelled others in the strength and power of that love while in the world, and who now live in the most blessed condition in their own heaven in the east, handed on commandments about marriage for us to keep. We are their descendants, and like fathers to sons they gave us rules of life, amongst which are these about marriage. "Children, if you wish to love God and the neighbour and to be wise and happy for ever, we advise you to adopt a monogamous life. If you depart from this commandment, all heavenly love will desert you, and along with it inner wisdom, and you will be banished". We have obeyed, as sons should, this commandment of our fathers, and we have seen how true it is. To the extent that anyone loves his wife alone, to that extent he becomes a heavenly and an inward person. To the extent that anyone does not love his wife alone, to that extent he becomes a natural and an outward person; and he loves only himself and the ideas he thinks up, becoming mentally unbalanced and foolish".

[5] 'This is why we in this heaven are all monogamous, and being so, we keep all the borders of our heaven closed to polygamists, adulterers and fornicators. If polygamists break in, they are cast out into the darkness of the north; if adulterers, into the furnaces of the west; if fornicators, into the deceptive lights of the south".

On hearing this I asked what he meant by the darkness of the north, the furnaces of the west and the deceptive lights of the south. He replied that the darkness of the north was darkness of mind and ignorance of truths; the furnaces of the west were loves for evil; and the deceptive lights of the south were falsifications of truth. These are types of spiritual fornication.

[6] After this he said, "Come with me to our treasure house". So we followed him, and he showed us the scriptures of the most ancient people;

they were on boards of wood and stone, and later on books of smoothed tablets. The second age wrote its scriptures on skins; and he brought a skin on which the rules of the earliest people had been copied from stone tablets, and among them was that about marriage.

[7] When we had looked at these and other things remarkable for their extreme antiquity, the angel said, "It is now time for us to leave". Then our host went out into the garden and plucked a few twigs from a tree, which he tied into a bundle, and gave it to is with these words, "These are twigs from a tree native and restricted to our heaven; its sap smells sweetly of balsam". We brought this bundle with us as we came down by a path close to the east, where there were no guards. The twigs we saw turn to shining bronze, and their tips to gold; this was a sign that we had visited the people of the third age, which is called the copper or bronze age.

Chapter Six—
The Israelite and Jewish Churches

Alternative concepts:

The Iron Age;

The Old Testament;

Winter; Evening; Adolescence;

A Natural Church.

By the Jews in the Word are meant all who are of the Church and acknowledge the Lord, and that by the land of Canaan, into which [. . .] they are to be led, is meant the Lord's Church.

Divine Providence §260

INTRODUCTORY

A new Church was established [. . .] among the descendants of Jacob. That which was called the Jewish Church was nothing other than a Church representative of charity and faith. In that Church, that is, among the descendants of Jacob, no charity or faith existed, and therefore no Church existed but merely the representative of a Church. This was so because direct communication of the Lord's kingdom in the heavens with any true Church on earth was not possible, and therefore an indirect communication by means of representatives was effected.

Arcana Caelestia §1850.3

[. . .] the Church of the Gentiles, [. . .] is represented by Esau, and the Jewish Church is represented by Jacob; and this is the reason for its being

so often said that the Jews should acknowledge the Gentiles as brethren; and in the Church of the Gentiles, or primitive Church, all were called brethren, from charity.

Arcana Caelestia §367.2

In this age the differentiation between the 'specific' and 'universal' churches was at its most pronounced. The Jews may have been encouraged to 'acknowledge the Gentiles as brethren', but they nevertheless regarded themselves as a separate and special people. In a sense Swedenborg took a similar attitude. He mentions the Iron Age in *Conjugial Love* and elsewhere. Also he makes more frequent references to the Church of the Gentiles around the Jewish period—which we mention later. But his main interest at this time was the small Jewish Church; doubtless because of the enormous influence it would have on later history. It was they who had 'the Word', and indeed, it was their destiny to actually act out its message in the symbolic sagas of the Old Testament.

But what exactly does Swedenborg mean us to understand by the Israelite or Jewish Church? He uses both terms and in general tends to use Israelite for the earlier phase and Jewish for the later period, but he may nevertheless use Jewish at any time—as in *Arcana Caelestia* §367 above.

I suggest that we today have three concepts of this Church. Firstly, there are the twelve tribes of Israel of the Old Testament.

Secondly, we have the 'post-Babylonian exile' Jews, the writers and readers of the Old Testament rather than its actors, basically the tribe of Judah which remained intact after the northern tribes had been dispersed by the Assyrians. It was the Jewish scribes who were the authors or editors of the Old Testament; who wrote down the history of their race as they interpreted it.

But archaeologists and historians have caused us to realize that, although the Old Testament epic is based on fact, the story has been 'mythologized' by the Jews. So thirdly we have the actual 'historic' Israelites, who probably lived out a somewhat different life to what is pictured in the Bible.

Swedenborg lived well before archaeologists led us to doubt the complete historic veracity of the Old Testament. He must nevertheless have realized the Bible was not pure history as he had other sources of information. In his *Spiritual Diary* he records meetings in the other world with Moses and with David (§§6107, 3674). In these reports Moses seemed to be a shadow of the dynamic leader of the Exodus, and David to exhibit the bad rather than good aspects of the biblical character. This inconsistency would not have unduly worried Swedenborg, however, as he realized the relative unimportance of the literal sense of Scripture, compared with its more essential purpose carrying the spiritual senses. The Jewish Church he offers us is a racially consistent body of people through the centuries, with limited spiritual aspirations. But he presents their story in the Old Testament as being much more than just a national history. It is also a symbolic saga of our spiritual development.

THE JEWISH CHARACTER
(at the time of the Jewish church, 1st Millenium BC)

> The character of that nation is such that they adore external things, and so idols, more than all other nations do; they have no desire whatever to know about internal things. For they are the most avaricious of all nations; and avarice, which with them is such that gold or silver is loved for its own sake and not for the sake of any useful purpose, is an extremely earthly desire.
>
> *Arcana Caelestia* §8301.6

How odd of God
To choose the Jews

So runs the epigrammatic couplet by Ogden Nash. Swedenborg had been brought up to feel much the same and frequently makes derogatory comments about them like that above. However, these observations were generalizations, often made to counteract any impression that the Jews were 'God's chosen people' because they were especially virtuous, rather than because they were obstinate and over-meticulous; the actual reason. A 'stiff-necked people' as Yahweh commented to Moses on more than one occasion. The other side of the coin, however, is that they valued tradition and obedience, even if they did not always practise those virtues. Occasionally Swedenborg does mention that there were good Jews, but generally he dwells on their weaknesses.

Anti-Semitism was common in eighteenth-century Europe and Swedenborg was a man of his times in this respect (although far less critical than Luther). But after all Moses, Samuel and the Prophets were equally critical of their race, if not more so. Perhaps the Jews were chosen for their bad image. The Old Testament is largely a parable about how evil attacks us and how easily we can fall prey to its wiles if we are not careful. The Lord therefore chose a nation susceptible to temptation and sensuality to act out such a story, a nation who would epitomize mankind's adolescence. So we should not be surprised by the less than complimentary comments which follow.

(Swedenborg does, however, express a good opinion of them for their faithful preservation of the letter of the Word, which is mentioned below. See also comments on the Jews in Chapters 7 and 8.)

> [The] Jewish nation [...] did not know what any of the symbolism [in the Word] signified; for they were altogether natural people, and therefore they were neither able nor willing to know anything about the spiritual person and his faith and love.
>
> *On the Sacred Scripture* §19

Moses won for that nation the concession that it should represent the Church even though they were by nature such that no [truly spiritual] Church could be established among them. No Church can exist among those whose interest lies in things on an outward level devoid of what is inward, because the Church resides [...] on an inward level and not on an outward one devoid of the inward. For a person is in contact with heaven and with the Lord through the inward level [...] But although the children of Israel were by nature such that it was impossible for them to have any contact with heaven through the inward level, they were nevertheless able to represent such things as belonged to the Church and heaven. This was accomplished solely by means of outward things to which inward ones correspond; and it was on account of this that they were accepted.

Arcana Caelestia §10698

They were such that they revered their fathers—Abraham, Isaac, and Jacob, and later on Moses and David—as demi-gods. In addition they venerated as being holy and Divine, and worshipped, every piece of stone or wood dedicated to their worship of God, such as the Ark, the tables there, the lampstand, the altar, Aaron's vestments, [. . .] and later on the temple. By means of outward things such as these, at that time, communication of the angels of heaven with mankind was in the Lord's providence made possible.

Arcana Caelestia §8588.4 (see also §3478)

If the only purpose of a church was to lead souls to heaven, Swedenborg seems to suggest that the Jewish Church was not very effective. However, as it was a 'specific church' it also had the role of providing the 'form' into which the Lord could pour the 'substance' of His Word. The essential task of the members of the Jewish Church was therefore to provide the means by which the Lord could reveal such a Word. However, as they lacked interest in spiritual matters, it was going to be difficult to involve them in such a project.

Therefore, just as He led them to perform physical rituals which symbolized spiritual activities, He involved them in the preparation of a national history of their entry into the Holy Land which would symbolize our path to heaven. They were to be the actors in a divine symbolic drama. Their battles would symbolize our battles with temptation. Swedenborg says the inner and outer layers of that story are symbolized by the two sets of tablets on which Jehovah wrote the Law and then gave to Moses. The first were hewn by Jehovah himself, but they were then broken by Moses (Exodus 32). Later, however, Jehovah authorized a second set of tablets, but they were hewn not by Jehovah, but by Moses (Exodus 34).

The breaking by Moses of the tablets which were the work of God, when he saw the calf and the dances, and the hewing by Moses, as commanded by Jehovah, of other tablets, which then had the same words inscribed on them (so that the tablets were no longer the work of God but the work of Moses, though the writing was still the writing of God), hold an arcanum [spiritual secret] unknown up to now.

The arcanum is that the literal sense of the Word would have been different if the Word had been written among another people, or if the character of the Israelite people had not been such as it was. For the literal sense of the Word is all about that people [...] as is evident from both the historical sections and the prophetical parts of the Word. They were a people steeped in evil because they were idolatrous at heart; yet in order that the internal sense and the external sense might be in agreement that people had to be highly acclaimed, and to be called God's people, a holy nation, and a peculiar treasure. Consequently the simple, who would be taught by means of the outward sense of the Word, would believe that that nation was all those things, as that nation itself also believes, and indeed as the majority in the Christian world do at the present day.

Furthermore most of the things that present themselves in and constitute the outward sense of the Word were ones that were permitted on account of their hardness of heart, such as those referred to in Matt. 19:8. [Jewish divorce laws.]

Arcana Caelestia §10453.3

Thus divorce, bloodshed, slavery, physical punishments, sexual discrimination and other questionable Jewish practices are presented as acceptable in the Old Testament. In the inner sense, however, such things represent the relationships of parts of our minds as we will find later when we examine the Jewish Word.

ESTABLISHMENT OF THE CHURCH

[...] the Jewish representative Church had its beginnings in Abraham and was re-established among his descendants from Jacob [...]

Arcana Caelestia §3778.1

> Jacob's actual sons did not constitute any Church but their descendants did, though not until after they had come out of Egypt, and in actual fact not until they entered the land of Canaan.
>
> *Arcana Caelestia* §4430.2

> The first state for the Children of Israel consisted in the Lord Jehovih's[1] appearing, calling, and making a covenant; and from the Word we learn that He did these three things first with Abram, secondly with Moses and thirdly with all the people.
>
> *Coronis* §49

> The third [church] was the Israelite Church, begun by the proclamation of the Ten Commandments on Mount Sinai, and continued through the Word written by Moses and the Prophets.
>
> *The True Christian Religion* §760

Just as religion takes time to develop in us as individuals, the picture we are given of the establishment of this Church is of a process so gradual that Swedenborg takes over ten volumes of the *Arcana* to comment upon it. The Jewish Church is not so much a new creation as a development from the Second Ancient or Hebrew Church to which Abraham belongs. Like Noah he represents the 'remnant' of the old church from which a new church will be formed.

Abraham, Isaac and Jacob are a celestial/spiritual/natural trine and as the Jewish Church is to be a 'natural' church it is not surprising that we hear little of Isaac and that the biblical story centres round Jacob. Jacob displays all the cunning that will be typical of many of his descendants, but he improves and is given the new name Israel, by which his descendants and their land will also be known.

Instruction

> The second state of this Church, following on in order from the first, consisted in instruction, for when anyone is called to the Church he must receive instruction in religious commands in accordance with which he will

conduct his life. The fact that the Children of Israel received such instruction after being called is evident from the announcement of the Law on Mount Sinai, which holds within itself all the commandments to do with love and belief in God and all those to do with love and faithfulness to the neighbour. After instruction concerning general commands about what to believe, there followed a public declaration of a large number of laws that were called judgements and statutes, which had regard to keeping the Sabbath holy, establishing feasts, sacrifices, the priesthood, the Tabernacle [. . .] all of which were natural representatives corresponding to spiritual realities.

Coronis §52

The instruction of the Israelites was carried out through Moses who was providentially saved for, and prepared for, the task with the help of Pharaoh's daughter as we read in Exodus Chapter 2.

Since it had been preordained that Moses should represent the Lord in respect of the law of God or the Word, [. . .] the incident therefore took place in which, when he was an infant, he was put in a box or little ark, though a crude one because that law was in its very earliest beginnings and because there was merely a representative of it lying there in the ark. But later on the real law of God, after it [. . . was made manifest on] Mount Sinai, was put in an ark, called the Ark of the Testimony.

Arcana Caelestia §6723.3

'[. . .] Pharaoh's daughter' means an affection for factual knowledge. [. . .] Factual knowledge is what those who are being regenerated must learn first, for that knowledge is the groundwork for things that compose the understanding, and the understanding is what receives the truth of faith, and the truth of faith what receives the good of charity. From this it may be seen that factual knowledge constitutes the first level to be laid down when a person is being regenerated.

Arcana Caelestia §6750

Fig. 16 An Egyptian Princess.

> '[I will call his name Moses] because I drew him out of the water' means a deliverance from falsities. This is clear from the meaning of 'the water', here the water of the river of Egypt, as falsities.
>
> *Arcana Caelestia* §6753

The Israelites still had many false ideas from the decadent Canaanite religions, but Moses is withdrawn from the Israelites and given to Pharaoh's daughter, in whose care he develops 'an affection for factual knowledge'. This will be the foundation upon which he can build a new understanding of spiritual truths for the Church.

On the other hand we learn in Exodus 4:10 that Moses was 'slow of speech and slow of tongue', and that it was therefore necessary for Aaron to speak for him. Again a reference to the divine truth (represented by Moses) being presented by the Jews (Aaron) in their own way.

We cannot be sure to what extent Moses wrote The Five Books of Moses, but it seems likely that he may well have laid the groundwork for the epic. It also seems likely that he received a good education in Pharaoh's court which prepared him for the task. There is even a case for suggesting that some biblical passages are drawn from Egyptian sources. As well as receiving education, being brought up as an aristocrat may have given him other advantages.

> 'And also you have found grace in My eyes' means that he was accepted because he had the ability to head that nation. [. . .] the Lord foresaw

that Moses would head the Israelite people. His foresight of this is evident from the fact that Moses was brought up in the court of Pharaoh the king where rule was exercised, and where he gained an air of authority over others. It was for this reason also that he was accepted to head that nation. In addition to this his character was such that he was better able than others from that nation to receive what would be uttered by the Divine, for the external in his case was not so separate from the internal as it was with that nation.

Arcana Caelestia §10563

Because Moses represented the Law he was allowed to go in to the Lord on Mount Sinai, not only to receive there the tablets containing the Law but also to hear the statutes and judgements belonging to the Law, and to enjoin these commands on the people. It is also said that the people should therefore believe in Moses forever.

Arcana Caelestia §6752.8

Entering Canaan

The land of Canaan [. . .] was to be given to them as a possession, for the reason that they might represent the celestial and spiritual things of the Lord's kingdom and Church and that among them a representative Church might be established, and because the Lord was to be born in that land.

Arcana Caelestia §1447

[. . .] all the wars that were being waged [. . .] against the idolatrous inhabitants of the land of Canaan represented the Lord's conflicts with hell, and consequently the conflicts of His Church, and of members of the Church.

Arcana Caelestia §1664.9

The reason the Church existed there [in Canaan . . .] was that the member of the Most Ancient Church, [. . .] was the kind of person who saw within every single object in the world something representative of the Lord's kingdom; the objects of the world being to him the means of thinking about heavenly things. Worldly objects were the things that enabled him to think about heavenly realities. This was the origin of all the representatives and meaningful signs that were afterward known in the Ancient Church [. . .] This is how it came to pass that every place, and also every mountain and river, in the land of Canaan, where the most ancient people dwelt, and likewise all the kingdoms round about, became representative. As the Word could not be written unless representatives and meaningful signs were used, including those connected with places, for the sake of this end the church was successively preserved in the land of Canaan.

Arcana Caelestia §5136.2

Canaan is the archetypal symbol of heaven. History suggests that the Israelite tribes had always lived in Canaan,[2] nevertheless the Bible highlights every occasion when members of the tribes migrated in or out of the land. Abram's entry, Jacob's return from Haran, Jacob's and Joseph's desire to be buried there, the Israelite conquest under Joshua, David's conquest of Jerusalem and extension of the Kingdom, and the Jews' return from Babylon are all given prominence. Their most important annual feast was the Passover celebrating the return to Canaan. So in symbolic stories we are shown the way to heaven. However, as these stories are so well known we will return to the central theme of the nature of the Jewish Church.

CONCEPT OF GOD

The Jews are often given the credit for establishing monotheism, and for our Christian culture this is largely true. But sadly for the Jews Swedenborg even denies them that credit. He had a wider time perspective and as we have already noted his Most Ancient and Ancient Churches were monotheistic, at least until they declined; a fact which anthropology now more generally supports.[3] He also points out that for much of their history the Israelites were polytheists. They preferred Jehovah, but assumed that other gods existed. True monotheism was only developed in its later stages in the time of Isaiah.

The Jewish Church [...] did in fact believe that Jehovah was Man as well as God, because He had appeared to Moses and the Prophets as a human being. [...] Yet their idea of Him was no different from ideas the gentiles had of their gods, though they preferred Jehovah God because He could work miracles.

Arcana Caelestia §4692.3

For Swedenborg monotheism is normality; it is polytheism that was invented.

[...] the nations in the world, who are possessed of religion and sound reason, insist that God is one: all the Mohammedans in their empires, the Africans in many kingdoms of their continent, and the peoples of Asia in several of theirs, not to mention the present-day Jews. The most ancient people of the Golden Age, those who had any religion, worshipped one God.

The True Christian Religion §9.2

Swedenborg comments that the frequent misunderstanding that our merciful God can ever be angry was especially common with the Jews; also that they misunderstood the concept of the Messiah as it developed in their Scriptures.

The Word attributes anger to Jehovah or the Lord because of the very general truth that all things come from God, thus the bad as well as the good. But this very general truth, which young children, older ones, and simple people need to have, must at a later stage be clarified. That is to say, it must be shown that bad things are assignable to man, though they may seem to be assignable to God, and have been declared to be so to the end that people may learn to fear God [...] and may then come to love Him. Fear must come before love in order that love may have holy fear within it.

[...] Furthermore it was by means of punishments that the Israelites and the Jews were compelled to fulfil the external and formal requirements of religious laws and commands. This led them to think that Jehovah was angry and punished them, when in fact they themselves through their idolatrous behaviour were the ones who brought such things upon themselves and cut themselves off from heaven. Their own behaviour brought about their punishments.

Arcana Caelestia §6997

[The Jews] had no other idea of the Messiah or Christ than one who would be a very great prophet, greater than Moses, and a very great king, greater than David, who would lead them into the land of Canaan to the accompaniment of amazing miracles. Of His heavenly kingdom they did not wish to hear anything at all, for the reason that they grasped none but worldly ideas since they were people separated from charity.

Arcana Caelestia §4692.3

WORSHIP

Sacrifices were the principal representatives in the worship of the Hebrew Church and after this of the Jewish Church. Their sacrifices were made either from the herd or flock, thus from various 'clean' animals, such as oxen, young bulls, goats, sheep, rams, kids, and lambs, besides doves and pigeons. All of these creatures meant the internal features of worship, [. . .] those from the herd meaning celestial-natural, those from the flock celestial-rational. Because both of these—natural things and rational things—are more and more interior and are various, so many genera and so many species of these creatures were therefore employed in sacrifices. This fact becomes clear also from its being laid down [in Leviticus etc.] as to which creatures were to be offered in burnt offerings and also which in every kind of sacrifice—the daily sacrifices; those offered on sabbaths and at festivals; those made as free-will, eucharistic, or votive offerings; and those offered in purifications, cleansings, and also in inaugurations. Which creatures were to be used, and how many, in each kind of sacrifice is mentioned explicitly. This would never have been done unless each one had had some specific meaning.

Arcana Caelestia §2180.2

CLEAN ANIMALS	UNCLEAN ANIMALS
Cattle	Camels
Sheep	Rabbits
Goats	Pigs
Deer	Weasels
Antelopes	Rats
Wild sheep and goats	Lizards
	Animals that walk on paws
Doves	Birds of Prey
Pigeons	Storks
	Herons
Fish with fins and scales	Water creatures without fins or scales
Locusts	Insects 'walking on all fours'
Crickets	Creatures which move on the ground
Grasshoppers	

Fig. 17 List of clean and unclean animals. List based on Leviticus 11 and Deuteronomy 14.

The practice of animal sacrifice was only accepted because it was traditional then (although it does seem to have offered scope for symbolic meaning). The offering of bread within the Tabernacle was more felicitous. But in time animal sacrifices did come to be questioned.

> Sacrifices were by no means acceptable to Jehovah, and so were merely permitted and tolerated [. . .] as is quite evident in the Prophets [. . .]
> In Micah:
> [. . .] *Will Jehovah be pleased with thousands of rams, with tens of*

thousands of rivers of oil? He has shown you, [. . .] *what is good; and what does Jehovah require of you but to carry out judgement, and to love mercy, and to humble yourself by walking with your God?* Micah 6:7-8.

Arcana Caelestia §2180.6

[Concerning washing, it was laid down] that Aaron and his sons should wash their hands and their feet when they entered into the Tent of Meeting, or came near unto the altar to minister; and in other places it is said that those who had become unclean should wash themselves and their garments, and so they would be clean. From this it can be seen that washing represented purification from evils; thus the washing of the body and the garments represented the purification of the heart and mind. Everyone [. . .] can see that the evils of the heart and mind were not wiped away by the washing, but only the uncleanness of the body and the garments; and that after this was wiped away the evils still remained; and that evils cannot possibly be washed away by water, but [only] by repentance.

From all this it is again evident that the things which were instituted among the Israelitish nation were external things that represented internal ones, and that these internal things were the real holy things of the Church among them, and not the external things without the internal things. But this nation nevertheless made all holiness to consist in the external things, and nothing of it in the internal things,

Arcana Caelestia §10235

The Books of Moses detail many other practices and rituals that often had no real value except as symbols. Nevertheless the Jews derived a superstitious satisfaction from the precise execution and repetition of these laws, which was a naïve expression of love on the external and natural level, and which could have been enough to prepare some Jews for entry to the lower heavens.

However, the laws, rituals, and details of the Tabernacle and priest's clothing, had the further value of giving the angels—and eventually the members of the New Church—

perfect symbolic models which could present, in concrete and memorable form, the wonderful and beautiful concepts of the mind of God.

THE HEBREW LANGUAGE

Angelic language has nothing in common with human languages except certain words that are the sounds of a specific affection. [. . .] I have been told that the first language of men on our earth was in agreement with angelic language because they had it from heaven; and that the Hebrew language agrees with it in some respects.

Heaven and Hell §237

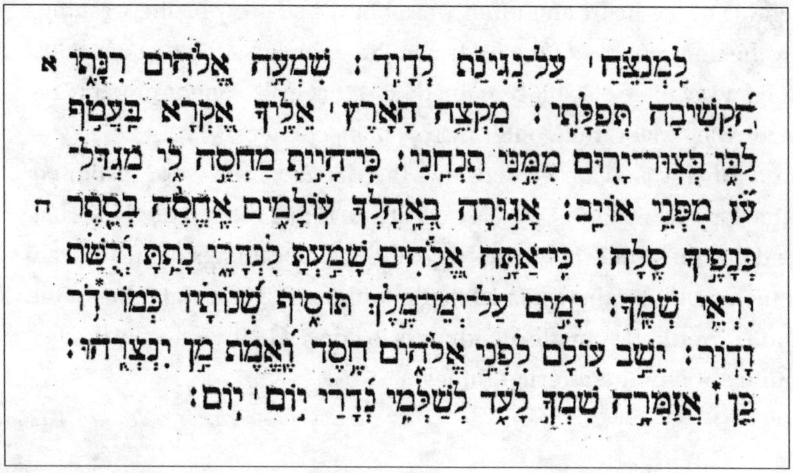

לַמְנַצֵּחַ ׀ עַל־נְגִינַת לְדָוִד ׃ שִׁמְעָה אֱלֹהִים רִנָּתִי א
הַקְשִׁיבָה תְּפִלָּתִי ׃ מִקְצֵה הָאָרֶץ ׀ אֵלֶיךָ אֶקְרָא בַּעֲטֹף
לִבִּי בְּצוּר־יָרוּם מִמֶּנִּי תַנְחֵנִי ׃ כִּי־הָיִיתָ מַחְסֶה לִי מִגְדַּל־
עֹז מִפְּנֵי אוֹיֵב ׃ אָגוּרָה בְאָהָלְךָ עוֹלָמִים אֶחֱסֶה בְסֵתֶר ה
כְּנָפֶיךָ סֶּלָה ׃ כִּי־אַתָּה אֱלֹהִים שָׁמַעְתָּ לִנְדָרָי נָתַתָּ יְרֻשַּׁת
יִרְאֵי שְׁמֶךָ ׃ יָמִים עַל־יְמֵי־מֶלֶךְ תּוֹסִיף שְׁנוֹתָיו כְּמוֹ־דֹר
וָדֹר ׃ יֵשֵׁב עוֹלָם לִפְנֵי אֱלֹהִים חֶסֶד וֶאֱמֶת מַן יִנְצְרֻהוּ ׃
כֵּן ׀ אֲזַמְּרָה שִׁמְךָ לָעַד לְשַׁלְּמִי נְדָרַי יוֹם ׀ יוֹם ׃

Fig. 18 Hebrew Script.

They have the Word in Heaven, and also books. In the spiritual heaven the writing is like writings in the world, with Roman letters; but they are not at all intelligible to those who are in the natural world, for they are in an entirely different language, which is a universal one. [. . .] They have the

Word, likewise; some, according to its internal sense, some, according to the external sense, but yet a more spiritual one [than with us].

In the celestial heaven, however, they have no such writing, but the letters are different, almost like the Hebrew; and there they see in the separate syllables, little jots and tittles.

The Spiritual Diary §§5561-2

As vowels are not essential to a language, but serve by means of tones to elevate the words to the various affections according to each one's state, so in the [original] Hebrew tongue the vowels were not written, and were also variously pronounced. From this a man's quality as to his affection and love is known to the angels. The speech of celestial angels is quite lacking in hard consonants, and it rarely passes from one consonant to another without the interposition of a word beginning with a vowel. This is why in the Word the particle 'and' is so often interposed, as can be confirmed by those who read the Word in the Hebrew language, in which that word is soft, beginning and ending with a vowel sound. Again, in the Word, in Hebrew, it can in some measure be known from the words used whether they belong to the celestial class or the spiritual class, that is, whether they involve good or truth. Those involving good partake largely of the sounds of *u* and *o*, and also somewhat of *a*, while those involving truth partake of the sounds of *e* and *i*.

Heaven and Hell §241

As we noted in the last chapter, the first alphabet was invented in Syria a little to the north of Israel; at the very least, a happy coincidence for the Hebrew word of the Old Testament.

It would seem that providence has moulded the Hebrew language to a form that would serve the needs of divine revelation. It has similarities with heavenly language and can express the discrete differences between the celestial and spiritual degrees. It also has no tenses, no future or past, which could be because it is intended to express 'eternal' truths. (When rendered into other languages with tenses, however, the translators have had to assume tenses from the context.)

That is why by the Lord's Divine providence those books have been kept intact, down to the last jot, from the time when they were written, by the care taken by many scribes who counted even the smallest details in them. This provision by the Lord was to guard the holiness which each jot, letter and word in them possesses.

Last Judgment §41.3

The Word is Divine in all its details, not only in the words, but also in the syllables and letters; and hence may be known what that signifies, that not the least jot or tittle should perish, and why the Jews have been made to count the separate letters. And that they have believed mysteries to be in every least constituent of a letter, although they have not been aware in what way.

The Spiritual Diary §5621

[The Jewish] nation has been preserved and dispersed over a great part of the world for the sake of the Word in its original language, which they more than Christians hold sacred; [. . .] for it is Divine Truth [. . .] proceeding from the Lord and by means of this the Word becomes the conjunction of the Lord with the Church and the presence of heaven with man. [. . .] This is the end which the Divine Providence has in view, in preserving and dispersing them over a great part of the world.

Divine Providence §260.3

Needless to say, the preservation of the Word is a matter of prime importance for the establishment and consolidation of the Church. The true message of the Ancient Word was gradually lost because those who copied it could not resist the temptation to modify it to suit their own purposes. A new strategy was required.

Given a new ethical and spiritual philosophy the Israelites would not have been aware of its value, except at the most practical level. Neither would they much value the sort of moral myths and fables that made up the Ancient Word. Such a new revelation would have then shared the fate of the Ancient Word. The Lord therefore gave them something they would value, a patriotic historic saga, something that they would identify with personally. Some of the myths of the Ancient Word were included in the early chapters of Genesis, but they appear with the addition of long genealogical tables which label such characters as Adam and Eve, and Noah, as being the Jews' own ancestors. They therefore came to reverence their history as holy. But within it there would be a symbolism that held a spiritual sense.

As Swedenborg quite correctly notes, even until quite recently, Jews believed there was some mysterious sense that must be preserved, which required the extreme measures the Masoretes took to preserve the exact text. For instance they counted and recorded the number of words in each chapter and each time they copied it they checked which was the 'middle' word.

REVELATION

The Word of the Old Testament contains heavenly arcana, with every single detail focusing on the Lord, His heaven, the Church, faith, and what belongs to faith; but no human being grasps this from the letter. Judging it by the letter or sense of the letter, nobody views it as anything more than a record, in the main, of external features of the Jewish Church. Yet at every point there are internal features that are nowhere evident in the external, apart from the very few which the Lord revealed and explained to the Apostles, such as that sacrifices mean the Lord; that the land of Canaan and Jerusalem mean heaven, which is therefore called Canaan and the heavenly Jerusalem; and that Paradise is similar in meaning.

Arcana Caelestia §1

As long as the mind confines itself to the sense of the letter alone one cannot possibly see that its contents are sacred. Take for instance these first sections of Genesis: From the sense of the letter the only subject matter people recognize is the creation of the world, and the Garden of Eden which is called Paradise, and Adam as the first man to be created. Who thinks anything different? These things contain arcana, however, [...] the subject of Genesis 1 in the internal sense is the new creation of man, [. . .] in general his regeneration, and in particular the Most Ancient Church.

Arcana Caelestia §4

So an eternal message was given to the Jews, but they did not understand its deeper import. As well as the Books of Moses recording their ancient history, the exodus from Egypt and their laws, further historical books and the prophesies were added: Joshua, Judges, the Books of Samuel and Kings, the Psalms and the Prophets. These all contained an inner sense and came to constitute the Jewish Canon as recognized in 200 BC. After the time of the Jewish Church, about AD 100, further books were added to the Canon but Swedenborg says they did not have a 'continuous spiritual sense', although some probably use correspondential language.

Swedenborg accepts the historical books as being good history, although as noted above he may have had doubts about the characters of Moses and David. Since Swedenborg's time historical and archaeological research has shown that other kings may not be quite as depicted. Solomon was not as great or magnificent, and on the other hand Ahab was quite a capable and successful ruler. Ahab is thoroughly criticized for marrying the foreign princess Jezebel, yet Solomon married hundreds of foreign wives—for whom he would have erected shrines—and is only mildly rebuked. It is apparent that the Jewish history is modified in order to contain the inner meaning. It is also evident in the many differences between the 'inspired' Books of Samuel and Kings when compared with the Books of Chronicles (which Swedenborg regarded as uninspired).

PROGRESS OF THE CHURCH

Having been given these instructions, the Children of Israel were allowed into the land of Canaan, and therefore into the Church, since the land of Canaan represented and consequently served to mean the Church. Furthermore that land was situated at the centre of the whole earth, for at the fore it looked towards Europe, on the left towards Africa, and at the rear towards Asia. But after they had arrived in that land the commands through Moses were supplemented through the [Former] Prophets [i.e., the Judges], and then through King David and at length through Solomon after the Temple was built, as is clear from the Books of Judges, Samuel and Kings. This therefore was the second state of the Church, that is, its advancement into light or its daytime.

Coronis §52

It should be realised, that the temple built by Solomon, and also the House of the Forest of Lebanon, both dealt with in Chapters 6 and 7 of Kings, served to mean the spiritual and celestial realities that constitute heaven and the Church.

Apocalypse Explained §220.12

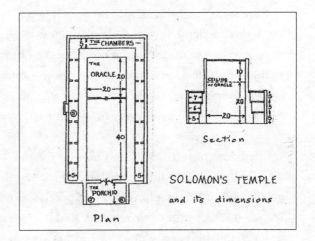

Fig. 19 Solomon's Temple. The Temple is described in considerable detail in Chapters six and seven of the Second Book of Kings. Its form and dimensions are carefully specified and Swedenborg notes in *Apocalypse Explained* §§220 and 700 that their correspondences are significant. He does not interpret them in detail, but notes that their symbolism is similar to those of the features of the Israelites' Tabernacle which he expounds at length in the last two volumes of the *Arcana Caelestia*.

Swedenborg sees the period from Joshua to Solomon as the primary period of spiritual progress. He was going by the text of the Old Testament, however, and, as noted before, the historical facts may be different. Historically, the Old Testament is 'political' rather than 'social' history.

From the time of Solomon Swedenborg sees decline setting in. But to resist this decline the Lord sent numerous prophets, whose message the Jewish scribes faithfully recorded and preserved. In their prophesies were enshrined some of the clearest statements of spiritual truth and doctrine, but also predictions of gloom. The period of 'vastation', that Swedenborg says concludes the history of churches, is setting in.

> But what vastation is, and how it came about with the people composing the Israelite Church, may be deduced from places where it is mentioned in the Prophets [. . .]
>
> The state of consummation of the Israelite Church is described in both the historical parts of the Word, and its prophetic parts: in the prophetic, by the atrocious deeds of the kings, first of those of the Israelites, and afterwards of those of the Jews, by whom and under whom the land is said to have been profaned.
>
> Here at the outset it should be mentioned that the following places in the Word 'the land' is used to mean matters of teaching; mountains, hills, valleys, rivers to mean formal things of the Church, and each according to the representation of the tribe in possession of it [. . .]
>
> Also 'vineyard' and 'field' in the following places—as in other passages in the Word—are used to mean the Church.
>
> From Coronis §§55, 56, 58
>
> O inhabitant of Jerusalem, and man of Judah, . . . what shall I do to My vineyard that I have not been doing? I looked that it should bring forth grapes, but it brought forth wild grapes. . . . I will make it a desolation, it shall not be pruned nor weeded, that the briar may come up; . . . and houses shall be a devastation; . . . for they regard not the work of Jehovah, neither see the operation of His hands (Isa. 5:3-12).
>
> Many shepherds have destroyed My vineyard, they have trampled My field, they have reduced the field of My desire to a desert of solitude; he has made it a solitude. . . . O desolate, desolate is the whole land, because no one lays it to heart. The vastators came upon all hills in the desert; . . . they have sown wheat, but have reaped thorns (Jer. 12:10-13).
>
> [. . .] In all your dwelling-places the cities shall be devastated, and the

high places shall be desolated; that your altars may be devastated and desolated, ... and your idols may cease, and your images may be cut down, and your works may be abolished (Ezek. 6:6).

[...] I saw the earth, and behold it was empty and void; and towards the heavens, and their light was not. (Jer. 4:23)

From *Coronis* §§56, 58

So as the people failed to support their religion, the 'specific' church of the Jews fell from grace, but even as it did so the prophets were inspired to record their messages as to the true nature of God and of His coming upon earth. But at the same time Swedenborg tells us about the continuance of the 'universal church', which, somewhat confusingly, he calls the Church of the Gentiles, during this period.

THE CHURCH OF THE GENTILES

Most of Swedenborg's mentions of the Church of the Gentiles are references to the text of the Bible, where this church is symbolized by characters in the stories. Usually they are in pairs, one character representing the Gentile Church and one the Jewish. Sometimes a larger group is involved. One has the impression that it was particularly important that both churches should be nurtured together; that the valuable influence of the small race should be spread more widely.

> **The Church of the Gentiles is represented by Esau and the Jewish Church by Jacob [referring to Genesis 27].**
>
> *Arcana Caelestia* §367.2
>
> **By the blear-eyed Leah is represented the Jewish Church, and by Rachael a new Church of the Gentiles.**
>
> *Arcana Caelestia* §422
>
> [...] 'the sons of Heth' means a new Church, or what amounts to the same, those who belong to that new Church. But that it was a new Church consisting of or drawn from the gentiles is evident from what Abraham

said to the sons of Heth, 'I am a stranger and an inhabitant among you', verse 4, which meant that the Lord was not known to them, yet He was nevertheless able to be with them, 2915. From this it is evident that 'the sons of Heth' means a Church consisting of gentiles. It cannot be said of any others that the Lord is not known to them.

Arcana Caelestia §2986

'Nebaioth, Ishmael's firstborn, and Kedar, and Abdeel, and Mibsam; and Mishma, and Dumah, and Massa; Hadad, and Tema, Jetur, Naphish, and Kedemah' means everything that constitutes the spiritual Church, in particular among the gentiles. This is clear from the representation of these individuals whose names are given. Some of them are mentioned again in the Word, in particular in the prophetical part, such as Nebaioth, Kedar, Dumah, and Tema. There they mean such things as constitute the spiritual Church, in particular among gentiles. This is in addition evident from the fact that there are twelve of them, and 'twelve' means all things that make up faith, and so the Church.

Arcana Caelestia §3268

The above passage is about Ishmael, the son of Abraham by Sarah's handmaid Hagar. A few pages before Swedenborg tells us more about the nature of the Gentile church; ideas that were very progressive for their time.

The Lord's spiritual Church [. . .] exists throughout the whole world, for it is not confined to those who possess the Word and from the Word have knowledge of the Lord and of some truths of faith. It also exists among those who do not possess the Word and therefore do not know the Lord at all, and as a consequence have no knowledge [. . .] of faith—for all truths of faith regard the Lord. It exists with gentiles remote from the Church. For among those people there are many who know from the light of reason that there is one God, that He has created and preserves all things; and also that He is the source of everything good and true; and that being the likeness of Him makes a person blessed. And what is more, they live up to their religion, in love to that God and towards the neighbour. From an affection for good they perform the works of charity, and from an affection for truth they worship the Supreme Being. Such people among the gentiles belong to the Lord's spiritual Church. And, although they do not know the Lord while they are in the world, they nevertheless have within themselves a worship and virtual acknowledgement of Him when good exists within them, for the Lord is present within all good. For this reason also they acknowledge the Lord in the next life without difficulty, and receive the truths of faith better than Christians.

Arcana Caelestia §3263.2

THE IRON AGE

Two days later the angel spoke with me again, saying, 'Let us complete the course of the ages. The last age remains, which is named after iron. The people of this age live in the north, on the western side, extending inward or in a latitudinal direction towards the interior. They all come from early inhabitants of Asia who had the Ancient Word and who worshipped according to it. Consequently they lived before the advent of our Lord into the world. This is apparent from the writings of ancient authors in which those times are given these names. The same ages are meant by the statue seen by Nebuchadnezzar [. . .].'

Conjugial Love §78 (This passage is quoted in full at the end of this chapter)

Although Swedenborg frequently equates the Golden and Silver Ages with the Most Ancient and Ancient Churches, he seems to avoid any direct identification of the Bronze and Iron Ages with the Hebrew and Jewish Churches. One assumes they must have had a certain amount in common nevertheless. The people in the *Conjugial Love* description of the Iron Age do not betray any sign of being Jews. In that they lived 'before the advent of our Lord into the world', one assumes they must be their contemporaries and probably members of the 'universal church' or Church of the Gentiles.

Those few references to the Iron Age that Swedenborg does make do seem to identify traits that are similar to those he attributes to the Jews; as in the following passage:

> Because members of the Most Ancient Church saw in everything belonging to the natural order something spiritual and celestial, so much so that natural things served them simply as objects for thinking about spiritual and celestial things, they were for that reason able to talk to angels and so be present with them in the Lord's kingdom in the heavens at the same time as they were in His kingdom on earth, which is the Church. Thus with them natural things were joined to spiritual and wholly corresponded. It was different however after those times, when evil and falsity began to reign, that is, after the golden age, when the iron age began. Because at that time correspondence did not exist any longer, heaven was closed. It ceased to exist so completely that men scarcely wished to know whether there was anything spiritual; indeed they did not wish at length to know that there was a heaven or a hell, or a life after death.
>
> *Arcana Caelestia* §2995

In the last sentence one assumes that Swedenborg particularly had in mind the attitude of the Jewish Sadducees, who rejected the concept of an afterlife, as mentioned in Matthew 22:23.

PRESERVATION OF THE JEWS

In *On the Sacred Scripture* §39, it tells us that the Jewish race has been preserved in order that the Hebrew Word should also be preserved. In the work known as *The Last Judgment (Posthumous)* Swedenborg makes other observations on the activities of the Jews at his time, both in the other world and in this.

> The Jews [those Swedenborg met recently arrived in the world of spirits below the heavens] still retain the worldly practice of carrying on trade,

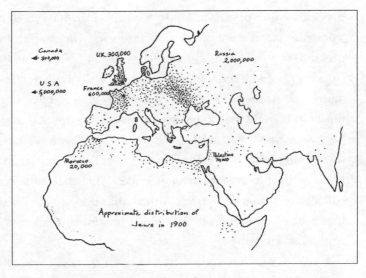

Fig. 20 The Jewish Diaspora. It has been the fate of the Jews to be constantly pushed around by rulers and governments and they are still very mobile. At various times in history their distribution has varied. For many centuries from Roman times onward there were many Jews in Spain and Portugal until they were expelled in the 15th century; largely towards France and the Low Countries. Over three million Jews have returned to Israel during the 20th century, but there are still twelve million living elsewhere so, as Swedenborg would expect, there are few cities where you cannot buy a Hebrew Old Testament.

especially in precious stones. These by certain methods they procure from heaven; for thence come precious stones, of which much more might be said. For in heaven are all things which are in the world. There is gold and silver there, also gold and silver in the form of coins, and also stones of every kind. Like all other things which appear before their eyes; they are from a spiritual origin, and hence are correspondences. They appear just as in the world. Divine Truths are their origin; and therefore, with those angels who are in truths, the decorations in the houses are resplendent with silver and gold, and diamonds. Precious things of this kind are given from heaven to those below who are studious of truths; and because of their origin they also remain forever. The Jews get them from these and sell them.

The reason why Jews have this business in the world, and also after their departure from the world, is because they love the Word of the Old Testament in the letter, and the literal sense of the Word corresponds to precious stones of various kinds. It is this sense that is meant by the twelve stones in Aaron's ephod, which were the Urim and Thummim; by the precious stones in Tyre, concerning which in Ezekiel; and by the precious stones with which the foundations of the wall of the New Jerusalem were adorned. Now because it was foreseen by the Lord that Christians would not hold the Old Testament so holy as do the Jews, therefore, the Jews have been preserved up to this day, and have been scattered throughout the whole Christian world, in order that the Word might still be in its holiness by means of correspondences. This also is the reason why it is still allowed the Jews to trade with similar things as in the world. If there had not been this reason, that whole nation, by reason of its perversity, would have perished.

Last Judgment (Posthumous) §254

*

SEXUAL RELATIONS IN THE IRON AGE
From Swedenborg's *Conjugial Love* §78

Two days later the angel spoke to me again and said: "Let us complete the cycle of the ages. All we have left is the last age, which is called after iron. The people of this age live in the north, deep inside on the west side. All of these are from the early inhabitants of Asia who had the old Word, and their worship was based on this; that is to say, before the Lord's coming into the world. This is clear from the writings of the ancients, in which this period is so named. The same periods are meant by the statue seen by Nebuchadnezzar, which had a head of gold, chest and arms of silver, belly and thighs of bronze, legs of iron, and feet of iron as well as clay (Dan. 2:32, 33)".

[2] The angel told me this on the journey, which was shortened and hurried on by changes produced in our mental state to match the

Chapter Six—The Israelite and Jewish Churches

characters of the peoples we passed through. For spaces and distances in the spiritual world are appearances dictated by mental states. When we lifted up our eyes, we found ourselves in a wood composed of beeches and two kinds of oak; and on looking around we saw bears to our left and leopards to our right. When I showed surprise at this, the angel said, "They are not bears or leopards, but people who act as guards for those who live in the north. They sniff out the spheres given off by the way passers-by live, and fly at all who are spiritual, because those who live here are natural. Those who only read the Word without drawing any teaching from it, look at a distance like bears, and those who confirm false ideas from the Word look like leopards". However on seeing us these creatures turned their backs and we passed through.

[3] After passing through the wood there were thickets, and then grassy plains, divided into plots with box-wood hedges. Then the ground sloped down into a valley, in which there was one city after another. We passed some by and went into a large one. Its streets were irregular, and so were its houses. The houses were built of bricks, with half-timbering and plastered walls. In the squares there were shrines built of ashlar limestone; they had an underground basement and a storey above. We went down into one of these by three steps, and saw the walls around us covered with idols of various shapes, and a crowd on their knees adoring them. In the centre was a choir, from which the head of the city's tutelary deity stood out. As we went out, the angel told me that among the ancients who lived in the silver age, as mentioned above, there were images to represent spiritual truths and moral virtues. When the knowledge of correspondences was lost from memory and became extinct, these images first became objects of worship, and after were adored as divinities. This was the origin of idolatry.

[4] When we had left the shrine, we examined the people and their dress. Their complexion was greyish, like steel, and they were dressed like clowns, with tabs around their hips hanging from a tunic which tightly

fitted the chest. On their heads they had sailors' cocked hats. "That's enough of this", said the angel. "Let us learn about marriage among the peoples of this age".

We entered the house of one of the leading citizens, who wore a top hat on his head. He made us welcome and said, "Come in and let us have a chat". We went into the entrance-hall and sat down there. I asked him about marriage in this city and region. "We", he said, "do not live with one wife. Some have two or three, some more. This is because we take pleasure in variety, obedience and being treated with the respect due to royalty. When we have several wives, we get this from them. With only one we should not have the pleasure of variety, but be bored with sameness; we should not be flattered by their obedience, but annoyed by their equal status. Nor should we have the satisfaction of controlling them and so being respected, but we should be bothered with quarrels about who was superior. And what about the woman? Surely she is by birth subject to her husband's will, intended to be a servant, not a ruler. Every husband here is treated in his house like a king. Since this is what we love, it is what makes our lives blessed".

[5] "But", I asked, "where then is conjugial love, which makes one soul out of two, linking minds and making people blessed? This love is indivisible; divided it turns into an ardour which cools off and disappears". "I don't understand what you mean", he replied to this. "What else makes a man blessed, if not the rivalry between wives to give the greatest respect to her husband?" On saying this the man went into the women's quarters and opened a double door. An odour of lewdness came out, stinking like filth; this was the result of polygamous love, which is marital and at the same time scortatory. So I got up and closed the doors.

[6] Then I said, "How can you keep living on this land, lacking as you do any truly conjugial love and adoring idols?" "As for marital love", he replied, "we are so jealous of our wives that we do not allow anyone to come further into our homes than the entrance-hall. Where there is jealousy,

there is also love. As for the idols, we do not adore them; but we cannot think about the God of the universe except by having some object before our eyes. For we cannot lift our thoughts above the sense-impressions of the body, or in thinking about God rise above His visual aspect".

Then I asked further: "Are your idols not of different forms? How can they suggest the vision of one God?" "This", he replied, "is one of our mysteries; each form contains some aspect of the worship of God". "You", I said, "are entirely sunk in the bodily senses. You have no love of God, nor love for a wife with any spirituality in it. These loves together make a person what he is, and can turn him from a creature of the senses into a heavenly one".

[7] When I said this, there was something like a flash of lightning seen through the doorway. "What is that?" I asked. "Such a flash of lightning", he said, "is for us a sign announcing the arrival of the Ancient Man of the East, who teaches us about God, as being one, alone and omnipotent, who is the First and the Last. He also warns us not to worship idols, but only to look on them as images representing the powers which proceed from the one God; these taken together make up His worship. This ancient man is our angel, whom we revere and listen to. He comes to us and sets us straight, when we slip into a dim way of worshipping God by indulging in fancies about images".

[8] When we had heard this speech, we left the house and the city, and as we journeyed we drew conclusions from what we had seen in the heavens about the ambit and development of conjugial love. Its ambit ran from the east to the south and from this to the west, and hence to the north. Its development was marked by a decrease as it moved around; in the east it was celestial, in the south spiritual, in the west natural, and in the north sensual. It also decreased in step with the love and worship of God. Our conclusion from this was that this love was in the first age like gold, in the second like silver, in the third like bronze, in the fourth like iron, and it finally ceased altogether. Then my angel guide and companion

said: "Yet I am still full of hope that this love will be revived by the God of heaven, who is the Lord, since it is capable of being revived".

Chapter Seven—
The Christian Church

Alternative concepts:

The New Testament;

The Age of Religions

(Buddhism, Confucius, Islam, etc.);

Adulthood;

A Spiritual Church.

CAUTIONARY NOTE

In case anyone might be dipping into this chapter before having read the introductory chapters, I should remind readers that the Christian Church Swedenborg is writing about is that existing between the first and eighteenth centuries. What he says need not be applicable to today's Christianity. (You can get a good idea of how he then saw the Roman Catholic and Protestant Churches in a twenty page summary of their beliefs he gives at the beginning of his *Apocalypse Revealed*.)

CONTINUITY BETWEEN OLD AND NEW TESTAMENTS

It is plain that the Lord fulfilled everything in the Word from a consideration of the passages where it is said that the Law and the Scripture were fulfilled by Him, and that everything was brought to completion, as where Jesus said:

Do not think that I have come to abolish the Law and the Prophets. I have come not to abolish, but to fulfil. Matt. 5:17, 18.

[. . .] He also taught His disciples, before He went away, that the whole Word was written about Him, and that He had come into the world to fulfil it, in these words:

He said to them, Foolish people and slow of heart to believe all that the Prophets have said! Surely this is what Christ ought to suffer, and enter into glory? Then beginning with Moses and all the Prophets, He explained to them the references to Himself in all the Scriptures. Luke 24:25-27.

The True Christian Religion §262

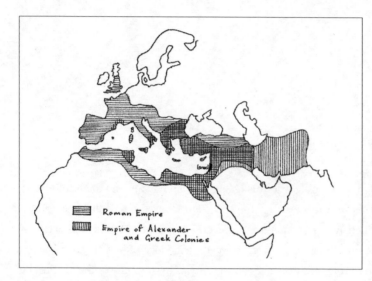

Fig. 21 **The Empires of Alexander and Rome.** The extensive spread of Greek and Roman influence and language provided wide opportunities for the dissemination of Christian teaching.

It is clear that Swedenborg looked upon the Old Testament and the events of the New Testament as being firmly linked in spite of the apparent time lapse between them. He believed the Jewish Scriptures, although different in some ways, were the firm foundation upon which our Lord built up his theological position. Indeed that the Old Testament had been designed for the use of the Lord Himself, and for future churches, quite as much as for the Jewish nation.

In passing I think it is useful to point out that, not only the Hebrew, but also the Greek and Roman cultures, seem to have been moulded by the hand of providence to serve the purposes of our Lord in His founding of the Christian Church. Greek culture was dominant in the eastern Mediterranean for many centuries. It provided the area with a felicitous and universally understood language and a philosophic discipline of thinking that would serve as a perfect vehicle for the New Testament. The Pax Romana offered a blanket of political protection under which the Church could both spread and consolidate itself in safety, even if some of the Emperors did throw Christians to the lions.

For Swedenborg the Old Testament is full of information about the Lord and the foundation of a new religion. It is not just in the prophecies but in the stories of Abraham, David, and in the Psalms, the 'inner senses' of which chart the progress of our Lord's spiritual development on earth. Swedenborg tells us there are three levels of meaning in the Word, the literal sense, a spiritual sense mirroring our mental experience, and the celestial symbolizing our Lord's living experiences of combating the hells on the plane of this material world. In the following quotation Swedenborg is speaking about the version of the Word used in the Celestial Heaven, but it could apply equally to the innermost of the three senses of the earthly Word:

> In this Word the Lord is read in place of Jehovah, and of Abraham, Isaac and Jacob; and also the Lord is named in place of David, Moses, Elijah and the rest of the Prophets; and His Divinity is distinguished by special marks. The names of the twelve tribes of Israel, and also the names of the Apostles, when read there, convey something about the Lord as regards the church; and so with all the rest. From this it became plain to me that the whole of the Sacred Scripture deals in its inmost sense with nothing but the Lord.
>
> *On the Sacred Scripture* §32

THE INCARNATION

> When no natural good was left among members of the Church [that of the Jews or Iron Age] the Lord came into the world and restored all things to order in the heavens and in the hells. He did this so that a person could receive influx from Himself out of heaven and have enlightenment, without the hells intercepting it and introducing thick darkness. At this point a fourth Church, called Christian, came into being.
>
> *Arcana Caelestia* §10355.5

God's omnipotence functions and works in the universe and all its parts in accordance with the laws of its order [. . .] Now since God came down, and He is order [. . .] He had, so as to become really man, to be conceived, be carried in the womb, be born, be brought up and learn items of knowledge one by one, and by their means be brought into a state of intelligence and wisdom. Therefore in His Human He was a child like any other child, a boy like any other boy, and so on, the only difference being that He achieved that progress more quickly, fully and perfectly than others. It is evident from this passage in Luke that He advanced thus in accordance with order:

The boy Jesus grew [. . .] and He advanced in wisdom, years and favour with God and men. Luke 2:40, 52.

The True Christian Religion §89

The Lord came into the world to subjugate the hells and to glorify His Human; and the passion on the cross was the last combat by which He fully conquered the hells and fully glorified His Human.

It is known in the Church that He conquered death, by which is meant hell, and that He afterwards ascended with glory into heaven. But it is not yet known that the Lord conquered death, or hell, by combating temptations, and at the same time glorifying His Human; the passion on the cross was only the last combat or temptation by which He effected this conquest and glorification. These combats are often mentioned in the Prophets and in the Psalms, but not so much in the Evangelists. These temptations, which He endured from childhood, are described in summary form by His temptations in the wilderness; and by the devil [as described in Matthew 4], and the final temptations by His sufferings in Gethsemane and on the cross.

Doctrine of the Lord §12

All temptation is an attack against the love present in a person, the degree of temptation depending on the degree of that love. [. . .] Destroying another person's love is destroying his very life, for his love is his life.

Chapter Seven—The Christian Church

The Lord's life was love towards the whole human race; indeed it was so great and of such a nature as to be nothing other than pure love. Against this life of His, temptations were directed constantly, and this was happening from earliest childhood through to His last hour in the world. The love that was the Lord's very life is meant by His being hungry and by the devil's saying,

If you are the Son of God, tell this stone to become bread. And Jesus answered, It is written that man will not live by bread alone but by every word of God. Luke 4:2-4; Matt. 4:2-4.

That He fought [. . .] against all that constitutes love of the world, is meant by the devil's taking Him on to a high mountain and showing Him all the kingdoms of the world in a moment of time and saying,

To you I will give all this power and their glory, for it has been given to me, and I give it to whom I will. If you, then, will worship before me, it will all be yours. But answering him Jesus said, Get behind Me, satan! for it is written, You shall worship the Lord your God, and Him only shall you serve. Luke 4:5-8; Matt. 4:8-10.

That He fought against self-love, and all that constitutes self-love, is meant by these words,

The devil took Him into the holy city, and set Him on the pinnacle of the temple, and said to Him, If you are the Son of God, throw yourself down, for it is written, He will give His angels charge regarding you, and on their hands they will bear you, lest you strike your foot against a stone. Jesus said to him, Again it is written, You shall not tempt the Lord your God. Matt. 4:5-7; Luke 4:9-12.

[. . .] To sum up, the Lord was attacked by all the hells from earliest childhood right through to the last hour of His life in the world, all the hells were confronting the Lord. He continually met, mastered and overpowered them, and this He did solely out of unselfish love towards the whole human race.

Arcana Caelestia §1690

Swedenborg tells us that God wants to leave people in freedom as much as possible, even if their ways are evil, and so He allows the hells to develop, although under the supervision of angels. If they threaten the heavens and the freedom of people in this world there is a need to restrain the hells' activities, as we have already noted in relation to previous eras.

So before the Christian Church could be introduced, the hells formed during the Iron Age would have to be confronted and put in order. In the latter days of the Most Ancient Church the hells had been resisted through the direct influence of angels and good spirits and the understanding of natural correspondences. When this ceased to be effective the Ancient Church was launched, when the hells were resisted through understanding of the correspondential teachings of the Ancient Word, which contained the spiritual sense of the Word. When this failed the Jews were given the Old Testament and helped to resist the hells by obedience to the literal sense of the Word. When even this was distorted by Jews, such as the Pharisees, a yet more powerful presentation of the truth was necessary—'the Word was made flesh'. Our Lord came on earth and was able to teach the truth, not only by word, but also by living example. The divine influence was felt directly in the material world, rather than via the heavens. His 'saving power', the influence of the Holy Spirit could be felt as a personal and immediate approach.

THE APOSTLES' ROLE

> [In the Word] The Lord's twelve disciples represented the church in all respects concerning truth and good or faith and love, in the same way as the twelve tribes of Israel. Peter, James and John represented faith, charity and the good deeds of charity. Peter stands for faith. Peter being given the keys of the kingdom of the heavens means that all power belongs to truth coming from good, or faith coming from charity which is from the Lord; and so that all power belongs to the Lord (AC 6344). A key is the power of opening and closing. Good has all power by means of truths, in other words, truths have all power from good which is from the Lord. A Rock in the Word means the Lord as regards Divine truth (AC 8581).
>
> Footnote to *Last Judgment* §57 (It does not appear in all translations)

> After the Apostles had been given the Holy Spirit by the Lord, they preached the Gospel throughout much of the world, and spread the news of it by word of mouth and by their writings. They did this of themselves from the Lord; for Peter taught and wrote in one way, James in another, John in another and Paul in another, each according to his own intelligence. The Lord filled them all with His Spirit, but each drew a contribution from that source which was determined by the nature of his perception, and they carried out their duty in a way determined by the nature of the ability of each. All the angels in the heavens are full of the Lord, for they are in the Lord and the Lord is in them; but still each speaks and acts in accordance with his own mental state, some simply, some wisely, and so with infinite variety, yet each one speaks of himself from the Lord.
>
> *The True Christian Religion* §154

These two passages define the roles the Apostles played on two planes. Their role as characters in the inspired Gospels was to symbolize spiritual characteristics of the Church. In actual life, however, they each followed their own personal convictions in spreading the gospel. In the Gospels Peter was important symbolically, but this does not mean the church he founded in Rome was any better than the churches founded by other disciples—although we can see the hand of Providence at work in taking Peter to the then political centre of the Western world.

DEFINING THE BOOKS WHICH CONSTITUTE DIVINE REVELATION; AND THE PRESERVATION OF THE OLD TESTAMENT

> The books of the Word are all those which have the internal sense. [...] The books of the Word, in the Old Testament, are the five Books of Moses, the Book of Joshua, the Book of Judges, the two Books of Samuel, the two Books of Kings, the Psalms of David, the Prophets Isaiah, Jeremiah, Lamentations, Ezekiel, Daniel, Hosea, Joel, Amos, Obadiah, Jonah, Micah, Nahum, Habakkuk, Zephaniah, Haggai, Zechariah, Malachi: and in the

New Testament, the four Evangelists, Matthew, Mark, Luke, John; and the Apocalypse. The rest do not have an internal sense.

The New Jerusalem §266

Groupings	"Books" *(Those in Italics are not in New Church Canon.)*	200BC	Jewish 100AD	250AD	Jerome 400AD	Luther 1525?	Swed'g 1750?
THE VARYING CANONS OF SCRIPTURE							
Ancient Word	Genesis Chapters 1-11	*	*	*	*	*	*
The Law	Genesis Exodus Leviticus Numbers Deuteronomy	*	*	*	*	*	*
Historical Books	Joshua Judges Samuel Kings	*	*	*	*	*	*
Major Prophets	Isaiah Ezekiel Jeremiah	*	*	*	*	*	*
Minor Prophets	Hosea Joel Amos Jonah Micah Nahum Habakkuk Zephaniah Haggai Zechariah Malachi	*	*	*	*	*	*
'The Books'	Psalms		*	*	*	*	*
	Proverbs Job		*	*	*	*	
'The Rolls'	Lamentations		*	*	*	*	*
	Song of Songs Ecclesiastes Ruth Esther		*	*	*	*	
The Histories	Daniel		*	*	*	*	*
	Ezra Nehemiah Chronicles		*	*	*	*	
The Apocrypha	*Tobit Judith Baruch The Book of Wisdom Maccabees I & II Ecclesiasticus*			*	*		
	I & II Esdras Sussanna Bel and the Dragon Maccabees III & IV The Prayer of Manasses The Song of the Three Children				*		
The New Testament	The Gospels of Matthew Mark Luke and John				*	*	*
	The Acts The Epistles of Paul The Epistles of James Peter John and Jude				*	*	
	Revelation				*	*	*

Fig. 22 **Canon of the Bible** The Old Testament 'books' that Swedenborg claims to have an 'internal sense' are the same as were accepted in our Lord's time, except that he adds Lamentations, Daniel and the Psalms; from which Jesus frequently quoted.

About 200 years before the time of our Lord, the Jewish scribes first laid down the 'Canon' of their Scriptures, deciding which books were sacred. It was these books which our Lord, during his ministry, would refer to as the 'Law and the Prophets'. Their list is almost identical to the above list drawn up by Swedenborg, except that Swedenborg adds Psalms, Lamentations and Daniel.

Chapter Seven—The Christian Church

Those three books, along with others were added to the Jewish Canon shortly after the fall of Jerusalem in AD 70 and the books of the Apocrypha were added by the Jews in AD 250.

As the Christian Church developed, it used these 'books', added the books of the New Testament and other writings now little known. When Jerome compiled the Latin 'Vulgate' he was more selective, but still accepted what we call the Apocrypha. Luther rejected it, however, so it is not found in Protestant Bibles.

(It is a matter of opinion whether Swedenborg set out an exclusive 'Canon' in the manner of Luther, defining the inspired and uninspired books. In *The New Jerusalem* §266 quoted above he is actually just listing books which have an 'internal sense'.) [1]

Though Paul's letters do not contain an internal sense, as is well known in the next life, they have been permitted to have a place in the Church. [. . .] Paul was not permitted to take a single parable, not even any teaching which the Lord had given, to display it or explain it. Everything came from himself. The Church indeed explains the Word of God, but it uses Paul's letters to do so. As a consequence of this the Church, wherever it exists, forsakes the good of charity and embraces the truth of faith which, however, the Lord did indeed teach, but to the end that the good of charity might be the all.

The Spiritual Diary §4824

Here Swedenborg may appear somewhat dismissive of Paul's Epistles. His comment that Paul shows little inclination to quote our Lord's teaching is valid. Although the Gospels were not existing during Paul's lifetime, the information used by the Evangelists must have been available. But while Swedenborg puts the Epistles in quite a different category from the books with an 'internal sense' he nevertheless valued their literal message. There are hundreds of references to them in his writings, particularly in *The True Christian Religion* and he uses them to confirm the teaching he draws from the 'internal sense'. The same is the case with the Epistles of John, the Book of Job and others. Although they have no internal sense, he nevertheless realized their particular value for the Christian Church, and their continuing usefulness for the New Church.

The Old Testament was retained by the Christian Church, but with varying degrees of enthusiasm as much of it was of no obvious value in its literal sense and little of the spiritual sense was realized. In order to preserve an interest in it the Lord therefore took special measures.

The Jewish Nation has been preserved and dispersed over a great part of the world for the sake of the Word in its original language, which they more than Christians hold sacred; and in every particular of the Word is the Divinity of the Lord, for it is Divine Truth united to Divine Good proceeding from the Lord, and by means of this the Word becomes the conjunction of the Lord with the Church and the presence of heaven with man [. . .] and there is the presence of the Lord and of heaven wherever the Word is read with reverence. This is the end which the Divine Providence has in view, in preserving and dispersing them over a great part of the world.

Divine Providence §260.3

A SUMMARY HISTORY OF THE CHRISTIAN CHURCH

The periodic changes which followed one another in the fourth Church, the Christian, are described in both Testaments within the Word; its Rise, or Morning, in particular, in the Gospels, and in Acts and the writings of the Apostles; its advancement towards midday, in the documents belonging to the history of the Church during the first three centuries; its decline or evening, in those belonging to succeeding centuries; and its destruction through to its consummation, that is its night, in the Book of Revelation.

Coronis, Summaries VII

The *Coronis* begins with a table of contents in Swedenborg's usual lengthy style, though perhaps hastily drawn up, as he didn't follow it in the first draft of his text (which is the only text we have). It gives us a simple picture, but one that we may find rather difficult to swallow, in that the Church appears to be on the decline before it reached what Western Christianity regards as its maturity. (Nevertheless a number of small denominations share Swedenborg's view.) It is also odd in that Swedenborg starts by referring us to the Gospels, then to 'history', and then reverts to the New Testament Book of Revelation. He will, however, justify his views in due course if we take the stages he lists one at a time.

THE EARLY CHURCH

In the earliest church parties took place among such people as called themselves brothers in Christ. They were therefore charitable parties, because there was a spiritual brotherhood. They served also as a consolation when the church encountered difficulties, as a celebration of its increase, and also to restore spirits exhausted by study and work, and for discussions of various matters. Since the source from which they sprang was spiritual love, their reason and morality had a spiritual origin.

The True Christian Religion §434

When a Church is raised up by the Lord it is faultless to begin with. At that time one person loves another as his brother, as is well known from the Primitive Church after the Lord's Coming. In those days all members of the Church lived with one another as brothers; they also called one another brothers, and loved one another mutually. In the course of time however charity faded and passed away, and as it passed away evils took its place, and along with the evils falsities too wormed their way in. From this schisms and heresies resulted, which would never have existed if charity had continued to reign and live. In those days they would not even call schism schism, or heresy heresy, but a matter of doctrine adhered to in accordance with the particular belief of that schism or heresy. That matter of doctrine they would leave to each individual's conscience, provided it did not deny anything fundamental, that is, the Lord, eternal life, or the Word, and provided it was not contrary to Divine order, that is, to the Ten Commandments.

Arcana Caelestia §1834.2

> [...] the Primitive Church, or that of the Gentiles, after the Lord's coming. In its beginning it had no other doctrine than that of love and charity, for this the Lord Himself taught. But after His time, successively, as love and charity began to grow cold, there arose the doctrine of faith, and with it dissensions and heresies, which increased as men came to lay stress on this doctrine.
>
> *Arcana Caelestia* §2417.3

Swedenborg paints a happy picture of the early Christian Church for two or three centuries. While we know a certain amount about the lives of the leading disciples and bishops, it is difficult to estimate quite how widely their teachings were received. Nevertheless, we know that by AD 300 the Emperor Constantine felt it politic to accept Christianity as the official religion of the Roman Empire, so a fair proportion of its citizens must by then have been Christians. At that time the Empire had a population of some 40,000,000, most of whom lived in the eastern parts of the Empire. There were also further Christians outside the Empire in Asia and Africa. Although the leaders of the church by then allowed their disputes to overshadow the charitable life, the faith of millions of simple people within the church may not have been affected for some time.

Nevertheless the disputes of the fourth century and the growth of political rather than spiritual considerations led to a decline in the quality of the Church, even though it was still continuing to spread. In spite of this apparent spiritual decline on earth, Swedenborg nevertheless speaks of a growing consolidation of the Christian community in the heavens.

THE DEVELOPING CHURCH

> In the final days of [a] Church, when there is no [true] faith because there is no charity, more internal truths contained within the Word are brought to light which will direct a new Church in its teachings and way of life. This is something which the Lord himself was carrying out when the final days of the Jewish Church were at hand. [...] But the reception of those more internal truths did not take place straight away, but only

> after a notable passage of time, as is well known from the history of the Church. The reason for this was that it was not possible for such truths to be received before the restoration to proper order of all things in the spiritual world. For that world is linked to people in the natural world, and therefore before the restoration of the spiritual world to proper order it was not possible for people in the natural world to understand and perceive the good aspects of love and the truths known through doctrine. This is why it took so long for the Christian Church to be established throughout Europe; for all effects that come about in the natural world have their origins in causes that exist in the spiritual world.
>
> Apocalypse Explained §670.2

Quite what timescale is involved here is not clear to me and may well have been unclear to Swedenborg too. One realizes, however, that although the Lord was doubtless caring for the church of that time He also had the long term vision in mind, preparing the foundation for the next stage of His eternal plan.

It was sad that the Early Church in the east declined, while the less charitably minded church of the west gradually overtook it in importance. Both groups would contribute to the consolidation and preservation of the Word, but it was the west that would eventually produce an environment in which the Word became freely available to members of the church at the individual level. As we shall see later, the hand of providence, working through the Christian heaven, seems to have created special conditions which enabled a new age to commence in Europe.

THE COUNCIL OF NICAEA

> The fourth [church] is the Christian church, which was established by the Lord through the evangelists and apostles. Of this church there have been two phases, one extending from the Lord's time to the Council of Nicaea, and the other from that Council to the present day [. . .]
>
> The True Christian Religion §760

After those times (of the Apostolic church) darkness settled upon the whole Christian world, first because of the spread of many heresies, and soon after by the deliberations and decrees of the Council of Nicaea respecting three Divine persons from eternity, and respecting the person of Christ as being the Son of Mary and not the Son of Jehovah God.

The True Christian Religion §206

It is said in heaven, that when the Nicene Council had finished its work, that had come to pass which the Lord foretold to His disciples:

The sun shall be darkened, and the moon shall not give her light, and the stars shall fall from heaven, and the powers of the heavens shall be shaken (Matt. 24:29);

and in fact the Apostolic church was like a new star appearing in the starry heaven. But the church after the two Nicene councils became finally like the same star darkened and lost to view, as has sometimes happened, according to the observation of astronomers, in the natural world.

The True Christian Religion §176

Swedenborg regarded the First Council of Nice or Nicaea, called by the Emperor Constantine in AD 329, as the turning point after which the Church as a spiritual organization started to run downhill. It was the point at which, as a potential state religion, its orientation became secular as much as spiritual. The general state of the church was at fault, but the specific decisions of the Council were the official confirmation.

Swedenborg especially criticizes the wording, and the later interpretations of the words, of the Nicene Creed in *Canons of the New Church*, *The Brief Exposition* and *The True Christian Religion*. His primary concern was the division of the Trinity into three persons, allowing such doctrines as the idea of 'a son from eternity' and the vicarious atonement to develop.

Swedenborg was not saying that the Christian Church was no longer of use, or that it would not continue to have an important role to play, but it would now be a less reliable channel of divine inspiration and teaching.

ISLAM or MOHAMMEDANISM

This form of religion was raised up [in the seventh century] by the Divine Providence of the Lord to destroy the idolatries of many nations [...] Previous to the religion of Mohammed the worship of idols was common throughout the whole world. This was because the Churches before the Coming of the Lord were all representative Churches. Such was the Israelite Church. In it the tabernacle, the garments of Aaron, the sacrifices, all things belonging to the temple at Jerusalem, and also the statutes, were representative. Moreover, among the Ancients there was the science of correspondences [...] This was especially cultivated in Egypt [...] From this science they knew the signification of animals, also of trees, and mountains, hills, rivers and fountains, and also of the sun, moon and stars; and as all their worship was representative, consisting wholly of correspondences, they celebrated it on mountains and hills, and also in groves and gardens. [...] Moreover, they made graven images of horses, oxen, calves, lambs and also of birds, fishes and serpents, and set them up in their houses and other places in an order according to the spiritual things of the Church to which they corresponded. They also placed similar objects in their temples that they might bring to remembrance the holy things which they signified.

[However] in the course of time, when the science of correspondences had been lost, their posterity began to worship the graven images themselves, as being holy in themselves, not knowing that their forefathers had seen no holiness in those things [...] Hence arose the idolatries which filled the whole world, Asia with its neighbouring islands, as well as Africa and Europe. In order that all these idolatries might be rooted out it was brought about by the Divine Providence of the Lord that a new religion should arise, adapted to the genius of Orientals, in which there should be something from both Testaments of the Word and which should teach that the Lord came into the world, and that He was a very great prophet, the wisest of all men, and the Son of God. This was effected by means of Mohammed, from whom that religion is called the Mohammedan religion.

By the Divine Providence of the Lord this religion was raised up [...] to the end that it might destroy the idolatries practised by so many nations and give the people some knowledge concerning the Lord before they entered the spiritual world. This religion would not have been received by so many kingdoms with power to extirpate idolatries if it had not been suited and adapted to the ideas of thought and life of them all. It did not acknowledge the Lord as God of heaven and earth because Oriental peoples acknowledged God as the Creator of the universe, but they could not comprehend that He came into the world and assumed the Human [...]

Hence it may be seen that the Mohammedan religion also arose from the Divine Providence of the Lord; and that all persons of that religion who acknowledge the Lord as the Son of God and at the same time live according to the precepts of the Decalogue, which they also have, by shunning evils as sins, come into a heaven called the Mohammedan heaven.

Divine Providence §255

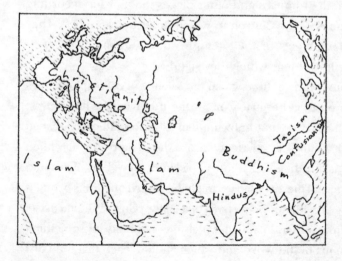

Fig. 23 **The Spread of Islam.** Swedenborg sees Mohammed and Islam as having a similar role to Christianity, 'among Orientals'; if a less perfect one. Had he been more aware of Hindu, Buddhist and Chinese religions he might have said the much the same of them.

The Mohammedan heaven lies outside the Christian heaven, and is divided into a higher and a lower heaven. None are raised to their higher heaven except those who forswear mistresses, and live with one wife, and acknowledge our Lord as the equal of God the Father, to whom dominion over heaven and earth is given.

Conjugial Love §342

There are well over a hundred paragraphs mentioning Islam in Swedenborg's writings, mostly in the *Divine Providence*, *The Last Judgment*, *Conjugial Love* and *The True Christian Religion*. He says Muslims have as good a chance of entering heaven as Christians, although their heaven has two levels. Those who practise monogamy enter the higher level, but polygamists are restricted to a lower one. Fully regenerate Muslims would enter the higher heavens where earthly religious divisions are of little or no significance.

It is of particular interest that we are told that: 'This religion was raised up to the end that it might destroy the idolatries practised by so many nations' (see *Divine Providence* §255 above). Muslim law particularly forbids the making of any image or picture and hence all realistic art. They even insist that all decorative art must be in the abstract, so that even textile and wall decoration patterns are free of animals or plants. This militant approach does seem to have eradicated idolatry in many lands where it was popular—it has been effective in West Africa as well as Asia.

Islam seems to be the only Eastern religion Swedenborg was fully aware of. He perhaps conceived it as being practised by most 'orientals'; a common view in eighteenth-century Europe, even though he occasionally talked to Indians and Chinese in the spiritual world. Had he been familiar with Hinduism, Buddhism and other faiths it seems not unlikely that he would also have seen in them the hand of divine providence creating other vehicles to nurture spiritual development. The following extracts from *Apocalypse Explained* seem to support this view. The word used for 'gentiles' here has also been rendered as 'heathen' by other translators.

The Lord provides each nation with a means of salvation common to all [. . .] This means exists in absolute fullness with Christians. It also exists, though not in fullness, with Muslims, and with gentiles as well [. . .]

The character of the good deeds which they are free to do or not to do, and of the truths which they are free to believe [...] Christians see from the Word, Muslims from the Koran, and gentiles from their religion [...] Gentiles [can] see from their religion that there is a God, that He is to be revered and worshipped, that what is good comes from Him, that there are a heaven and hell, that there is a life after death, and that the evils mentioned in the Ten Commandments must be shunned. If they shun those evils and believe those which they see they are saved. And because the majority of gentiles see God to be human and this God-Man is the Lord, therefore after death they receive instruction from the angels, accept the Lord, and after that receive truths from Him which they hadn't known before.

from *Apocalypse Explained* §1180

THE CHRISTIAN HEAVEN

This may be an appropriate moment to remind readers of Swedenborg's teaching about the basic relationship between the spiritual world and the natural; between heaven and the Church.

Man is totally unaware of the fact that the Lord is governing him by means of angels and spirits, and that at least two spirits and two angels are present with everyone. By means of the spirits he is in communication with the world of spirits, and by means of the angels with heaven. Without this communication with the world of spirits by means of the spirits, and with heaven by means of the angels, and so by means of heaven with the Lord, a person cannot exist at all.

Arcana Caelestia §50

I also perceived at that time, by communication, the joy of the angels who are in the Christian heaven; from which it was manifest that there was a communication of the whole of heaven, originating in the Christian Heaven where the Word is; and, thus, that it is the Word from which are wisdom and interior joy. The communication is like the communication of light, and like the communication of all the viscera in the human body from the heart and lungs.

The Spiritual Diary §5947

As the above passage shows, the Christian heaven, because it nurtured the Word, was truly heavenly. It performed the role of a 'good influence', transmitting love and wisdom to people on earth. But, in the process of time, as in the case of the previous dispensations, problems arose.

The heavens, which were derived from the Christian world after the Lord's coming, gradually declined, as happens on earth. At first those in them acquired heaven inside themselves and worshipped the Lord, and so had heaven around them—as is meant to be. But gradually the heaven inside them grew dimmer and eventually disappeared. Then they wanted to have the heaven, which they knew, still around them, and called that heaven, even though it was no longer inside them. And it was allowed them to have an outward heaven, one of amazing, indescribable magnificence— palaces, colonnades, decorations, ornamental gardens, also in being honoured and suchlike, in the splendour of many servants, thus in high rank only, and in outward self-adoration because of these things.

At length, when they could not obtain such things from the Lord, because they regarded themselves, not him who provided their wealth, then they got them by fantasies and arts unknown in the world, of which there are many, and so they went on continually. Those who were from the first resurrection were not like this, only those who came later; for, as these came into heaven, the Lord in his providence removed the earlier ones, or hid them there, so that they would not be seen. Hence, when the only things that mattered to the others were outward splendours and pleasures, then at last came the judgment already mentioned.

The Spiritual Diary §5749

MARRIAGE

The state of marriage in the Christian Church also had good and bad aspects. The next quotation, taken from Swedenborg's chapter on polygamy in his *Conjugial Love*, accords Christians a unique respect for marriage, although this could just possibly be because he was under the impression that polygamy was universal outside Europe. However, the second quotation reporting on the state of marriage in a decadent society in the spiritual world in Swedenborg's time, shows that for some Christians, monogamy was upheld only in word and disregarded in deed. Even so, Swedenborg correctly identifies monogamy as highly desirable for moral stability, and that therefore monogamous societies have a sounder social foundation.

> **Truly conjugial love with all its happiness cannot be granted except to those who belong to the Christian church.**
>
> The reason why conjugial love, [...] is only possible for those who belong to the Christian Church, is that the Lord is the only source of that love, and the Lord is not so known elsewhere that He can be approached as God. It is also because that love depends upon the state of the church with the individual, and the proper state of the church can only come from the Lord, so that it is not found except with those who receive it from Him.
>
> [...] The reason, however, why truly conjugial love is rare in the Christian world, is that few people there approach the Lord; and these include some who while believing in the church do not live in accordance with its teaching. [...] But it remains none the less true that truly conjugial love is only possible for those who belong to the Christian church. For this reason too polygamy has been utterly banished from it.
>
> *Conjugial Love* §337

Nevertheless, Swedenborg says some men wanted to rebel against monogamous laws, as he found out on a visit to a society of people who I assume to have lived in the second millennium AD.

> We went into some houses here and there, and saw in each a man with his woman. So we asked whether they all live in their own homes with only one wife. To this they replied with a whistle, 'Why do you say with one wife? Why not with only one trollop? What is a wife but a trollop? Our laws do not allow us to fornicate with more than one woman; still there is nothing indecent or improper in doing it with more, so long as it is not at home. We boast about this among ourselves, thus taking more delight and pleasure in it than polygamous people. Why is it that we are not allowed to have several wives, when it used to be allowed, and is still today in all parts of the world around us? What is living with only one woman, but being shut up and imprisoned? But we are breaking down the bars of this prison, rescuing ourselves from slavery and setting ourselves free. No one can be cross with a prisoner who grabs his freedom when he can.'
>
> *Conjugial Love* §79.5

ACCEPTANCE OF THE WORD IN THE EIGHTEENTH CENTURY

In our new age the Bible is spread around the world in almost every language, but the situation was different in Swedenborg's time.

> The numbers of those who have the Word are small compared with those who do not have it. The Word exists only in Europe among what are called the Reformed Christians; among the Roman Catholics the Word certainly exists, but it is not read, and there are kingdoms devoted to this religion such as France, Spain, Portugal, Italy, more than half of Germany and also of Hungary, as well as Poland. The Word is also little read in Russia, but it is still believed to be holy. Only in Britain, Holland, certain duchies in Germany, and in Sweden and Denmark is the Word taught and preached. But the peoples of Asia, Africa and the Indies are ignorant of the Word, numerous as they are compared with the Reformed Christians.
>
> *On the Sacred Scripture* §39

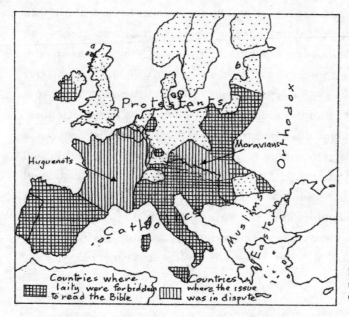

Fig. 24 Access to the Bible in the 18th Century

THE ROMAN CATHOLIC CHURCH

Swedenborg wrote extensively about the Roman Catholic Church, but he was of course speaking of the Church of his own time. Most of what he says is condemnatory in tone, but as Swedenborg was the son of a Lutheran bishop this should not surprise us. The assumed faults of the Roman Church would have been frequently drawn to the attention of Lutheran congregations. Protestants needed to do so in order to justify their still fairly recent separation from the Roman Catholic Church.

The most critical passages will be found in Swedenborg's book *Apocalypse Revealed*. There, in accordance with Lutheran ideas of the time, he identifies the Catholic Church with the wicked Babylon, described in the Book of Revelation. However, he does also state in many passages that Babylon symbolizes the 'love of self and the love of dominion over others', which fault many besides Catholics entertain (see *Doctrine of Life* §79, *Doctrine of Faith* §49, *Divine Providence* §231, etc.). It is not surprising that Swedenborg should associate the loves of self and dominion with the Roman Catholic Church of his time. For many years most popes had been largely interested in furthering family interests and building opulent churches and palaces. In France many abbés were demolishing the noble abbeys their predecessors had erected and using the stone to build extravagant mansions. It is all very similar to what Swedenborg reported above of the decadence in heaven (*The Spiritual Diary* §5749).

Swedenborg's criticism is aimed primarily at the Church and priesthood rather than the people. As I mentioned in Chapter Two it is the 'specific church' element in that decaying organization, rather than the 'universal' element that is being criticized. He often comments that, once disabused of 'Romanist superstition', Catholics are more easily led to heaven than the Reformed.

All those of the Catholic religion, on realising that they are living after death, if in the former world they have thought more about God than the Papacy, and have performed charitable deeds out of simplicity of heart, are easily led away from the superstitions of that religion, once they have been taught that here the Lord Himself, the Saviour of the world, is King.

The True Christian Religion §821

Swedenborg was particularly critical of the Catholic Church's disregard for the Bible and their preventing lay people from reading it. He also rejected the claim that the popes had been appointed as Christ's 'vicar' on earth and the belief that Papal Bulls (edicts issued by the Pope) were as authoritative, possibly more important, than the teaching of the Word. He realized, however, that many Catholics, particularly in France, did not fully support those views.[2] His balanced view is perhaps presented most succinctly in the following 'interview' he claims to have had with Pope Sixtus V, whom he found leading a society of Catholics in the world of spirits. Sixtus V was the son of a washerwoman, but rose rapidly through administrative skills to become pope in 1585. He then did much to reform the Vatican organization, issued a revision, if not a very good one, of the Roman Catholic Latin Bible, and also improved the roads and water supply of Rome.

To these things I will add this memorable occurrence. I was allowed to speak with the Pope Sixtus V. [. . .] He told me that he was appointed as chief governor of a society gathered together from Catholics who excel the rest in judgement and activity. He became their chief governor on account of his having, for half a year before his death, believed that the vicarship was an invention for the sake of dominion; and that the Lord the Saviour, because He is God, only ought to be adored and worshipped; also that the Sacred Scripture is Divine, and is thus holy above the edicts of Popes. He said that until the end of his life he remained firm in the faith of these two principles of religion. He said also that their saints are not anything. He was astonished when I related that it had been decreed in a synod, and confirmed by a bull, that they should be invoked [by praying]. He said that he is leading a similar life to that he had lived in the world; and that every morning he proposes nine or ten things to himself which he wants to have accomplished before the evening.

I asked whence he obtained within so few years such a great treasure as he laid up in the Castelo del Angelo [a fortress beside the Vatican]. He replied that he wrote with his own hand to the rulers of rich monasteries to send of their wealth as much as they would from choice because it was for a holy use; and that because they were afraid of him they sent abundantly. And when I said that that treasure is still in existence, he said, 'What use is it now?' In the course of speaking with him I related that since his time the treasure at Loretto has been immensely augmented and enriched, and so likewise have the treasures in certain monasteries, especially in Spain. And I added, that they are keeping them without any useful purpose other than the pleasure of possessing them. And when I related this, I also said that they are such as the infernal gods, which the ancients used to call Pluto. When I mentioned Pluto, he replied, 'Hush! I know.' He said again that no others are admitted into the society that he is set over but those who excel in judgement, and are able to receive [the truth] that the Lord Only is the God of heaven and earth, and that the Word is the Divine Holy (*Sanctum Divinum*); and that under the Lord's auspices he is perfecting that society every day. He also said that he has spoken with so-called saints, but that they become foolish when they hear and believe that they are saints. He was even calling stupid those Popes and cardinals who wish to be adored as Christ—although not in person—and who do not acknowledge the Word as Divine Wisdom itself, in accordance with which one ought to live.

He wishes me to say to those who are living today [approx. 1765] that Christ is the God of heaven and earth, and that the Word is Holy; also that the Holy Spirit does not speak through anyone's mouth, but Satan does as he wishes to be adored as God. Also that those who do not give heed to these things, as the stupid, go away to their own kind and after a time enter hell, with those who labour under the fantasy that they are gods and these have no other life than the life of a wild beast. To this I said, 'Perhaps these things are too harsh for me to write.' But he replied, 'Write, and I will sign them, for they are true.' And then he went away from me into his own society, and he signed one copy and transmitted it as a Bull to other societies attached to the same religion.

Apocalypse Revealed §752

THE REFORMED CHURCH

It will be noted from the passages above that Swedenborg was especially concerned that members of the Roman Catholic Church were not respecting the Word. As a result he says they could no longer fulfil the proper role of the Church on earth and so the need arose for a 'reformed' church as he explains in the *Doctrine of the Sacred Scripture*.

It will now be shown how the Lord and heaven are present, and how conjunction with them is effected throughout the whole earth by means of the Word. The whole heaven is, in the sight of the Lord, as one man. [. . .] In this Man the Church, where the Word is read and by means of which the Lord is known, is like the heart and lungs: [...] As from these two fountains of life in the human body all the other members and organs subsist and live, so also do all those throughout the world who have a religion, worship one God and live good lives, thereby forming part of this Man. They represent the members and organs outside the chest in which are the heart and lungs, and they subsist and live from the union of the Lord and heaven with the Church by means of the Word. For the Word in the Church, although it is with comparatively few, is life to the rest [of the world] from the Lord through heaven, just as the members and organs of the whole body receive life from the heart and lungs. The manner of communication between them is also similar; and for this reason Christians among whom the Word is read constitute the breast of this Man. They are in the centre of all, and round about them are the Roman Catholics; around these again are the Mohammedans [...] After these come the Africans, while the nations and peoples of Asia and the Indies form the outermost circumference.

[...] From these considerations it may be evident that the Word as it is in the Church of the Reformed, enlightens all nations and peoples by spiritual communication; and further, that the Lord provides that there should always be on earth a Church where the Word is read, and the Lord thereby made known. When therefore the Word was almost totally rejected by the Romish Church, through the Divine Providence of the Lord the Reformation took place, in consequence of which the Word was again received. It was also provided that the Word should be regarded as holy by an eminent nation among the Roman Catholics.

Doctrine of the Sacred Scripture §§105 and 110

This explains why it has come about that certain Churches have set themselves apart from the Babylonish, which Churches recognize the Lord's Divine power over heaven and earth to be equal to God the Father's power, and also attribute Divine holiness to the Word alone. The Lord has made this provision to prevent the Christian Church in Europe from falling into total ruin.

Apocalypse Explained §1069

Chapter Seven—The Christian Church

This refers to the period of Swedenborg's life and is not necessarily true today. The translation of the Word into the North European languages did a great deal to revive and democratize religion. The 'eminent' nation referred to above in *Doctrine of the Sacred Scripture* §110 is France where the rights of laymen to read the Bible were defended by Louis XIV in spite of the restrictive attitude of the popes.

But in spite of their championship of the Word, Swedenborg was equally critical of the Reformed Church. The Medieval Church had been practising the sale of 'indulgences'; offering places in heaven upon payment of appropriate sums of money. It was one of the prime reasons that had inspired Luther to instigate the Reformation. The Protestant reaction perhaps went too far, however. Swedenborg suggests that for many eighteenth-century Protestants 'works' [of charity] had little to do with salvation and that 'faith alone' qualified one to enter heaven.

For Swedenborg this point of view was as disastrous as the Catholic's disinterest in the Word. He insisted on the need for both faith and charity—the marriage of good and truth, and the desirability of a balance of these values in a life of usefulness. The attempt to separate them was the final reason for the failure of the Christian Church as it existed in the eighteenth century.

It is a law of Divine order that good and truth should be linked and not kept separate, so that they make a single unit, not two. For linked they proceed from the Divine, linked they are in heaven and therefore linked they should be in the church. In heaven the linking of good and truth is called the heavenly marriage, for all there are linked in this marriage. This is why heaven in the Word is likened to a marriage, and the Lord is called bridegroom and husband, while heaven is called bride and wife; and these same terms are used of the church. The reason why heaven and the church are so called is that those in them receive Divine good in truths.

The New Jerusalem §13

Swedenborg recounts the reasons for the decline of the first Christian Church at great length in his works the *Apocalypse Explained* and *Apocalypse Revealed*. In the unpublished draft of his *Coronis* however, we do find convenient summary notes of the situation as he was seeing it. But they are only notes, probably for headings, and are therefore more strongly worded than the considered text he might have written later. (Again it may be necessary to point out it should not be assumed that it is fully applicable today.)

The falsities which have up to now desolated, and have at length consummated, the Christian Church, have been chiefly the following:

Christians have departed from the worship of the Lord preached by the Apostles, and from faith in Him.

They have separated the Divine Trinity from the Lord, and transferred it to three Divine Persons from eternity, consequently to three Gods.

They have divided saving faith among these three Persons.

They have separated charity and good works from that faith, as not at the same time saving.

They have deduced justification, that is, forgivness of sins, regeneration, and salvation, from that faith alone, apart from man's co-operation.

They have denied that man has free-will in spiritual things, thus asserting that God alone operates in man, and on the other hand that man does nothing.

From this predestination necessarily flowed forth, by which religion is abolished.

They have made redemption consist in the passion of the cross.

From these heresies, falsities crept forth in such abundance that there does not remain any genuine truth which has not been falsified, consequently, neither any genuine good which has not been adulterated.

The church knows nothing at all about this, its desolation and consummation, nor can it know, until the Divine Truths revealed by the Lord in the work entitled, *The True Christian Religion*, **are seen in light and acknowledged.**

The Word has been so obscured and blotted out, that not a single truth any longer appears in it.

Coronis, Summaries XL-XLIX

So the Christian Church of the eighteenth century is roundly condemned, but it is mainly the theologians and establishment of the Church that are being condemned (again perhaps the 'specific church' element). In the following passage Swedenborg notes that the people of the Church did not necessarily understand the Church's teaching in the way that most priests did and, after appropriate adjustment of ideas, could still enter heaven.

THE STATE OF THE 'PEOPLE' OF THE CHURCH

Among the people of the Church there are two states of faith and consequent life or of life and consequent faith. The first has its origins in doctrine, the second in the Word or rather sermons preaching the Word [. . .] Now I must speak about these states existing with the people of the Church [. . .] Most of those born within the Churches that have accepted the doctrine of faith alone or of justification through this do not know what is really meant by faith alone or by justification. So when they hear these terms used in sermons they think that a life in keeping with God's commands in the Word is meant by them, this being what they believe faith and also justification to be. They do not go into the deeper matters lying hidden within the doctrine. Furthermore, when they are being taught about faith alone and justification they do no other than believe that faith alone means thinking about God and salvation, and how to lead their lives, and that justification means doing so in the sight of God. All within the Church who are being saved are maintained by the Lord in that way of thinking and believing, and after leaving this world they are enlightened with truths, for they are able to receive such enlightenment.

Apocalypse Explained §233.3

The following paragraphs also remind us that a church should not be judged by its doctrinal position, but rather by love in the hearts of its members. Those Christians who could agree to differ and concentrate on love to the Lord and the neighbour were part of the Lord's kingdom on earth, despite the attitudes of the establishments of the churches.

By itself doctrine does not constitute the external aspect of the Church, still less the internal, as stated above. Nor on the Lord's part is it its teachings that make one Church distinct and separate from another, but its life in accordance with those teachings, all of which regard charity as their basic principle. What else does doctrine do but teach men the kind of people they ought to be?

In the Christian world it is their doctrines that cause Churches to be distinct and separate, and because of these they call themselves Roman Catholics, Lutherans, Calvinists or the Reformed, and Evangelicals, among other names. It is solely by reason of their doctrines that they are called by these names. This situation would never exist if they were to make love to the Lord and charity towards the neighbour the chief thing of faith. In this case their doctrinal differences would be no more than shades of opinion concerning the mysteries of faith which truly Christian people would leave to individual conscience, and in their hearts would say that a person is truly a Christian when he lives as a Christian, that is, as the Lord teaches. If this were so all the different Churches would become one, and all the disagreements which stem from doctrine alone would disappear. Indeed the hatred one man holds against another would be dispelled in an instant, and the Lord's kingdom on earth would come.

Arcana Caelestia §1799

The Summaries of the *Coronis*, quoted above continue by looking to the future:

For many reasons this New Christian Church is not being established through any miracles as the previous Church was.

But, instead of them, the spiritual sense of the Word is revealed, and the spiritual world disclosed, and the nature of both heaven and hell manifested; also, that man lives as man after death; which things surpass all miracles.

Coronis, Summaries L-LI

So, although Swedenborg often says that in principle the old church must be consummated before the new can begin, at least, he talks of a New Christian Church and so indicates that the next church will be built upon the foundations of the old; that there was within eighteenth-century Christendom a remnant who would receive the call to build a new age.

*

SEXUAL RELATIONS IN LATER TIMES
From Swedenborg's *Conjugial Love* §79

The angel who had previously been my guide and companion on my visits to the people of antiquity, who had lived in the four ages, golden, silver, copper and iron, came to me again and said: "If you want to see what the age which followed those ancient ones was and still is like, follow me and you will see. These are the people of whom Daniel prophesied: There shall arise after those four a kingdom in which iron will be mixed with common clay. They will mix together by the seed of man, but one will not stick together with another, even as iron will not mix with clay. Dan. 2:41-43".

"The seed of man", he said, "by which iron will be mixed with clay, but without sticking together, means the truth of the Word falsified".

[2] After this speech I followed him, and on the way he informed me: "They live on the border between the south and the west, but a long way behind those who lived in the four earlier ages, and also lower down". We travelled through the south until we came to the region bordering the west, and passed through a terrifying forest. For it had lakes in it, from which crocodiles raised their heads, gaping at us with their wide, toothy jaws. Among the lakes there were frightening hounds, some with three heads like Cerberus, some with two; all with horrid jaws, watching us pass with their savage eyes. On entering the western sector of this region we saw dragons and leopards, as described in Rev. 12:3, 13:2.

[3] "All these beasts", the angel told me, "which you have seen are not beasts at all, but correspondences and so forms which represent the lusts of the inhabitants we are to visit. The lusts themselves are represented by those horrid hounds, their tricks and cunning by the crocodiles, their falsities and erroneous attitude to religious matters by the dragons and leopards. But the inhabitants, of whom they are a picture, live not near the end of the forest, but across a great intervening desert, so that they can be kept apart and separated from the peoples of earlier ages. They are too of quite an alien and different nature from them. Admittedly they have their heads above their chests, their chests above their hips, their hips above their feet, like the primeval people. But their heads contain not a scrap of gold, their chests not a scrap of silver, and their hips not a scrap of bronze; nor indeed is there a scrap of unmixed iron in their feet. But their heads contain iron mixed with clay, their chests iron and clay mixed with bronze, their hips the same too mixed with silver, their feet these mixed with gold. This inversion has turned them from human beings into sculptures of human beings, lacking all internal cohesion. For what was highest has become lowest, the head has become the heel and vice versa. As we look from heaven they seem like clowns who stand upside down and walk on their hands; or like animals that lie flat on their backs, lifting their feet in the air, and burying their heads in the ground, to look up to the sky.

[4] Crossing the forest we entered the desert, which was no less frightening. It was composed of heaps of stones, with ditches between them, out of which crept poisonous snakes and vipers, and fiery serpents flew out. The whole of this desert kept sloping downwards, and we went down a long descent, finally reaching a valley inhabited by the peoples of that region and age.

Here and there we saw huts, which eventually seemed to come together and join up to form a town. We went into it and found the houses were built of tree-branches, charred and stuck together with mud; they were roofed with black slates. The streets were irregular, all of them narrow to begin with, but opening out as you went on, and widening out at the end to form squares. So there were as many squares as were streets.

On entering the town it grew dark, as the sky was not to be seen. So we looked up and light was granted us to see by. Then I asked any I met on the way, "Surely you can't see, since the sky is not to be seen above you?" "What sort of a question is that?" they answered, "we can see clearly, we walk in broad daylight". On hearing this the angel told me: "Darkness is light to them, and light is darkness, just as it is for night birds. They look down and not up".

[5] We went into some houses here and there, and saw in each a man with his woman. So we asked whether they all live in their own homes with only one wife. To this they replied with a whistle, "Why do you say with one wife? Why not with only one trollop? What is a wife but a trollop? Our laws do not allow us to fornicate with more than one woman; still there is nothing indecent or improper in doing it with more, so long as it is not at home. We boast about this among ourselves, thus taking more delight and pleasure in it than polygamous people. Why is it that we are not allowed to have several wives, when it used to be allowed, and is still today in all parts of the world around us? What is living with only one woman, but being shut up and imprisoned? But we are breaking down the bars of this prison, rescuing ourselves from slavery and setting ourselves free. No one can be cross with a prisoner who grabs his freedom when he can".

[6] We replied to this: "Friend, you speak as if you had no knowledge of religion. Is there anyone with any rationality, who does not know that adultery is profane and hellish, and that marriage is holy and heavenly? Surely adultery is to be found among the devils in hell, and marriage among the angels in heaven? Haven't you read the sixth commandment, or Paul's statement that adulterers can by no means reach heaven? [1 Cor. 6:9]".

This amused our host so much he roared with laughter, looking on me as a simpleton and almost crazy. But then suddenly a messenger arrived from the chief man of the town, who said: "Bring the two newcomers to the court, and if they refuse, drag them there. We have seen them in the shades of light; they have crept in secretly to spy on us".

The angel said to me: "They saw us in shade, because the light of heaven we brought with us is shade to them; their light is in the shade of hell. This happens because they think nothing of sinning, not even of committing adultery, so that falsity to them looks exactly like truth. Falsity shines brightly before the satans in hell, and the truth darkens their eyes like the shades of night".

[7] "We shall not", we told the messenger, "be forced, much less dragged, to court, but we shall go with you of our own free will". So we went and found there a large crowd. Some lawyers detached themselves from the crowd and whispered in our ears: "Take care not to say anything against religion, our kind of government and good behaviour". "No", we replied, "we shall not say anything against them, but speak in their favour and as they dictate".

"What". we asked, "is the rule of your religion about marriage?" This produced a murmuring among the crowd, "What business of yours are marriages?" they said, "marriages are marriages".

We asked another question: "What is the rule of your religion about licentious conduct?" Again there was a murmur from the crowd. "What business of yours is licentious conduct?" they said. "Licentiousness is licentiousness. Let him who is without guilt throw the first stone".

Our third question was: "Surely your religion teaches that marriages are holy and heavenly and that adulteries are profane and hellish?" This made many in the crowd cackle, laughing and making fun of us. "Address", they said, "your questions on religion to our priests, not to us. We fully accept their pronouncements, because no religious matters fall within the scope of intellectual judgment. Surely you have been told that the intellect is deranged when it comes to mysteries, and these are what religion is all about. And what have actions to do with religion? Isn't it heartfelt mumbling about expiation, satisfaction and imputation which make souls blessed, not deeds?"

[8] Then some men came up sent by the so-called wise men of the town, who said: "Leave here at once. The crowd is growing angry and there will soon be a riot. Let us have a talk about this subject by ourselves. Behind the courthouse there is a walk, where we can be private. Come with us".

So we followed them, and then they asked us where we came from and what our business was there. "We came", we said, "to learn about marriage, whether like the ancient peoples of the golden, silver and copper ages you regarded marriages as sacraments or not". "Sacraments indeed!" they answered, "Aren't they the work of flesh and darkness?" "Aren't they too", we replied, "the work of the spirit? Isn't what the flesh does under the direction of the spirit itself spiritual? Everything the spirit does is directed by the marriage of good and truth. So isn't it this spiritual marriage which enters into the natural marriage, that between husband and wife?"

To this the so-called wise men replied: "You are being too sharp and lofty in your treatment of the subject. You are going beyond the realm of reason into the spiritual realm. How can anyone start there, and come down from there to make any judgment?" They added with a mocking grin, "Perhaps you have eagle's wings so that you can soar to the heights of heaven and spy such things out? We cannot".

[9] Then we asked them to tell us, from their height, that is, the region where the volatile ideas of their minds flit about, whether they knew or could know of the existence of the conjugial love of one man with one wife, a love on which are conferred all the blessedness, bliss, pleasures, charms and gratifications of heaven; this love being given by the Lord in proportion to one's ability to receive good and truth from Him, and so depending on the state of the church.

[10] On hearing this they turned away and said: "These men are crazy. They soar about the atmosphere with their judgments, and indulge in the folly of playing with toys". Then turning back to us, they said: "We will give you a straight answer to your vain and vacuous prognostications. What connexion is there between conjugial love and religion or Divine inspiration?

Surely everyone has this love in proportion to his sexual potency? Don't those outside the church feel it just as much as those inside? The heathen just as much as Christians? In fact, the irreligious as much as the religious? Doesn't the strength of that love depend on heredity, state of health, self-discipline or climate? It can also be strengthened and aroused by drugs. Isn't it shared with animals, especially with birds, which form loving pairs? Surely it is a fleshly love. What has the flesh to do with the spiritual state of the church? When it comes to the effects at the lowest level, there is surely not the slightest difference between a wife and a trollop. The lust is the same and the delight felt is the same. It is therefore disrespectful to derive the origin of conjugial love from the holy things of the church".

[11] On hearing this we told them: "Your reasoning arises from the goadings of lewdness, not from conjugial love. You are totally ignorant of what conjugial love is, because for you it is cold. Your remarks have proved to us that you come from the age named after a mixture of iron and clay, which do not hold together, as prophesied by Daniel (2:43). You make conjugial love and scortatory love one and the same. Can these two hold together any more than iron and clay? You think you are wise and you have that reputation, yet you are in fact anything but wise".

On hearing this they shouted out in fury and summoned the crowd to throw us out. Then by the power given us by the Lord we held out our hands, and at once fiery serpents, poisonous snakes and vipers, and also dragons, appeared from the desert, moving into and filling the town, so that the inhabitants were terrified and fled.

The angel said to me: "Newcomers from earth are daily arriving in this region, and the earlier inhabitants are from time to time banished and cast into quagmires in the west. These look from a distance like lakes of fire and brimstone. All the people there are both spiritually and naturally adulterers".

Chapter Eight—
The New Church

Alternative concepts:
The Book of Revelation;
Maturity;
The Modern World
(Enlightenment, Freedom, Communication,
Science, Technology, Global Unity,
Tolerance, Variety, Education, Love, etc.);
Potentially a Celestial Age.

Once when I was meditating on the Lord's second coming, there suddenly appeared a beam of light, so powerful as to dazzle my eyes. So I looked up, and saw the whole heaven above me full of light; and from east to west I heard a long series of voices glorifying God. An angel came close and said: 'This is the glorifying of the Lord on account of His coming, uttered by the angels of the eastern and western heavens.' [. . .] This glorifying and praising was taken from the Word.

[. . .] I looked again to the east of heaven, and the light was growing from the right; the brightness spread into the expanse of sky to the south, and I heard a sweet sound. I asked the angel what glorifying of the Lord was taking place there. He said it was with these words from Revelation:

I saw a new heaven and a new earth; and I saw the holy city New Jerusalem coming down from God out of heaven, prepared like a bride for her husband. And I heard a mighty voice out of heaven saying: Behold the tabernacle of God is with men, and He will dwell with them. And the angel spoke with me and said: Come, I will show you the bride, the wife of the Lamb. And he carried me away in the spirit onto a great and high mountain, and showed me the holy city, Jerusalem. Rev. 21:1-3, 9, 10.

Also with these words:

I, Jesus, am the bright star of the morning; and the Spirit and the bride say, Come. And He said, I am coming soon. Amen; even so, come, Lord Jesus. Rev. 22:16, 17, 20.

After this and more I heard a general glorifying from the east of heaven to the west, and also from the south to the north. I asked the angel what this was. He said it was these words from the Prophets:

[The angel then quoted from: Daniel 2:43, Daniel 7:13, Isaiah 9:6, 25:9, 40:3, 44:6, 49:26, and 54:5, from Jeremiah. 23:5,6, and 33:15,16 and Zechariah 14:9.]

On hearing and understanding this my heart leaped for joy and I went home rejoicing; and there I came back from the state of the spirit into that of the body, in which state I wrote down these things I had seen and heard.

The True Christian Religion §625

It is good that Swedenborg shares such experiences, celebrating the coming of the new age, predicted in the biblical books of Revelation, Daniel and others, with us, but I must also turn your attention to what he tells us in his normal textbook style. In one sense nearly everything Swedenborg wrote was about the New Church. His writings are its foundation. Certainly they are the foundation of the 'specific New Church' and probably the conscious or unconscious inspiration of the evolving 'universal new church'. On the other hand, however, because he died soon after it began he can tell us little. It is surprising that if you look in the index he himself prepared for the early *Arcana Caelestia* there is no entry for 'New Church', although there are in fact a small number of references.[1] The significance of the Last Judgment and the New Jerusalem are only mentioned towards the end of the *Arcana*. In the later six volume *Apocalypse Explained* and two volume *Apocalypse Revealed* the new church is discussed at length and in great detail, but such is the extent of the information that for present purposes it is Swedenborg's shorter books that are most useful.

Chapter Eight—The New Church

PREPARATIONS ON EARTH

> The Lord sees to it that on this earth there is always a church where the Word is read. When therefore [in the sixteenth century] the Word was more or less rejected by the Roman Catholics, by the Lord's Divine Providence the Reformation took place; and there the Word was again accepted [. . .]
>
> *On the Sacred Scripture* §42
>
> Because they [spirits in the other world from another solar system] wished to know what revelation is like on our planet, I told them that it is accomplished by means of writing and of preaching from the Word [. . .] I told them that what is written can be made public by means of printing, which can be read and understood by congregations of people throughout the world, whose lives can thereby be amended. They were utterly amazed by the existence of such a device totally unknown anywhere else [. . .]
>
> *Arcana Caelestia* §10384

Although Swedenborg thought the Reformed Church was mistaken in several of its beliefs, he points out that it prepared the ground for the New Church by translating the Bible into many languages, asserting the book's authority and encouraging all to read it. Swedenborg also seems to have been aware that the invention of printing was a necessary step before the New Church, the church of the 'open Word', could be established on this earth. Printing would also be necessary for the distribution of Swedenborg's writings and it was perhaps providential that several of the earliest readers of Swedenborg's writings were printers and publishers.

Perhaps the most important preparatory requirement was the preparation of Swedenborg's mind to digest the new form of revelation. This is too vast a subject to cover here, but plenty of information can be gathered from any of the numerous biographies of Swedenborg.[2] The essential difference was that whereas revelation for previous ages had been more or less by 'dictation', for the new rational age it was desirable that its recipient, Swedenborg, should fully understand what was being revealed and then express it in his own words. This required a highly intelligent and enquiring mind, well stocked with as much knowledge as was then possible, which could then be gently introduced into awareness of the spiritual plane.

Fig. 25 Emanuel Swedenborg.

Swedenborg was always free to think and write whatever he wished, whether true or not, as can be seen from the occasional scientific slips that can be found, where his knowledge was less up to date than current science. In spiritual matters, however, he claimed that he was always guided by the hand of providence as the following passages show:

> Since the Lord cannot show Himself in person, as has just been demonstrated, and yet He predicted that He would come and found a new church, which is the New Jerusalem, it follows that He will do this by means of a man, who can not only receive intellectually the doctrines of this church, but also publish them in print. I bear true witness that the

Lord has shown Himself in the presence of me, His servant, and sent me to perform this function. After this He opened the sight of my spirit, thus admitting me to the spiritual world, and allowing me to see the heavens and the hells, and also to talk with angels and spirits; and this I have now been doing for many years without a break. Equally I assert that from the first day of my calling I have not received any instruction concerning the doctrines of that church from any angel, but only from the Lord, while I was reading the Word.

The True Christian Religion §779

[You ask] my opinion concerning the writings of Boehme. I have never read them, and I was forbidden to read dogmatic and systematic books in theology before heaven was opened to me, and this for the reason that otherwise unfounded opinions and notions might easily have insinuated themselves, which afterwards could have been removed only with difficulty. When heaven was opened to me I had therefore first to learn the Hebrew language, and also the correspondences of which the whole Bible is composed, and this led me to read through the Word of God many times. And since the Word of God is the source from which all theology must be taken, I was thus enabled to receive instruction from the Lord, who is the Word.

Letter to Beyer, February 1767

Swedenborg tells us that, in the year 1744, he began to be enabled to make contact with the spiritual world. At first we find him jotting down impressions in *The Spiritual Diary* (also called *Spiritual Experiences*) and then compiling more composed works, which, however he did not publish. Then in 1748 he began his commentary on Genesis and Exodus, the *Arcana Caelestia*, at the beginning of which he tells us this:

By way of introductory remarks it can be disclosed that in the Lord's Divine mercy I have been allowed constantly and without interruption for several years now to share the experiences of spirits and angels, to listen to them speaking and to speak to them myself. I have been allowed therefore to hear and see astounding things in the next life which have never come to any man's knowledge, nor even entered his imagination. In that world I have learned about different kinds of spirits, about the state of souls after death, about hell (the miserable state of people who do not have faith), about heaven (the very happy state of those who do have faith), and above all else about the doctrine of the faith that is acknowledged in the whole of heaven.

Arcana Caelestia §5

PREPARATIONS IN HEAVEN, THE LAST JUDGMENT (CONSUMMATION OF THE AGE)

Swedenborg was probably one of the first to point out that the Medieval Christian concept of a 'Last Judgment' is not biblically sound. A 'judgment' is mentioned, but not a last or final one. Swedenborg prefers the term 'consummation of the age', but he nevertheless went on using the term 'Last Judgment' quite freely. Most modern Christians wisely avoid the subject, but it was a fairly common belief in Swedenborg's day. I should therefore remind readers that the last judgments mentioned by Swedenborg are only the last judgment of the particular ages and not of humankind for ever. Swedenborg does not anticipate an end to the world.

The Last Judgment is not to take place on earth, but in the spiritual world, where all are gathered who have lived since the beginning of creation. This being so, no one [on earth] could possibly be aware when the Last Judgment took place. For everyone expects it to happen on earth, with everything in the visible sky and on the earth being changed at the same time, and affecting human beings on earth. So to prevent people in the church living with that belief out of ignorance, [...] which would eventually result in people disbelieving what the literal sense of the Word says about it, [...] I have been allowed to see with my own eyes that

the Last Judgment has now taken place. I have seen the wicked cast into the hells, and the good raised to heaven, thus restoring all to order and so re-establishing the spiritual equilibrium between good and evil, or between heaven and hell. I was allowed to see how the Last Judgment took place from beginning to end; [. . .] and then again how the new heaven was formed, and the new church meant by the New Jerusalem was set up in the heavens. I was allowed to see all this with my own eyes so that I could bear witness. This Last Judgment started at the beginning of last year, 1757, and was fully completed by the end of the year.

Last Judgment §45

Before the Last Judgment was carried out [. . .] much of the communication between heaven and the world, and so between the Lord and the church, was blocked. All of a person's enlightenment is from the Lord by way of heaven, and it comes in by an internal route. So long as there were groups [believing that faith alone was sufficient for entry to heaven] between heaven and the world, or between the Lord and the church, people could not be enlightened. It was as when the sun's rays are blocked by a dark intervening cloud; or when the sun goes into eclipse by the interposition of the moon and its light is blocked. If therefore any revelation had been made by the Lord, [by way of heaven] either it would not have been understood, or, if it was understood, it would still not have been accepted, or, if it was accepted, it would still afterwards have been choked. Now, since all these interposed groups were scattered by the Last Judgment, [. . .] communication was restored between heaven and the world or between the Lord and the church.

Continuation of the Last Judgment §11

Before a new dispensation or church could be established, in the natural world, preparations had to be made in the spiritual world. The world of spirits between heaven and earth had to be set in order for the influence of the Lord to be fully effective. Problems were being caused by Catholic spirits who believed they could buy their way into heaven with 'works'. On the other hand, some Protestants were claiming all that was necessary was 'faith', even if they had done no good works. Both groups failed to acknowledge the importance of love and they were managing to persuade other charitable but credulous souls to join their groups. Both groups set up what Swedenborg calls 'false heavens' and were causing a sort of 'traffic jam' below the true heaven.

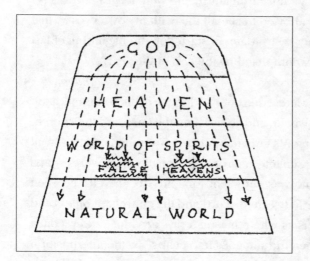

Fig. 26 **Divine Influx to the World.** Good influx flows down from the Lord through the heavens and world of spirits to the world. Its quality will be modified according to quality of the spirits passing it to earth.

However, as the next quotation shows, it should not be thought that the whole, or larger part, of the world of spirits was composed of these obstructionist groups, although they may have constituted an influential minority.

> The first heaven [as mentioned in Revelation 21:1, 'Then I saw a new heaven and a new earth, for the first heaven and first earth had passed away'] was a gathering of all on whom the last judgment took place. It did not take place on those in hell, nor on those in heaven, nor on those in the world of spirits; and not on any person still alive; but only on those who had made themselves a similitude of heaven, mostly on mountains and rocks. These are also those whom the Lord meant by the goats, which He placed on the left (Matt. 25:32, 33).

> [. . .] They were those who in the world had put on an outward show of a holy life, though lacking any inward basis. Those who had been upright and honest [only] because they were compelled by civil and moral laws, but not the laws of God. Thus they were external or natural people, not internal or spiritual people. They included those who possessed the church's teachings and were able themselves to teach, though they did not live in accordance with what they taught; also those who held various offices and performed services, though not for the sake of being of service.
>
> *Last Judgment* §69

Swedenborg not only explains this course of events, but says he saw them happen. This is one of Swedenborg's more provocative claims and one which readers would probably like to know more about. As, however, Swedenborg wrote more than one book on the subject, and as it concerns the end of the Christian Church, rather more than the beginning of the New Church, I trust I will be forgiven if I do not quote much from these books here.

One of the startling things in the above passages is that Swedenborg gives a fairly precise date for this occurrence; the year 1757. It is not a year that is picked out in older history books, even though it was the year in which the Seven Years War, which had begun the year before between Prussia and Austria, escalated into becoming the first 'world war'. That war created the opportunity for Britain to become a 'global' power, so changing the course of world history. Within recent times, however, many historians have begun to regard the period as one of crucial change.[3]

A NEW HEAVEN (REVELATION 21)

> By the new heaven and the new earth which he [John] saw, after the first heaven and the first earth passed away, are not meant a new star-bearing sky visible to human eyes, nor a new earth on which people dwell. Rather a new existence of the Church in the spiritual world and a new existence of the Church in the natural world are meant.
>
> *Doctrine of the Lord* §62

After the completion of the Last Judgment, a new heaven was created, that is, formed by the Lord. This heaven was formed from all those who, from the time of the Lord's coming down to the present, have lived a life of faith and charity, since these alone were in heaven's image.

[...] These facts enable us to know from whom the new heaven was made, and also its nature, as being totally of one mind. For anyone who lives a life of faith and charity loves another as himself, and he links the other to himself by love, so that the other loves him in turn. Love is a linking in the spiritual world; so when all act alike, then the association of many, or rather countless, people, in keeping with the form of heaven, brings about unanimity and they become as one. For there is nothing to separate and divide them, but everything links and unites them.

Since this heaven has been formed from all who were such as described, from the time of the Lord down to the present, it is clear that it is composed as much of non-Christians as of Christians. For the greater part it is composed of all the children throughout the world, who have died since the Lord's time; for all of these have been taken in by the Lord and brought up in heaven. They have been taught by angels, and then kept so as to constitute together with the rest the new heaven. That will give some idea how large that heaven is.

It must further be appreciated that this new heaven is distinct from the ancient heavens, which existed before the Lord's coming. Still the former ones fall into such a pattern with this that taken together they make up a single heaven.

The New Jerusalem §§2–4

After the completion of this book [*The True Christian Religion*], the Lord called together His twelve disciples, who had followed Him in the world; and a day later He sent them all forth throughout the spiritual world to preach the Gospel, that the Lord God Jesus Christ is king, and His kingdom shall be for ever and ever, as foretold by Daniel (7:13, 14) and in Revelation (11:15):

Chapter Eight—The New Church

Blessed are they who come to the wedding supper of the Lamb. Rev. 19:9.

This happened on the nineteenth of June in the year 1770. This was meant by the Lord's saying:

He will send his angels, and they will gather together His chosen people from the bounds of the heavens on one side as far as the bounds of the heavens on the other. Matt. 24:31.

The True Christian Religion §791

One day a magnificent church building appeared to me; it was square in plan with a roof like a crown, with arches above and a raised parapet running around. Its walls were all windows made of crystal, its door of a pearly substance. Inside on the south side towards the west there was a platform, on which the open Word lay at the right surrounded by a blaze of light, so bright as to spread round and light up the whole platform. In the middle of the church was a shrine with a curtain in front of it; but this was now raised and there stood a golden cherub with a sword which he brandished in all directions in his hand.

When I caught sight of all this, as I meditated, the meaning of each of the details came flooding into my mind. The church meant the new church; the door of a pearly substance, entry into it; the windows of crystal, the truths which enlighten it; the platform, the priesthood and their preaching; the Word on it, open and lighting up the top of the platform, the revelation of its internal, or spiritual, sense; the shrine in the middle of the church, the link of that church with the heaven of angels; the golden cherub there, the Word in its literal sense; the sword brandished in his hand meant that this sense can be turned in different ways, so long as it is made to refer to some truth. The lifting of the curtain in front of the cherub meant that now the Word was laid open.

Later, when I got closer, I saw there was an inscription over the door: NOW IT IS PERMITTED. This meant that now it is permitted to enter with the understanding into the mysteries of faith.

The True Christian Religion §508

So a new heaven is created and is ready to take over the surveillance of the earthly plane. A new breed of open-minded rational angelic spirits can help to inspire the minds of earth's people. As a result the world will be freed from the tyranny of the early eighteenth-century culture imposed by absolute monarchy, feudal aristocracy and dogmatic church organizations. As J M Roberts comments of that time 'the weight of the past was everywhere enormous and often it was immovable', but soon 'a world once regulated by tradition was on a new course'.[4]

THE SECOND COMING AND THE CLEARER CONCEPT OF GOD

> [. . .] no one until now has known what the Consumation [close] of the Age may be, or why the Second Coming of the Lord is necessary, or that the arrival of a New Church is about to take place. Yet these three matters are dealt with in the Word, both in the Prophets and in the Gospels, and fully in the Book of Revelation. [. . .] without knowledge regarding the Consumation of the Age, the Second Coming of the Lord, and the New Church, the Word is shut away, so to speak [. . .]
>
> *Coronis* §1

Swedenborg identifies three subjects—the Consummation of the Age (Last Judgment), the Second Coming, and the New Church—as essential to the understanding of the new age. For better or worse I have introduced the Second Coming last as it is perhaps the more difficult to grasp, although possibly the most important concept.

> It is written in many places that the Lord will come in the clouds of heaven.[5] And as no one has hitherto known what is meant by 'the clouds of heaven,' it has been believed that the Lord would appear in them in person. Until now it has not been known that 'the clouds of heaven' mean the Word in the sense of the letter, and that the 'glory and power' in which He is then to come (Matt. 24:30), mean the spiritual sense of the Word [. . .]
>
> *The True Christian Religion* §776

Chapter Eight—The New Church

Fig. 27 **Christ in Majesty, Coventry Cathedral.** This mid twentieth-century cathedral is dominated by Graham Sutherland's large tapestry depicting a 'risen' Christ still wrapped in grave cloths, in a position where it had been usual to place a 'crucified' Christ.

The Coming of the Lord is revealed, in the end of a church. At the end of the Jewish church, the Lord Himself came into the flesh, and He then revealed Himself as being God or Jehovah who was to come, as written in the Prophets, and still further, that He it is who rules heaven with the earth, and who is the only one God. This, in the Gospels (Matt. 24), also is called His Coming. Thus far, however, He has been practically neglected, because in thought and idea He has been regarded as an ordinary man; concerning whom there was scarcely any thought of anything of the Divine, for the reason that men have in their idea placed the Divine outside of Him and not within Him, as undoubtedly He teaches. By the Divine outside Him, most men have understood the Father, and thus another person; so that the Lord was practically neglected in the world, at the end of the Church. Consequently His new and Second Coming is made.

Athanasian Creed §173

Swedenborg suggests that despite Jesus's Coming as a man on earth, as a loving and understanding being, the old image of a stern and distant patriarch was still dominant. So there was going to be a need for a Second Coming for the people of the new age, the basis and spirit of which was already laid down in the Word, but hidden in the 'clouds of heaven', the letter of the Word (Matthew 24:30). The well-prepared yet modest recipient of this revelation was Swedenborg. As we have noted he was allowed to see into the heavens, but he would also see the earth from a new perspective.

The concept of a trinity of persons introduced at the Council of Nicaea needed to be clarified. The Latin word *persona* simply means a mask, such as Greek actors held in front of their faces. So, in this context, the word 'person' should be understood as personality or role. God presents himself to us in different ways, but remains the same person beneath the appearances. The schizophrenic idea that the 'Father' was angry with mankind, yet that the 'Son' was merciful, needs to be expunged. Although this is still accepted doctrine among fundamentalists, compared with the eighteenth-century situation, much has changed. The nineteenth century is said to have seen the 'death of God',[6] nevertheless Christianity is still alive and Jesus has come much more to the fore in the twentieth century. The idea of the crucified Jesus suffering physical torment, cherished by the Roman Medieval Church, is fading and the more positive image of the risen Christ is gaining ascendancy.

THE NEW EARTH (AS IN REVELATION 21)

> Until now it has remained unknown that a new earth means a new church on earth, because everyone has understood earth in the Word as meaning the earth, when it really means the church. In the natural sense earth is the earth, but in the spiritual sense the church. The reason is that those who grasp the spiritual sense, those, that is, who are spiritual like the angels, do not understand the actual earth when earth is mentioned in the Word, but the people on it, and their worship of God.
>
> *Last Judgment* §3

By the holy city, [New] Jerusalem, is meant this new Church as to its

Chapter Eight—The New Church

teaching. It was therefore seen coming down from God out of heaven, for the doctrine of genuine truth comes only from the Lord through heaven. Because the Church as to doctrine is meant by the city, New Jerusalem, it is therefore said:

Prepared as a bride adorned for her husband. Rev. 21:2.

[. . .] It is well known that by the bride and wife are meant the Church when the Lord is meant by the Bridegroom and Husband. The Church is a bride when she is willing to receive the Lord, and a wife, when she has received Him. It is evident that the Lord is here meant by the husband; for it is said, the bride, the Lamb's wife.

Doctrine of the Lord §63

To put the beginning of the New Church on earth into focus timewise, I should remind readers that Swedenborg's spiritual sight was opened in 1743; that he began the *Arcana Caelestia* in 1748; he witnessed the Last Judgment in 1757 and reported that the Lord's disciples were sent out into the heavens in 1770.

By 1756 the last volume of the *Arcana* had been published and by 1771 we know the entire stock of several hundred volumes had been dispersed over Britain, the Netherlands, Germany and Sweden.[7] Swedenborg had expressed disappointment that the response to his efforts had been small, but his writing continued unabated. As he tells one of the first receivers of the doctrines, Dr Beyer of Gothenburg, in letters written in 1766 and 1769:

[In 1766] the time has not yet come when the essentials of the New Church can be received. The clergy who have confirmed themselves in their dogmas at the universities will be convinced only with difficulty, for all confirmations in theological matters are as if glued fast in the brain, and are budged only with difficulty; and so long as they remain there is no room for real truths. Moreover, the New Heaven of Christians from which the New Jerusalem is to descend from the Lord, Rev. 21:1-2, is not yet fully established.

Letter to Beyer, 25 September 1766

[In 1769] I am asked concerning the New Church, when it will come; and to this I reply that it will come gradually as the doctrine of justification and imputation is uprooted, which should be done by means of this treatise [the *Summary Exposition*]. It is known that the Christian Church did not come into its own immediately after the ascension of Christ, but increased gradually; which is also meant by these words in the Book of Revelation: And the woman flew into the wilderness, into her place, where she is nourished for a time, and times, and half a time, from the face of the serpent, chap. 12:14. The serpent or dragon is that doctrine [of justification and imputation].

Letter to Beyer, 15 March 1769

The doctrines of Justification and Imputation were defined by the Roman Catholic Council of Trent, and the Reformed Church's *Formula Concordiae* (drafted after the Augsburg Confession). Both claimed that salvation was dependant only on faith in the Lord or Grace, regardless of whether they had lived a good or evil life.

Something of the situation around that time can be gathered from a conversation with angels that Swedenborg reports in *The True Christian Religion* published in 1771:

I was once carried up in my spirit to the heaven of angels, and to one community there. Then some of their wise men came to me asking, 'What is the news from earth?' I told them that the Lord has revealed secrets far exceeding in excellence any so far revealed since the church began.

'What are these?' they asked. I said that they are:

(1) In every detail the Word contains a spiritual sense corresponding to the natural sense, and by means of that sense the Word forms a link between people in the church and the Lord; it also creates an association with angels, and the holiness of the Word resides in that sense.

(2) The correspondences of which the spiritual sense is composed have been disclosed. 'Did not the inhabitants of the earth,' asked the angels, 'previously know about correspondences?' I told them that they knew

nothing at all and these had been lost to sight for thousands of years, in fact, since the time of Job. [...]

(3) I went on to say that at the present time the Lord had made a revelation about people's life after death. 'What about life after death?' said the angels. 'Surely everyone knows that a person lives after death?'

'They do and they do not,' I replied. 'They say that what lives on is not the person, but his soul, and this lives as a spirit. Their notion of a spirit is that it is like the wind or the ether; and they say that the person will only live after Judgment Day. [...]

(4) The angels asked, 'What do they know of our world and about heaven and hell?' I replied that they know nothing, but that at the present time the Lord had disclosed what the world is like where the angels and spirits live, and so what heaven and hell are like. It had also been revealed that angels and spirits are linked with human beings, and many other surprising facts. The angels were glad that the Lord had been pleased to disclose such matters, so that mankind should no longer be impelled by ignorance to doubt its own immortality.

The True Christian Religion §846

In case any readers are not familiar with Swedenborg's descriptions of heaven and hell, it should be said that they appeared, at first sight, to be identical to this material world, even though the underlying reality is spiritual and not material. His book entitled *Heaven and Hell* is the most accessible description that he gives on the subject.

THE FUTURE OF THE CHURCH

As Swedenborg was making his last journey in 1771 to London, he paused in Amsterdam to see *The True Christian Religion* through the press. There he wrote to Dr Beyer saying:

Of this I am certain, that when this book has been published the Lord our Saviour will operate mediately as well as immediately to establish the

New Church, which is founded on this Theology, throughout Christendom. The new heaven, from which the New Jerusalem is to descend, will now soon be completed, see Revelation 21:1-3.

Letter to Beyer, 30 April 1771

The book Swedenborg referred to was *The True Christian Religion*, his last major work. Quite what he means by 'mediate' and 'immediate operation' we cannot be sure. However, an interesting fact about *The True Christian Religion* is that soon after its publication in Holland in Latin in 1771, Swedenborg brought copies to England and one fell into the hands of an eminent Church of England minister and capable Latin scholar, the Revd John Clowes. Within the decade, he had translated it into English, well before most of Swedenborg's writings were translated.

Swedenborg died in 1772 and so was unable to provide any direct information. In his books on the Last Judgment, however, he did venture some predictions as to the future.

The future state of the world will be exactly the same as it has been up to now; for the mighty change which has taken place in the spiritual world does not cause any change in the external appearance of the natural world. So just as before there will be politics, peace-treaties, alliances and wars, and all the other general and particular features of society. When the Lord said:

> There will be wars, and then nation will rise up against nation, and kingdom against kingdom; and there will be famines, plagues and earthquakes in various places. Matthew 24:6, 7

He did not mean such events in the natural world, but corresponding ones in the spiritual world. For the Word in its prophecies is not concerned with kingdoms on earth or the peoples on it, so not with their wars either; nor is it concerned with famine, plague and earthquakes on earth, but with the events in the spiritual world which correspond to them.

Last Judgment §73.1

Chapter Eight—The New Church

Some new churches and Religious developments after 1757.

1787	New Church (Swedenborgian)
1795	Methodism (Separated from Anglicans)
1790s	Revolution frees French Catholic Church
1800s	Evangelical groups forming
1800s	Reformed Judaism developing
1802	Swaminarayan Movement (India)
1825	Unitarians
1830	Latter-Day Saints (Mormons)
1833	Anglo-Catholicism
1844	The Baha'i Faith
1847	Christadelphians
1876	Christian Science
1875	Theosophy
1882	Parsee Theosophy
1890s	New Sufi Orders

Fig. 28 Post 1757 religious developments.

Intriguingly in the very next section of *Last Judgment* (§74) Swedenborg tells us he 'had various talks with angels about the future state of the church. They said that they did not know what would happen, because the Lord alone knows the future.' For better or worse this was borne out, as around the very time Swedenborg was writing, his suggestion that catastrophes were not imminent proved doubtful. The Lisbon earthquake—the worst known in Europe—occurred and the Seven Years War—the first 'world war' involving hundreds of thousands of deaths—was getting under way.

However in the second part of the above quotation from *Last Judgment* §73, concerning the church rather than the world, he got much nearer the truth, even though it took some time for his predictions to become fully apparent:

The future state of the church, however, will not be the same. It may seem much the same in outward appearance, but inwardly it will be different.

In outward appearance the churches will be divided from one another as before, their teachings will differ as before, and so will the religious systems of the heathen. But people in the church will henceforward have more freedom in thinking about matters of faith, and so about the spiritual matters which have to do with heaven, because of the restoration of spiritual freedom. For now everything in the heavens and the hells has been restored to order. It is from there that all thinking about Divine matters or against them is influenced; from the heavens when the thoughts favour what is Divine, from the hells when they oppose it.

But people will be unaware of this change of state, since they do not reflect on it, nor indeed do they know anything about spiritual freedom or influences from the spiritual world. [. . .] It is because people have had their spiritual freedom restored that the spiritual sense of the Word has now been disclosed, and by this means Divine truths of a more inward kind have been revealed.

Last Judgment §73.2

The change is most easily recognized in America and to a lesser extent Britain, where the established church found itself seriously challenged by many 'religious denominations' exercising 'freedom in thinking about matters of faith'. They had their own ideas on the interpretation of Scripture and church government. In continental Europe this was soon to take a more dramatic form when during the French Revolution the Roman Catholic Church was theoretically abolished and the 'Cult of Reason' instituted. This was soon modified, but the authority of the church was never fully re-established and priests had to swear loyalty to the state, and most did so even though the Pope forbade it. All over Europe the authority of churches was questioned. Churchgoing dropped and dropped, yet most people still classed themselves as Christians; but they wanted the freedom to make their own moral judgements rather than be dictated to from the pulpit.

Thus Swedenborg predicted that the material things of the world would be unaffected by the Judgment, but that spiritual matters would. There are between these extreme cases many other planes of activity, such as literature, sociology, education, and the various arts.

Insofar as these activities have a spiritual interest, it could be assumed that they would be influenced by the influx of freer thinking from the New Heaven. It has, for instance, long been believed that music is inspired by heavenly influence; this belief is in fact the reason for its name. Music is that which is inspired by the 'Muses', Zeus's daughters, patronesses of the arts. Swedenborg more or less confirms the belief that musical 'inspiration' comes from above:

> **It is well known that some types of musical instruments are used to express one kind of natural affections and other types to express another kind, and that when a fitting melody is played they in actual fact stir the affections. Skilled musicians know all about this and also make proper use of it. [. . .] Mankind at first learned about it not from science and art but through the ear and its keen sense of hearing. From this it is plain that the ability does not have its origin in the natural world but in the spiritual world; it springs from the correspondence of things in the natural world [. . .] with realities in the spiritual world.**
>
> *Arcana Caelestia* §8337.2
>
> [. . .] fullness of joy within the heart manifests itself in singing. The reason why it does so in singing is that when the heart is filled with joy, and consequently the mind also, it bursts out into singing. The actual joy within the heart is expressed in the singing, the consequent joy within the mind in the words of the song. [. . .] All this flows spontaneously from the actual joy [. . .] From this it is evident that the ability of the lyrical qualities of the singing, and also the art of music, to express various kinds of affections, has its origins in the spiritual world and not in the natural.
>
> *Apocalypse Explained* §326.1

We might therefore expect to see a change in the quality of music about this time, and in fact we do. In the last decades of the 'old Christian era', the 1740s and 50s, there was a relative shortage of good music, yet suddenly about 1760 there was an explosion of new music, much of it of a joyful exuberant nature. Haydn who was approaching thirty and had composed little of interest until then, was now suddenly inspired to fully develop the string quartet and the symphony, as we now know them. On the other hand Mozart, though scarcely out of his cradle, started to compose with quite exceptional prolificity. Gluck, who had been composing trivial operas to show off falsetto voices, turned serious and produced his *Orpheus and Eurydice*, sometimes called the first true opera, where the music is truly expressive of the feelings of the characters in the opera.

Another form of art that may, because of its abstract nature, be easily influenced by the heavens is architecture (sometimes poetically called 'frozen music'). Architecture too undoubtedly changed in the latter half of the century, with the sudden dismissal of the elaborate and rather frivolous rococo style and its replacement by the simple and pure neoclassical style (for Englishmen 'Regency' style). Here the year 1757 has significance, as the Panthéon (or Church of St Geneviève) in Paris, was conceived that year. Its story is interesting:

Great symbolic significance could be placed on the fact that in 1757, the year of the Last Judgment, Louis XV, king of France, then the most powerful man in the world, appeared to be dying—the despair of his doctors. He did not lack faith, however, and turned to God, vowing to rebuild the ruined Church of St Geneviève if he could live on. Perhaps God was impressed;[8] certainly Louis survived and began the construction of the church. (It was completed after the French Revolution, when the atheist government decided to use it as a mausoleum for the heroes of their 'new age' and called it the Panthéon, by which name it is now known.)

Within a few decades buildings in the pure simple neoclassical style appeared all over Europe, and America too. The style also inspired furniture design, clothes fashion, painting and sculpture. In the latter cases we can claim some Swedenborgian connection, as John Flaxman, the first Professor of Sculpture of the Royal Academy and a founder member of the Swedenborg Society's Committee, was one of its most influential exponents. His books of illustrations to Homer, in simple confident line drawing, became the standard textbook in art schools all over Europe and his designs for Wedgwood pottery are famous. Swedenborg's influence on Flaxman's fellow student William Blake, who championed artistic freedom and independence, is also well known.

I could go on at considerable length about the changes that came about in the fields of literature, education, science and technology at this time. I might comment on how the population rose dramatically, or how the 'global village' began to take shape, but this is Swedenborg's book and he says little about such matters. He had of course died before such changes became obvious. Nevertheless it should be remarked that he himself did a considerable amount to extend scientific knowledge and technological progress, especially in his native land.

SOME CULTURAL CHANGES IN THIS NEW WORLD?

We should also note other comments that Swedenborg made about the future of certain racial groups in the other world at the time of his Last Judgment. Here Swedenborg is describing the 'geography' of the world of spirits in 1757.

> **The arrangement in the spiritual world of all the nations and peoples who were judged was seen to be as follows. In the centre were gathered those who are called the Reformed, and they were divided into groups according to their native countries: the Germans were towards the north, the Swedes towards the west, the Danes in the west, the Dutch towards the east and south, the British in the middle. Surrounding this centre, where all the Reformed were, the Roman Catholics were to be seen gathered, most of them in the western quarter, but some in the southern. Beyond them were the Mohammedans, also grouped according to their native countries; they were all to be seen in the west bordering on the south. Beyond them were gathered immense numbers of the heathen, who thus made up the outermost ring. [. . .] The reason the nations were thus arranged by districts was that their position depended upon the shared ability of each group to receive Divine Truths.**
>
> *Last Judgment* §48

The better of the British nation occupy the very centre of the Christians. The reason they are in the centre is that they have inward intellectual light. No one can see this in the natural world, but in the spiritual world it is

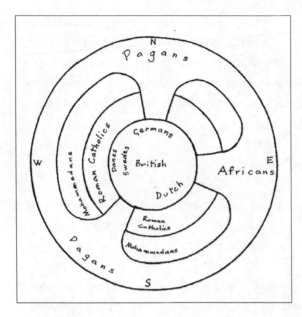

Fig. 29 'Map' of the world of spirits shortly after 1757. Swedenborg's description is only of what he calls the 'world of spirits', not of the heavens and, although it probably changed soon afterwards, can be taken as an interesting comment on the mental culture of the 19th century.

plain to see. They get this light from the freedom they have to think, and so to speak and write. In the case of others who do not have the same freedom, that light is blocked, not having any outlet.

Continuation of the Last Judgment §40

The Reformed Christians have been allotted places in this centre depending on how they receive spiritual light from the Lord. [. . .] Since the Dutch have that light very closely connected with their natural enlightenment, [. . .] they have been given dwellings in the Christian heartland in the east and south, in the east because of their ability to receive spiritual heat, which gives them charity, in the south because of their ability to receive spiritual light, which gives them faith.

[. . .] Another reason why they occupy those quarters of the Christian heartland is that the aim of their love is directed to trading and to money as the means to that aim, and this is a spiritual love. [. . .] The Dutch above others have the spiritual love just mentioned; regarded in itself it is a

shared good containing and advancing the good of their native country.
Continuation of the Last Judgment §48

Britain and Holland were, as it happens, the two countries Swedenborg spent most time in, apart from his Swedish homeland. They were the only European countries with 'free presses' where Swedenborg could publish his theological works without ecclesiastical interference. However, there is no reason to think he therefore allowed himself to show bias. The primary reason he gives for their superiority, at the time he writes, was their 'freedom to think, and so to speak and write'. This for him was an essential quality for regeneration in the new spiritual age now dawning. The blind obedience to dogma demanded by Rome, and to some extent by Protestantism, failed to allow people to adopt truths and live by them of their own freewill, but many in Britain and Holland were moving away from that situation.

It is interesting that Swedenborg saw 'trade' as having spiritual potential, but as it encouraged personal intercourse and sharing, particularly on an international level, one can see why. It would be a lever that would lead to the spreading of the Bible to many nations who would benefit from its teaching.

One could also comment that in the eighteenth century few people would have considered Britain to be exceptional. France was dominant in most fields and Austria and the decaying Italian states cultural leaders in other ways. It is remarkable that Swedenborg should have, perhaps unknowingly, picked as the centre of his other world environment, the culture that in years to come, through the British Empire and later the United States, was to lead the world in so many fields.

Swedenborg wrote in Latin, the language then understood by most scholars. The only language he chose to have his writings translated into was English; although no one then imagined it would overtake Latin, French and Spanish as the most widely acceptable international language.

It was only in Swedenborg's 'world of spirits' that Britain held such a position of course; in the heaven above it nationality would be of little importance. There was also another race who might have qualities that others would not have deemed of much importance. Swedenborg shows an unexpected interest in the Africans.

The African people are more capable of enlightenment than all other peoples on this earth, because they are of such a character as to think interiorly and thus to accept truths and acknowledge them. Others, such as Europeans, think only externally, receiving truths in their memory, but not seeing them interiorly in any light of the understanding, a light which they also do not acknowledge in matters of faith.

Last Judgment (Posthumous) §119

The heathen, who know nothing about the Lord, are to be seen surrounding those who do. [...] Those, however, who acknowledge one God and are scrupulous in observing the kind of precepts that are in the Ten Commandments, are to be seen in the upper region, and are thus in more direct communication with the Christians in the heartland, for this prevents communication being cut off by the Mohammedans and the Roman Catholics. The heathen too are grouped according to their characters and their ability to receive light from the Lord through the heavens. Some live further in, some further out; this does not depend on their native country, but on their religion. The Africans are further in than the rest.

Continuation of the Last Judgment §73

Since Swedenborg wrote, Western cultural influence has spread round the world and become dominant in many, if not most fields. Western Christianity has sent out its missionaries wherever it saw opportunities to spread the gospel, but their success has been less even geographically than that of other Western influences. Missionary progress in the Middle East and Asia has been disappointing, but on the other hand enormous headway has been made in Africa, where Christianity is now the dominant religion. Not only have Africans accepted European Christianity, they have created an African Christianity; they have formed their own churches which often seem to have more spirit and life than the organizations they derived from. This is very much as Swedenborg would have expected. One should also mention that Swedenborg's ideas on Africans inspired the pioneering slavery abolitionist Charles Wadstrom, who inspired the movement to establish colonies such as Sierra Leone and Liberia for repatriated slaves in West Africa.

Swedenborg might have been more surprised to know that African music would become the most significant new influence in twentieth-century music. As the proud owner of a chamber organ and a proficient musician himself, he would nevertheless probably have been pleased and interested. Highbrows may frown on the blues or jazz, but they have spread around the world more rapidly than any other music and have had a strong influence on 'classical' composers too.

SOCIAL CHANGE IN A NEW WORLD

Swedenborg made no predictions about social change in the future, but we know from his writings that he believed it would happen; and it is indeed happening. In particular what he wrote in his *Conjugial Love* about sexual relations and marriage suggests that a return to the ideals of the Silver and Golden Ages could be hoped for. He frequently tells us about marriage relationships in heaven and how different they were from those of his own time, particularly when compared with the marriages arranged for largely financial or social reasons among his own class.

> **Since the Lord's [second] coming He is reviving conjugial love as it was among the ancient peoples, because that love comes only from the Lord, and is present with those who are under His guidance becoming spiritual by means of the Word.**
>
> *Conjugial Love* §81.4

As heaven is from the human race, and consequently the angels there are of both sexes, and from creation woman is for man and man is for woman, thus the one belongs to the other, and this love is innate in both, it follows that there are marriages in heaven as well as on the earth. But marriages in heaven differ widely from marriages on the earth.

[. . .] Marriage in heaven is a conjunction of two into one mind. It will first be explained what this conjunction is. The mind consists of two parts, one called the understanding and the other the will. When these two parts act as one they are said to be one mind. In heaven the husband acts the part called the understanding and the wife acts the part called the will. When this conjunction, which belongs to man's interiors, descends into the lower things pertaining to the body, it is perceived and felt as love, and this love is conjugial love. From this it is clear that conjugial love has its origin in the conjunction of two into one mind. This in heaven is called cohabitation; and it is said that they are not two but one. So in heaven a married pair is spoken of, not as two, but as one angel.

Heaven and Hell §§366-7

This is one of Swedenborg's most revolutionary concepts and there is much more one could quote, but we must not stray from our main theme. The essential point to note is the change today from the male-dominated eighteenth-century situation, where women were considered inferior, marriage primarily a business contract and sexual relations mostly a matter of physical pleasure.[9] Swedenborg supported sexual equality and the sacred and psychological nature of marriage. Considerable changes have taken place in attitudes to women and to sexual relationships. Sexual promiscuity and the rise in the divorce rate may not seem to indicate progress, but even they reflect the freedom of thinking that Swedenborg said would be characteristic of the new age. But note that while supporting sexual equality, Swedenborg insisted on the psychological differences between the sexes, which complement one another, and so help create a more efficient, understanding and loving partnership.

Also in *Conjugial Love* Swedenborg comments on children's need for support and affection, a subject considered of little interest at his time. There is a whole chapter on the subject, but we have only space for a few lines of his introductory summary.

There are two universal spheres proceeding from the Lord designed to keep the universe in the condition in which it was created. One of these is the reproductive sphere, the other the sphere of the protection of what is procreated.

These two universal spheres make one with the sphere of conjugial love and that of the love of children. [. . . They] influence [. . .] everything in heaven and in the world, from first to last. The sphere of the love of children is one which protects and supports those who are unable to protect and support themselves.

This sphere affects the wicked as well as the good, making every individual disposed to love, protect and support his own offspring as the result of his particular love. This sphere chiefly affects the female sex, that is, mothers, but is passed on by them to the male sex, that is, to fathers.

[...] The more innocence in children withdraws, the more affection and bonding decline; and this continues gradually until it results in separation. [...] The love of small and older children is different in the case of spiritual married couples and natural [materially minded] ones.

Conjugial Love §385

Swedenborg says that parental love is a divine gift, which spontaneously develops in even the most unlikely people. The nurturing and education of children has been essential for the development of the new age. While good parents always did their best, now society as a whole is also concerned with the welfare of children.

The last point is particularly interesting; once the child is mature, the wise parent will have the good sense to allow them their freedom, while the self-centred parent will try to continue to exert a dominant influence. Once again this declares freedom to be a keynote of the new age and tends to condone the parental permissiveness considered acceptable in the later twentieth century.

IS THERE A 'SPECIFIC' NEW CHURCH?

I know of no definite mention of a 'specific' New Church in Swedenborg's writings. Nevertheless we have the indefinite and general passage already quoted in Chapter two:

[...] the Lord's church exists throughout the whole world, although it is especially located where the Lord is acknowledged and the Word is known.

The New Jerusalem §244

The phrase 'Word is known' could also be translated as 'where the Word is understood'. In that the Bible has been the world's best-selling book ever since it was first printed it is indeed widely known. How well it is understood, however, could be a subject for endless argument.

It seems reasonable to suggest that a 'specific church' now exists wherever Jews

Fig. 30 **Bryn Athyn Cathedral.** The Cathedral, near Philadelphia, is part of the headquarters of the General Church of the New Jerusalem.

fully appreciate the message of the Psalms, or where Christians understand our Lord's teaching in the New Testament. Swedenborgians, at least those belonging to 'New Church' organizations,[10] may be more choosy, however, and claim that an understanding of the symbolic sense of the Bible as explained by Swedenborg is essential for membership of the specific New Church. They would probably add the need to worship Jesus as the only God and to have some understanding of Swedenborg's theology.

Although Swedenborg's writings are not standard reading—yet some have been included in comprehensive libraries such as the Everyman's series—they are quite widely read. They have been in print ever since he died and have been translated into most modern languages. Some of those who studied their less than easily read pages, such as Blake, Flaxman, Crompton,[11] Balzac, Strindberg, Coleridge, the Brownings, Emerson, Baudelaire, Burnham,[12] Deakin,[13] Yeats, Helen Keller, Borges, and others too numerous to mention, have been particularly instrumental in encouraging progress in their fields. Nevertheless I do not wish to suggest that the influence of Swedenborg's writings has been the essential factor in establishing the new age. It is the quiet influence of angels and good spirits, no longer impeded by the barrier of the 'false heavens', dispelled after the Last Judgment, that has led and will lead us to build Jerusalem 'in England's green and pleasant land' and all over the world. Always remembering of course, that heaven is a state of mind, not a physical construction. We must remember the story of the Tower of Babel.

CONCLUSION

We are still only at the beginning of Swedenborg's 'New Age', but much has already happened and great changes can be seen. They may not be the changes people expected. Certainly no celestial events in the sky above us. Neither has any religious organization been able to assume temporal or even moral authority on an international scale. Authority has passed from rulers and churches to the people in general, and, as far as their own affairs are concerned, to individuals in particular.

Swedenborg often notes that the perfection of heaven is dependant upon its variety (*Heaven and Hell* §§56, 71, 469). Doubtless the New Heaven will have such a variety and certainly the world today displays a variety of human activity never seen before. Surely this will provide the potential for a better world, something nearer heaven on earth. But the Lord has given us our freedom, and so for better or worse, hell is also developing new ways to tempt us. Earth is the imperfect 'school' or even 'battleground' necessary to prepare us for heaven. While we are free, however, we will always be able to reject hell's advances, if we so wish. We should not be deterred from working towards a better spiritual environment because some people allow selfishness and hatred to enter their thinking. Divine revelation in one form or another is available to help us.

As we have already noted, neither we nor the angels can see into the future. However, the Book of Revelation does offer a 'timeless' prophecy of what can happen in the world in general. Swedenborg would also remind us it is equally about what can happen to the 'personal church' hopefully developing in each one of us at any time. In the following selected passages taken from the closing pages of Swedenborg's *Apocalypse Revealed*, he gives us some interpretations of the final chapters of the Bible which tell us much about the nature of the New Church to come in the minds of good and honest people.

And I John saw the holy city New Jerusalem coming down from God out of heaven signifies the New Church going to be set up by the Lord at the end of the former one, which [New Church] in companionship with the New Heaven will be in Divine truths as to both doctrine and life.

Prepared as a bride [adorned] for her husband signifies that Church conjoined with the Lord by means of the Word.

[. . .] *To the thirsting one I will give of the fountain of the water of life freely* signifies that to those who desire truths on account of any spiritual use, the Lord out of Himself, by means of the Word, is going to give all the things that conduce to that use.

[. . .] *Having a great and high wall* signifies the Word in the sense of the letter, from which the doctrine of the New Church will be derived.

Having twelve gates signifies the knowledge of truth and good there by means of which people are introduced into the Church.

[. . .] *And the city was pure gold like unto pure glass* signifies that consequently everything of that Church is the good of love inflowing together with light out of heaven from the Lord.

Apocalypse Revealed (§876)

And he showed me a pure river of water of life, shining crystal clear, going forth out of the throne of God and of the Lamb signifies the Apocalypse now opened and expounded as to the spiritual sense, where Divine Truths in abundance have been revealed by the Lord for those who will be in His New Church, which is the New Jerusalem.

In the midst of the street and of the river on this side and on that is a tree of life bearing twelve fruits [. . .] *each month yielding its own fruit* signifies that the Lord produces goods with people in accordance with every state of truth with [them].

And the leaves of the tree are for the healing of the nations signifies the rational truths therefrom by means of which those who are in evils and consequently in untruths are led to thinking soundly and living properly.

[. . .] ***Blessed are those doing His commandments, that their authority may be in the tree of life, and they may enter in by the gates into the city*** signifies that they have eternal happiness who live in accordance with the Lord's precepts to the end that they may be in the Lord and the Lord in them by means of love, and that they may be in His New Church by means of knowledge concerning Him.

Apocalypse Revealed (§932)

So the student of the Word is given this delightful sparkling vision of the church, with its gates open to pilgrims from every direction—from every spiritual persuasion—and truths of every variety available for us to study. The walls of the city are transparent crystal and yet perhaps we feel much of this truth is obscured in the symbolic clouds of heaven. We may never understand all its wealth and complexity. In the times of previous churches there were 'wise men' or 'universal geniuses' who seemed to know everything, but in the new age we have such a wealth of truth this is no longer possible. The situation is rather that that Swedenborg mentions above. If we sincerely wish and have a genuine need to understand some matter, we will be able to find the answers in the Word:

To the thirsting one I will give of the fountain of the water of life freely signifies that to those who desire truths on account of any spiritual use, the Lord out of Himself, by means of the Word, is going to give all the things that conduce to that use.

Apocalypse Revealed (§876)

Endnotes

—

Appendix

—

Index of Quotations

—

Index

Endnotes

Chapter Two

1. The question is discussed at length in an article by George de Charms, 'How Many "Last Judgments" Have There Been?', in *New Church Life*, vol. C, no. 6, June 1980, pp. 265-8.

Chapter Three

1. A series of articles on 'The Preadamites', by Alfred Acton II can be found in *New Church Life*, vol. XCIX, nos. 1-4, January-April 1979, pp. 26-32, 64-71, 109-15, 154-9.
2. W Schmidt, *The Origin and Growth of Religion: Facts and Theories*, tr. H J Rose (London: Methuen & Co. Ltd., 1931), pp. 45, 266; Karen Armstrong, *A History of God* (London Mandarin: 1994).
3. Laurens Van der Post, *The Lost World of the Kalahari* (London: Hogarth Press, 1958); Colin Macmillan Turnbull, *The Forest People* (London: Chatto & Windus, 1961); Farley Mowat, *People of the Deer* (London: Michael Joseph, 1952).
4. Bruce Chatwin's Australian travelogue *The Songlines* (London: Cape, 1987) is largely devoted to the subject.
5. Ovid, *The Metamorphoses of Ovid*, tr. Mary M Innes (Harmondsworth: Penguin, 1955), p. 31.
6. Ibid., p. 32.
7. Laurens Van der Post, *The Lost World of the Kalahari*, p. 246.
8. Robert Winston, *human instinct* (London, New York, Toronto, Sydney, Auckland: Bantam Press, 2002), p. 292.

Endnotes

9 Benjamin Walker, *Foundations of Islam: The Making of a World Faith* (London: Peter Owen, 1998), ch. 3, sec. 1, p. 56.

Chapter Four
1 See Michael Grant, *The History of Ancient Israel* (London: Weidenfeld and Nicolson, 1984), pt. 3, ch. 8, pp. 93-4.
2 Sogdian was spoken in the first millenium AD in the area around Samarkand. Being on the Silk Road it became the medium by which many ideas were transmitted between east and west. See Andrew Dalby, *Dictionary of Languages: The Definitive Reference to more than 400 Languages* (London: Bloomsbury, 1998), p. 426.
3 See David M Rohl, *Legend: The Genesis of Civilisation* (London: Century, 1998), p. 237.
4 See John Sassoon, *From Sumer to Jerusalem: The Forbidden Hypothesis* (Oxford: Intellect, 1993), pp. 26, 17, 60, 93.

Chapter Five
1 Jonathan N Tubb, *Canaanites* (London: British Museum Press, 1998), in the Peoples of the Past series, is a useful introduction to the subject.
2 James B Pritchard (ed.), *The Times Atlas of the Bible* (London: Times, 1987), p. 44.
3 The dates for both papyrus and parchment are taken from H E L Mellersh, *Chronology of the Ancient World: 10,000 BC-AD 799* (London: Barrie and Jenkins, 1976).

Chapter Six
1 This is not a misprint for Jehovah. Although the word Jehovih is not found in English translations it is in the Hebrew. Swedenborg discusses its use in *Arcana Caelestia* §§1793, 2923, noting that it is used in connection with temptations and supplications.
2 Jonathan N Tubb, *Canaanites*, p. 16.
3 See Karen Armstrong, *A History of God*, p. 9.

Chapter Seven
1 There is no reflection of this differentiating passage in his *Doctrine of the Sacred Scripture* or *The True Christian Religion*, where such a matter could have been raised, if it was essential doctrine. Undoubtedly the books listed in *The New Jerusalem* are the biblical books he most frequently refers to, but he nevertheless often quotes from books not on his list, especially from Job and the Epistles of Paul. As I noted in Chapter four, the Song of Solomon is 'written in the ancient style' of the Ancient Word, but is nevertheless set aside by Swedenborg because of 'improper' subject matter (*Arcana Caelestia* §3942). Few people would worry about its improprieties today.
2 See Swedenborg's *Apocalypse Explained* §1070.

Chapter Eight

1. N.b. The term 'new church' is of course very frequently used in the *Arcana* to apply to other new churches than the 'modern' New Church, as the Ancient Church, the Jewish, Christian and other churches were all new at one time.
2. The most accessible and comprehensive biography is Cyriel Odhner Sigstedt, *The Swedenborg Epic* (London: Swedenborg Society, 1981). The most recent biography, written by a knowledgeable fellow countryman of Swedenborg's, is Lars Bergquist, *Swedenborg's Secret* (London: Swedenborg Society, 2005). A shorter one is George F Dole and Robert H Kirven, *A Scientist Explores Spirit* (West Chester, PA: Swedenborg Foundation, 2006).
3. In J M Roberts, *History of the World* (Harmondsworth: Penguin, 1980), the author begins his Book Six entitled 'The Great Acceleration' in the middle of the eighteenth century. Arnold Toynbee, in *Mankind and Mother Earth: A Narrative History of the World* (New York and London: Oxford University Press, 1976), p. 562, chooses 1763 to date the beginning of the Industrial Revolution and other social changes. In his 1996 television series *A History of British Art*, Andrew Graham-Dixon said that, during the late eighteenth century, Western civilization changed profoundly and forever. He also says a new spirit of ambition and dissent entered British art sometime around the middle of the eighteenth century. Although discussing a rather longer period of time, Roy Porter's *Enlightenment: Britain and the Creation of the Modern World* (London: Allen Lane, 2000) details the changes of these times most effectively.
4. See J M Roberts, *History of the World*, p. 657.
5. Matt. 17:5; 24:30; 26:64; Mark 14:62; Luke 9:34, 35; 21:27; Rev. 1:7; 14:14; Dan. 7:13.
6. This is well documented in A N Wilson, *God's Funeral* (London: John Murray, 1992).
7. See Swedenborg's letter to the Landgrave of Hesse-Darmstadt, 18 June 1771, in John Elliott (ed.), *Small Theological Works and Letters of Emanuel Swedenborg* (London: Swedenborg Society, 1975), p. 299.
8. Intriguingly, Swedenborg met Louis XIV in the other world and learnt that he kept a great-grandfatherly eye on Louis XV and may have been able to influence him. See *Continuation of the Last Judgment* §60.
9. The situation is well documented in Roy Porter, *Enlightenment*, ch. 14, 'Did the mind have a sex?'.
10. Organized 'New Churches', based on Christian forms but following Swedenborg's teachings, are to be found in Britain, Continental Europe, North America, Australia, South and West Africa and elsewhere. The oldest is the British General Conference of the New Church. The Swedenborgian Church of North America is almost as old. The more recent General Church of the New Jerusalem is also based in North America, but has congregations in many other countries. In Africa, New Churches are less organized, but have many members.
11. Samuel Crompton was the inventor of 'Crompton's Mule', a machine which revolutionized Lancashire's cotton industry.

Endnotes

[12] Daniel Burnham designed the Chicago city plan; the Flatiron Building—New York's first skyscraper; and also Selfridges department store in London, a more revolutionary building than is generally recognized. See Irving D Fisher, 'An Iconology of City Planning—The Plan of Chicago', in Erland J Brock (ed.), *Swedenborg and his Influence* (Bryn Athyn, PA: The Academy of the New Church, 1988), pp. 449-64.

[13] Alfred Deakin, the first Attorney General of Australia and three times its Prime Minister, wrote a 'Gospel According to Swedenborg' for the guidance of early settlers. See Al Gabay, 'Alfred Deakin and Swedenborg: An Australian Experience', in Erland J Brock (ed.), *Swedenborg and his Influence*, pp. 381-403.

Appendix: World Age Patterns

The table on the following page is given to indicate how widespread the five or six world age idea is. It is common in mythology and found in the Bible. Prophets of several world religions have adopted it into their philosophies. Although the usual archaeological system essentially relates to the nature of the artefacts found in the various levels of excavations, it does echo the classical pattern. Historians use different terms, but the basis is still there, although they think in terms of many more ages.

COMMENTARY TO WORLD AGES CHART

Swedenborg's age patterns have of course been described in the main text of the book in Chapter one.

Hesiod's ages can be found in his 'book' *Works and Days* lines 105-203. His insertion of an age of 'Heroes' is unusual and can be accepted as a patriotic Greek quirk. The Greek heroes are in fact typical Bronze Age characters and are happily accommodated in that age. For Hesiod the periods are 'races'. The 'golden race' lived in the time of 'Kronos, king of heaven'. Was he perhaps their only god? '...they lived with happy hearts, untouched by work or sorrow...All good things were theirs; ungrudgingly, the fertile land gave up her fruits unasked'. Certainly a Paleolithic rather than Neolithic lifestyle.

Appendix

Swedenborg's Patterns

Swedenborg I	Most Ancient	Ancient	Jewish	Christian	New	
Swedenborg II	Most Ancient	1st Ancient	2nd Ancient	3rd Ancient	Christian	New

'Aryan' Patterns

Hesiod 700 BC	Gold	Silver	Bronze/Heroes	Iron		
Ovid AD 1	Gold	Silver	Bronze	Iron	'Present'	
Norse	Gold	War of the Gods		Twilight	New	
Persian	Creation of Heaven	Creation of Earth		Creation of Evil	Zoroaster	New Age
Hindu	Krita Yuga	Treta Yuga	Dvapara Yuga	Kali Yuga	New Age	

Biblical Patterns

St Augustine AD 400	Adam	Noah	Abraham	David/Captivity	Incarnation	'Present'
Mohammed AD 600	Adam	Noah	Abraham	Moses	Jesus Christ	Mohammed
Swedenborg	Adam	Noah	Heber	Moses	The Gospels	Revelation
Mappa Mundi	Eden	Babylon	Jerusalem	Rome	P. of Hercules	

Other Concepts

Amerindian	Ocelots (light?)	Water	Air	Fire	Motion	
Astrology	Cancer	Gemini	Taurus	Aries	Pisces	Aquarius
Ages of Man	Infancy	Childhood	Youth	Adulthood	Maturity	

Modern Ideas

Archaeological	Palaeolithic	Neolithic	Bronze	Iron Age		
Historical		Agricultural Revolution	Urban Revolution	Iron Age	Common Era	Industrial Revolution
Approx Dates for Mid East & Western Europe	< 8000 BC	8000 BC >	3000 BC >	1500 BC >	AD 0-1757	AD 1757 >
Creative Process	Conception	Planning		Execution	Assessment	Enjoyment

The races of silver, bronze and heroes follow in sequence, each of lesser worth until Hesiod's own time of the iron race, of which he comments, 'I wish I were not of this race, that I had died before or had not yet been born'. He then decries the many faults of the race of iron. As far as I am aware Hesiod sees history only as going downhill, there is no hope of any return to the golden age, as we find elsewhere.

Ovid's version occurs in his poem *Metamorphoses*. It is particularly interesting for the vivid description of the Golden Age, comparable with the Palaeolithic, as mentioned in our Chapter three. He emphasizes the ages' peaceable lifestyle with no need of city walls or trumpets calling men to arms.

The **Norse** versions occur in the Icelandic *Voluspa* (The 'book' of the prophetess Vala). It is the last part of what is called the *Elder Edda*. Although a verbal saga of apparently very ancient origin it had never been committed to writing until Christian monks came into contact with it in the 11th century AD. A discussion of the 'correspondences' within this myth can be found in J J Garth Wilkinson's book on the subject entitled *Voluspa and its Correspondences*.

The **Persian** concept is found in Persian Zoroastrian literature, which is derived from earlier mythology. It has a more optimistic pattern than most ancient series, after three declining ages things are put right in the fourth and fifth ages.

The **Hindu** Yugas were first mentioned in the Vedas and are claimed to be cyclic, repeating like reincarnation. The four Yugas are a declining series, but then in the new fifth age the good state of the first Krita Yuga is restored.

St Augustine of Hippo's version was based on a Jewish concept (which I have not been able to trace) and used until medieval times but is now largely ignored.

Muhammad had a concept of a succession of 'Great Prophets' who gave successive revelations of truth, each being superseded by its successor.

The **Mappa Mundi** in Hereford Cathedral shows the world as a disk divided by an 'equator' punctuated with five locations deliberately misplaced to make a straight equatorial line. At the centre of the world is Jerusalem a feature common to many medieval maps. At the eastern end of the equatorial line is the Garden of Eden and halfway between them is Babylon, the two seeming to have a similar symbolism to the Most Ancient and Ancient dispensations. Balancing them along the western equator are Rome and the Pillars of Hercules (straits of Gibraltar) seeming to symbolize the Christian and New ages.

The **Amerindians** have a legend of four 'suns' or ages which came to disastrous ends caused by black jaguars, flood, wind and volcanic eruptions, before the age of 'motion'.

Astrology claims that a new age begins approximately every 2000 years as the constellations rotate above the earth. An idea which probably stems from knowledge of correspondences in earlier times.

Appendix

There is a long standing idea that we pass through 'ages' during our lives. 4, 5, 7 & 10 have been suggested, but 5 suited **St Gregory** and fits modern psychological ideas best.

Modern scholarship finds a mere five ages too imprecise and has little use for the concept, but terms that are closely comparable are still used, particularly Bronze Age and Iron age.

More detail can be found in my article 'Round the World in Five Ages' in the *Swedenborg Society Magazine* no 2, December 1986.

Index of Quotations from the Works of Swedenborg

Apocalypse Explained

§176.	p. 18	§326.1.	p. 203	§799.1.	p. 36
§220.12	p. 131	§659.18	p. 35	§1069.	p. 170
§233.3.	p. 173	§670.2.	p. 157	§1180.	p. 162

Apocalypse Revealed

§752.	p. 169	§896.	p. 8	§932.	p. 215
§876.	pp. 214, 215				

Arcana Caelestia

§1...	p. 129	§442.	p. 53	§640.	pp. 57, 82
§4...	p. 130	§422.	p. 133	§641.	p. 82
§5...	p. 188	§483.	p. 53	§660.	p. 55
§50..	p. 162	§483.2.	p. 40	§§669-79..	p. 72
§82..	p. 10	§527.	p. 55	§743.	p. 72
§190-1.	p. 52	§605.	p. 69	§765.	p. 67
§337.	p. 53	§605.	p. 71	§920.	p. 34
§367.2...	pp. 112, 133	§607.2.	p. 48	§1002.	p. 40

Index of Quotations

§1067	p. 73	§2722.1	p. 74	§6065	p. 7
§1068	p. 73	§2897	p. 79	§6723.3	p. 118
§1069	p. 73	§2916	p. 83	§6750	p. 118
§1083	p. 8	§2986	p. 134	§6752.8	p. 120
§1083.3	p. 66	§2995	p. 136	§6753	p. 119
§1102.1	p. 36	§3035	p. 32	§6846	p. 70
§1118	p. 44	§3263.2	p. 22, 135	§6905	p. 100
§1122	p. 47	§3268	p. 134	§6997	p. 123
§1123	p. 43	§3596	p. 86	§7636	p. 33
§1238.2	p. 98	§3667	p. 70	§7840	p. 24
§1293	p. 37	§3778.1	p. 116	§8118	p. 42
§1327	pp. 6, 65	§3893	p. 49	§8301.6	p. 113
§1327.2	p. 90	§3942	p. 79	§8337.2	p. 203
§1343.1	p. 32	§4060.4	p. 17	§8588.4	p. 115
§1356	p. 104	§4149.2	p. 66	§8762	p. 24
§1447	p. 120	§4328	p. 44	§8944.2	p. 87
§1551	p. 18	§4430.2	p. 117	§9353	p. 50
§1664.9	p. 120	§4447.2	p. 56	§10099.3	p. 84
§1690	p. 149	§4454	pp. 7, 32, 44	§10235	p. 125
§1799	p. 174	§4489.2	p. 101	§10355.5	p. 147
§1834.2	p. 155	§4493.3	pp. 33, 74	§10384	p. 185
§1850.3	p. 111	§4517	pp. 35, 100	§10453.3	p. 116
§2144	p. 45	§4680.2	p. 89	§10563	p. 120
§2180.2	p. 124	§4680.3	p. 97	§10643.1	p. 74
§2180.6	p. 125	§4692.3	pp. 122, 123	§10698	p. 115
§2417.3	p. 156	§5136.2	p. 121		

Athanasian Creed

§173	p. 195	§153	p. 70	

Conjugial Love

§75	p. 57	§77	pp. 103, 105	§205	p. 40
§75.3	pp. 36, 39	§78	pp. 135, 138	§337	p. 164
§76	p. 90	§79	p. 175	§342	pp. 68, 161
§76.4	p. 85	§79.5	p. 165	§385	p. 211
		§81.4	p. 209		

Index of Quotations

De Conjugio   §119 . . . pp. 18, 43

Continuation on the Last Judgment
§11 . . . . p. 189   §48 . . . . p. 207   §73 . . . . p. 208
§40 . . . . p. 206

Coronis
§1 . . . . p. 194   §43 . . . . pp. 75, 88   Summaries II-III . p. 19
§2 . . . . pp. 5, 6   §49 . . . . p. 117   Summaries VII . p. 154
§37 . . . . p. 18   §52 . . . . pp. 118, 131 Summaries XL-XLIX p. 172
§39 . . . . pp. 67, 87   §55 . . . . p. 132   Summaries L-LI . p. 174
§41 . . . . p. 66   §56 . . . . pp. 132, 133
§41.3 . . . p. 105   §58 . . . . pp. 132, 133

Divine Providence
§215.2 . . p. 41   §255 . . . p. 160   §328 . . . p. 26
§215.4 . . p. 39   §260 . . . p. 111
§245 . . . p. 23   §260.3 . . p. 128, 154

The Divine Wisdom
§121 . . . p. 48

Doctrine of the Lord
§12 . . . . p. 148   §62 . . . . p. 191   §63 . . . . p. 197

Doctrine of the Sacred Scripture
§102 . . . p. 104   §105 . . . p. 170   §110 . . . pp. 20, 170

Heaven and Hell
§56 . . . . p. 23   §168.3 . . p. 11   §306 . . . p. 46
§57 . . . . p. 23   §237 . . . p. 126   §366 . . . p. 210
§115 . . . p. 46   §241 . . . p. 127   §367 . . . p. 210

Last Judgment
§3 . . . . . p. 196   §48 . . . . p. 205   §69 . . . . p. 191
§41.3 . . . p. 128   §57 (note) . p. 150   §73.1 . . . p. 200
§45 . . . . p. 189   §59.1 . . . p. 26   §73.2 . . . p. 202

Index of Quotations

Last Judgment (Posthumous)
§119 . . . . p. 208 §254 . . . . p. 138

Letters to Beyer
p. 187. p. 197. p. 198, p. 200

The New Jerusalem
§2 . .	. . p. 192	§13 . .	. . p. 171	§244 .	. . pp. 20, 211
§3 . .	. . p. 192	§242 .	. . p. 21	§261 .	. . p. 27
§4 . .	. . p. 192	§243 .	. . p. 21	§266 .	. . p. 152

On the Sacred Scripture
§18 . .	. . pp. 68, 77	§36 . .	. . p. 77	§39 . .	. . p. 165
§19 . .	. . pp. 8, 114	§37 . .	. . p. 77	§40 . .	. . p. 17
§32 . .	. . p. 147	§38 . .	. . p. 77	§42 . .	. . p. 185

The Spiritual Diary
§1587 .	. . p. 84	§5561 .	. . p. 127	§5749 .	. . p. 163
§3390 .	. . p. 31	§5562 .	. . p. 127	§5947 .	. . p. 163
§4824 .	. . p. 153	§5621 .	. . p. 128	§5999 .	. . pp. 50, 85

The True Christian Religion
§9.2 . .	. . p. 122	§262 .	. . p. 146	§764 .	. . p. 4
§89 . .	. . p. 148	§275 .	. . p. 36	§776 .	. . p. 194
§154 .	. . p. 151	§279.3 .	. . p. 80	§779 .	. . p. 187
§176 .	. . p. 158	§434 .	. . p. 155	§791 .	. . p. 193
§201 .	. . p. 79	§508 .	. . p. 193	§821 .	. . p. 167
§202 .	. . p. 54	§625 .	. . p. 183	§846 .	. . p. 199
§205 .	. . p. 76	§760 .	. . pp. 3, 117, 157		
§206 .	. . p. 158	§762 .	. . p. 10		

White Horse Appendix
p. 50

Worlds in Space
§54.2 . . . . p. 48

Select Bibliography

BOOKS

Emanuel Swedenborg, *The Coronis* or *Appendix to the True Christian Religion* (London: Swedenborg Society, 1931). Swedenborg's incomplete, posthumous work on the five churches.

—*Arcana Caelestia,* Vol. II (London: Swedenborg Society, 1984). §§1114-1129 contain a short, but full, description of the Most Ancient Church. In a wide sense the whole of the *Arcana Caelestia* deals with the first three churches.

—*Divine Providence* (London: Swedenborg Society, 1949). §328 has a concise summary of the Five Churches.

—*The Last Judgment* and *Continuation on the Last Judgment* (London: Swedenborg Society, 1992). Swedenborg's account of the consummation of the 'first' Christian Church in 1757.

—*The Last Judgment in Retrospect* (West Chester: Swedenborg Foundation, 1996). George Dole offers an edited colloquial translation, with an introduction by James Lawrence.

Samuel M Warren, *A Compendium of the Theological Writings of Emanuel Swedenborg* (London: Swedenborg Society, 1939). Within this extensive work Warren has collected a comprehensive selection of passages concerning the Five Churches.

Ernst Benz, *Visionary Savant in the Age of Reason* (West Chester: Swedenborg Foundation, 2002). Chapter 29 is on Swedenborg's 'Ideas on the History of Humankind'.

Lars Bergquist, *Swedenborg's Secret: A Biography* (London: Swedenborg Society, 2005). Chapter 22 emtitled '*Arcana Caelestia*, the Fall and the Ages of Man', is largely about the first and second churches.

Select Bibliography

Philip H Johnson, *Revelation Through the Ages* (London: Swedenborg Society, 195?). Booklet concentrating on the type of revelation given to each age.

Brian Kingslake, *Swedenborg Explores the Spiritual Dimension* (London: Seminar Books, 1981). Chapter 22, entitled 'Ecclesiastical History', is a quick up to date summary of the Five Churches concept.

William R Kintner, *The Role of Ancient Israel, Written with the Finger of God* (Vantage Press, New York). A Swedenborgian perspective of the history of the Israelites from Abraham to Jesus.

Carl Th. Odhner, *The Golden Age* (USA: Academy Book Room, 1978). 'The story of the Most Ancient Church'.

Carl Th Odhner, *The Mythology of the Greeks and Romans* (USA: Academy Book Room, 1978). Explores the application of Swedenborg's 'Science of Correspondences' to ancient myths. Written around 1900 its scholarship may be outdated, but the themes are sound.

Hugo Lj Odhner, *The Divine Allegory* (USA: Academy Book Room, 1954). 'The story of the peoples and lands of scripture and their spiritual significance as revealed in the writings of Emanuel Swedenborg.

The Ancient Church Conference, (Bryn Athyn: General Church Press, 2008).

MAGAZINE ARTICLES

Alfred Acton II. 'The Preadamites', *New Church Life,* Jan-Apr 1979 (USA: General Church of the New Jerusalem). A series of four articles.

Patrick L Johnson, 'The Pattern of Time', *Lifeline Magazine,* Aug 1997-March 1998 (London: General Conference of the New Church.). A series of seven articles relating Swedenborg's five church concept to archaeology and history.

Eric E Sandstrom, 'An Age-old Advent', *New Church Life,* Jan-Mar 1991 (USA: General Church of the New Jerusalem). A series of three articles discussing evidence of the Lord's Advent and purposes through the five ages.

Covenant, 'A journal devoted to the study of the Five Churches' (Bryn Athyn: Glencairn Museum). Issues 1,2 & 3 have articles on the Ancient, Jewish and Christian Churches.

The New Philosophy, July-Sept 2008, 'The World Transformed Conference'. This issue of the magazine contains some of the papers given at this Conference on the subject of *The Last Judgment.*

Index

Aaron, 115, 119, 125, 138, 159
Abdeel, 134
Abel, 13, 52, 53
Aborigine(s), 33, 34, 37, 44, 45, 46, 49, 51, 56; Aboriginal, 13, 41
Abraham, 12, 69, 83, 104, 105, 115, 116, 117, 133, 134, 147; Abram, 104, 117, 121
Adam, 5, 6, 12, 13, 18, 31, 32, 52, 53, 56, 129; *see also* church
Aesop, 77
affection(s), 4, 8, 11, 24, 41, 45, 47, 72, 76, 86, 118, 119, 126, 127, 135, 203, 210, 211
Africa, 3, 67, 77, 87, 130, 156, 159, 165, 208; African(s), 21, 44, 122, 170, 207, 208, 209; West Africa, 161, 208
ages; Bronze Age, 6, 12, 13, 27, 76, 83, 84, 87, 90, 102, 105, 108, 135, 141; classical, 7, 12; Copper Age, 6, 9, 18, 57, 102, 105, 106, 108, 175, 179; Five Ages, 6, 10, 11, 12, 13; Golden Age, 6, 9, 12, 13, 18, 19, 36, 38, 42, 45, 57, 61, 122, 135, 136, 141, 175, 179, 209; Industrial, 12; Iron Age, 6, 9, 12, 13, 18, 27, 53, 57, 112, 135, 136, 138, 141, 147, 150, 175; Neolithic Age, 12, 13, 40, 53, 73, 74, 76, 83, 87; New, 4, 157, 165, 175, 184, 185, 194, 196, 204, 207, 210, 211, 213, 215; Palaeolithic Age, 12, 13, 19, 36, 37, 38, 40, 41, 43, 53; Age of Religions, 12, 14; Silver Age, 6, 9, 12, 13, 18, 38, 57, 85, 90, 91, 92, 94, 135, 139, 141, 175, 179, 209; six ages, 6, 12, 13; Stone Age, 39; *see also* church
agriculture, 37, 38, 68
Agricultural Revolution, 73
Ahab, 130
Ahura Mazda, 71
Akkadian, 89, 90
Alexander the Great, 146
Alexandria, 86
altar, 100, 101, 115, 125, 133
America, 87, 202, 204; *see also* United States
Amorites, 78
Amsterdam, 199
ancients, 7, 18, 36, 43, 46, 49, 50, 69, 70, 74, 75, 76, 78, 83, 84, 85, 86, 103, 135, 138,

Index

139, 159, 168, 175, 179, 209; *see also* church
Ancient Word, 67, 76, 77, 79, 80, 82, 87, 102, 104, 128, 129, 135, 150, 152
angel(s), 26, 27, 39, 40, 43, 45, 46, 47, 48, 55, 57, 58, 59, 68, 76, 80, 82, 84, 90, 92, 94, 102, 103, 105, 106, 108, 115, 125, 127, 135, 136, 137, 138, 139, 140, 141, 149, 150, 151, 162, 175, 176, 177, 178, 180, 183, 184, 187, 192, 193, 196, 198, 199, 201, 209, 210, 213; angelic, 34, 47, 49, 126, 194
Anglicans, 201
Anglo-Catholicism, 201
animist, 57
anthropology, 40, 121; anthropologist(s), 42, 45, 46, 49
Apostles, 3, 129, 147, 150, 151, 154, 157, 172; *see also* disciples
Ar, 78
Arabia, 54, 67, 68, 76, 86, 103
Aramaic, 80
arcana, 79, 116, 129
archaeology, 83; archaeological, 4, 88, 130; archaeologists, 37, 38, 43, 51, 112
architecture, 69, 204
Arctic, 40
Aristotle, 48
Ark, the, 115; Noah's, 68, 71, 72, 73, 82; of the Testimony, 118
Arnon, 78
Artemis, Temple of, 75
Asia, 3, 50, 67, 68, 76, 77, 80, 85, 86, 92, 102, 104, 106, 122, 130, 135, 138, 156, 159, 161, 165, 170, 208; (central), 13; Asiatic, 54, 88, 102, 106; South-East, 87
Assyria, 54, 67, 68, 76, 86, 103; Assyrians, 112
astrology, 7
Athens, 77, 86
atonement, 158
Augsburg Confession, 198
Augustine, St, 7
Australia, 13, 34; Australian, 33, 37, 56

Austria, 191, 207
Ayers Rock, *see* Uluru

Baal, 88
Babel, *see* Tower of Babel
Babylon, 68, 88, 121, 166; Babylonish, 170; Babylonian exile, 112
Baha'i Faith, 201
Bahrain, 83
Baiame, 33
Balzac, Honoré de, 212
Baudelaire, Charles, 212
Beyer, Gabriel, 187, 197, 198, 199, 200
Bible, 5, 12, 13, 22, 73, 99, 112, 121, 133, 153, 165, 166, 167, 171, 185, 187, 207, 212, 214; Acts, 154; Amos, 73, 151; Apocrypha, 153; Chronicles, 130; Corinthians, 177; Daniel, 3, 5, 12, 138, 151, 152, 175, 180, 184, 192; Deuteronomy, 124, 152; Epistles of Paul, 153; Exodus, 60, 105, 113, 115, 118, 119, 187; Ezekiel, 133, 138, 151; Five Books of Moses, 3, 78, 79, 117, 119, 125, 130, 151; Genesis, 6, 10, 11, 12, 13, 40, 51, 52, 53, 54, 55, 56, 57, 66, 68. 69, 71, 72, 73, 77, 78, 89, 100, 104, 105, 129, 133, 187; Habakkuk, 151; Haggai, 151; Hosea, 151; Isaiah, 73, 121, 132, 151, 184; Jeremiah, 79, 132, 133, 151, 184; Job, 35, 79, 153, 199; Joel, 151; John, 73, 152, 153; Jonah, 151; Joshua, 80, 104, 105, 121, 130, 131, 151; Judges, 105, 130, 131, 151; Kings, 130, 131, 151; Lamentations, 151, 152; Leviticus, 123, 124, 152; Luke, 146, 148, 149, 152; Malachi, 151; Mark, 152; Matthew, 73, 116, 136, 145, 148, 149, 152, 158, 190, 193, 194, 195, 196, 200; Micah, 125, 125, 151; Nahum, 151; New Testament, 5, 12, 54, 145, 146, 147, 152, 153, 154, 155, 159, 212; Numbers, 78, 79, 80, 102, 106; Obadiah, 151; Old Testament, 5, 12, 53, 54, 74, 78, 79, 103, 112, 113, 114, 116, 127, 129, 131, 137, 138, 145, 146, 147, 150, 151, 152, 154, 159; Prophets, 3, 78,

Index

79, 103, 114, 117, 122, 124, 130, 131, 132, 145, 146, 147, 148, 151, 152, 184, 194, 195; Proverbs, 80; Psalms, 130, 147, 148, 151, 152, 212; Revelation (Apocalypse), 5, 11, 12, 20, 152, 154, 155, 166, 175, 183, 184, 190, 191, 192, 193, 194, 196, 197, 198, 200, 213, 214; Samuel, 80, 114, 130, 131, 151; Song of Songs, 79, 80; Vulgate, 153; Zechariah, 151, 184; Zephaniah, 151; *see also* Sacred Scripture; Word, the

biblical, 5, 7, 8, 13, 41, 56, 98, 100, 113, 117, 119, 184, 188

Black Sea, the, 67, 87

Blake, William, 204, 212

Boehme, Jacob, 187

Borges, Jorge Luis, 212

brain, 40, 197; (right), 82; (left), 82

breathing, 47, 48, 49; (internal), 48, 49

Britain, 165, 191, 197, 202, 207; British, 205

British Empire, 207

bronze, 6, 13, 18, 101, 108, 138, 141, 176; *see also* ages

Brownings, the, 212

Bryn Athyn Cathedral, 212

Buddhism, 7, 161; Buddhist, 14, 160

burial, 83; buried, 121; *see also* graves

Burnham, Daniel, 212

Bushmen, 13, 34, 45, 49, 56

Cain, 13, 52, 53

Calvinists, 174

Canaan, 35, 54, 56, 67, 68, 76, 77, 83, 86, 87, 97, 98, 99, 103, 104, 105, 111, 117, 120, 121, 123, 129, 130; Canaanite(s), 88, 98, 99, 100, 101, 103, 119

Canon, the, 130, 152, 153

Castelo del Angelo, 168

Catholic(s), 145, 165, 166, 167, 168, 169, 170, 171, 174, 185, 189, 198, 201, 202, 205, 208

cavemen, 38

celestial, 7, 8, 9, 12, 27, 31, 32, 35, 42, 43, 44, 45, 52, 56, 74, 79, 86, 101, 103, 117, 120, 123, 127, 131, 136, 141, 147, 213; heaven, 8, 9, 127, 147; *see also* church

Celts, 7

Chaldaea, 54

charity, 6, 20, 21, 24, 53, 66, 67, 72, 74, 76, 81, 82, 86, 88, 89, 97, 111, 112, 118, 123, 135, 150, 153, 155, 156, 171, 172, 174, 192, 206; charitable, 73, 155, 156, 157, 167, 190

Chemosh, 78

child, 148; childhood, 9, 45, 58, 148, 149; children, 9, 39, 40, 41, 43, 58, 76, 88, 107, 122, 192, 210, 211; *see also* offspring

Children of Israel, *see* Israel

China, 80; Chinese, 83, 160, 161

Christ, 123, 146, 155, 158, 167, 169, 192, 195, 196, 198

Christadelphians, 201

Christendom, 56, 175, 200

Christian(s), 4, 5, 13, 14, 22, 116, 121, 128, 135, 138, 145, 146, 147, 154, 156, 157, 158, 161, 162, 163, 164, 165, 170, 172, 173, 174, 180, 188, 192, 197, 202, 203, 205, 206, 208, 212; Christianity, 145, 155, 156, 160, 196, 208; *see also* church

Christian Science, 201

church; Adamic, 5, 12, 13, 31, 51, 54, 98; Ancient (*Ecclesia Antiqua*), 3, 4, 5, 6, 8, 9, 12, 13, 20, 33, 35, 50, 65, 66, 67, 68, 69, 70, 72, 73, 74, 79, 80, 82, 84, 85, 86, 87, 88, 90, 97, 98, 100, 102, 121, 135, 150; Apostolic, 158; Celestial, 7, 43, 66; Christian Church, 3, 4, 5, 8, 10, 12, 66, 84, 145, 146, 147, 150, 153, 154, 156, 157, 158, 164, 170, 171, 172, 173, 174, 175, 191, 198; Church of the Gentiles, 22, 111, 112, 133, 134, 136, 156; First Ancient, 5, 12, 65, 87, 89, 97, 102; Five Churches, 4, 6, 8, 10, 11, 12, 19; four churches, 3, 4, 5, 7, 9, 10, 19, 54; Hebrew Church, 35, 97, 100, 117, 123, 135; Israelite, 3, 5, 12, 105, 112, 117, 132, 159; Jewish, 5, 6, 8, 10, 12, 18, 20, 56,

111, 112, 113, 115, 116, 117, 121, 122, 123, 129, 130, 133, 135, 156, 195; Lord's Church / Church of the Lord, 20, 22, 87, 111, 211; Medieval, 171, 196; Most Ancient (*Ecclesia Antiquissima*), 3, 4, 5, 7, 9, 12, 13, 18, 19, 20, 31, 32, 33, 35, 36, 42, 46, 48, 50, 51, 52, 53, 54, 55, 56, 57, 65, 66, 67, 73, 81, 82, 84, 90, 101, 120, 121, 130, 135, 136, 150; new / New Church, 4, 5, 8, 9, 12, 19, 20, 71, 82, 97, 98, 105, 111, 117, 125, 133, 153, 156, 158, 174, 175, 184, 185, 186, 189, 191, 193, 194, 196, 197, 198, 200, 201, 211, 212, 214, 215; Noachian, 5, 6, 12, 67, 86; Reformed, 165, 167, 169, 170, 171, 174, 185, 198, 205, 206; representative, 23, 27, 75, 111, 116, 120, 159; Second Ancient, 6, 12, 65, 90, 97, 98, 102, 104, 105, 117; 'specific', 19, 20, 21, 22, 36, 56, 99, 112, 115, 133, 167, 173, 184, 211, 212; Spiritual, 6, 7, 8, 21, 23, 43, 66, 67, 73, 100, 114, 134, 135, 159, 180; Third Ancient, 6, 12, 65; 'universal', 17, 19, 20, 21, 22, 36, 56, 99, 112, 133, 136, 167, 184; *see also* ages; Catholic(s); Christian(s)
Church of England, 200
Church of St Geneviève, 204
classical, 7, 12, 75, 78, 86, 209; *see also* neoclassical
Clowes, John, 200
Coleridge, Samuel Taylor, 212
Confucian, 14
Congo, 35, 41
conjugial love, 42, 57, 60, 79, 92, 93, 107, 140, 141, 164, 179, 180, 209, 210
conscience, 32, 44, 45, 67, 68, 82, 155, 174
Constantine, 156, 158
Consummation of the Age, 20, 188, 194
copper, 106; *see also* ages
Corinthian, 75
correspondences, 12, 39, 45, 46, 49, 50, 54, 68, 75, 76, 77, 79, 80, 85, 86, 88, 91, 92, 93, 102, 103, 130, 131, 136, 137, 138, 139, 150, 159, 176, 187, 198, 200, 203; *see also* representatives
Council of Nicaea, 157, 158, 196
Council of Trent, 198
covenant, 60, 117
Coventry Cathedral, 195
Creation, 3, 9, 129, 188, 209
Creator, 10, 33, 160; *see also* God; Lord
Crompton, Samuel, 212
Cult of Reason, 202

David, 23, 83, 113, 115, 121, 123, 130, 131, 147, 151
Deakin, Alfred, 212
death, 10, 26, 36, 48, 55, 82, 136, 148, 162, 167, 168, 174, 188, 196, 199, 201; dead, 83
Decalogue, 160; *see also* Ten Commandments
degrees (discrete), 7, 8, 12
Denmark, 165; Danes, 205
devil, the, 148, 149, 177
Dibon, 78
Dinah, 56
disciples, 145, 150, 151, 156, 158, 192, 197; *see also* Apostles
divorce, 116, 210
dominion, 161, 166, 167, 168; *see also* power
dreams, 3, 5, 18, 46, 47
Dreamtime, 46, 51
Dumah, 134
Dutch, *see* Holland

earth, 3, 8, 9, 10, 17, 19, 20, 23, 27, 34, 36, 38, 40, 43, 45, 50, 72, 84, 89, 106, 111, 126, 130, 133, 136, 147, 150, 156, 160, 161, 163, 167, 168, 169, 170, 173, 174, 180, 185, 188, 189, 190, 194, 195, 196, 197, 198, 200, 208, 209, 213; new, 183, 190, 191, 196; *see also* world
East, 14, 141; Eastern, 161
Eber, *see* Heber
Ebla, 99
economic development, 12
Eden (Garden of), 52, 53, 56, 129

Index

Egypt, 50, 54, 67, 68, 76, 77, 83, 86, 88, 91, 99, 103, 105, 117, 119, 130, 159; Egyptian(s), 50, 68, 71, 79, 80, 90, 105, 119
Elijah, 147
Emerson, Ralph Waldo, 212
England, 200, 213; English, 200, 207; Englishmen, 204
Enoch, 50, 53, 54, 68, 85
Enosh, 53, 54, 56
Ephesus, 75
Esau, 111, 133
Eskimos, 49
Ethiopia, 67, 77, 86
eucharistic, 123
Euphrates, 99
Europe, 7, 114, 130, 157, 159, 161, 164, 165, 170, 201, 202, 204; Europeans, 44, 83, 171, 207, 208
Evangelicals, 174, 201
Evangelists, 3, 148, 152, 153, 157; *see also* Bible
Eve, 13, 52, 129
Everyman's (library), 212
evil, 25, 26, 55, 57, 72, 81, 82, 100, 107, 114, 116, 125, 136, 150, 155, 160, 162, 189, 198, 215
external(s), 8, 23, 24, 26, 27, 33, 34, 35, 46, 48, 66, 73, 74, 89, 97, 101, 104, 113, 116, 120, 122, 125, 127, 129, 174, 191, 200, 208

fables, 50, 69, 77, 128; Aesop's, 77
facial expression, 44, 45, 47, 48, 49
faith, 6, 8, 17, 21, 23, 24, 26, 52, 53, 55, 67, 72, 73, 88, 111, 114, 118, 129, 134, 135, 150, 153, 156, 161, 168, 171, 172, 173, 174, 188, 190, 192, 193, 198, 202, 204, 206, 208; faith alone, 21, 171, 172, 173, 189
family, 35, 41, 42, 55, 70, 167; nuclear, 9
farmer, 13; farming, 53
feminine values, 9
festivals, 123

Flaxman, John, 204, 212
Flood, the, 3, 5, 7, 20, 55, 65, 71, 72, 90
food, 36, 37, 38, 40, 72, 73, 86
Formula Concordiae, 198
France, 137, 165, 167, 171, 204, 207; French, 201, 207
freedom, 44, 48, 52, 150, 162, 165, 177, 202, 204, 206, 211, 213; (of thought), 186, 202, 206, 207, 210; (of press), 207
freewill, 44, 100, 123, 172, 178, 207
French Revolution, 201, 202, 204
Fujiyama, 34

General Church of the New Jerusalem, 212
gentile(s), 21, 22, 56, 112, 122, 133, 134, 135, 156, 161, 162; *see also* church; heathen
geography, 205; geographical(ly), 66, 99, 208
Germany, 165, 197; Germans, 205
Gluck, 204; *Orpheus and Eurydice*, 204
God, 4, 8, 10, 11, 17, 20, 21, 22, 25, 26, 32, 33, 36, 42, 52, 69, 70, 71, 72, 77, 80, 87, 102, 104, 105, 106, 107, 113, 115, 116, 118, 121, 122, 125, 126, 133, 134, 135, 141, 142, 148, 149, 150, 153, 158, 160, 161, 162, 164, 167, 170, 172, 173, 183, 187, 191, 194, 195, 196, 197, 204, 208, 212, 214; (image/likeness of), 21, 25, 32, 135; gods, 33, 70, 76, 88, 90, 104, 115, 121, 122, 168, 169, 172; *see also* Creator; Lord, the
gold, 6, 18, 60, 108, 113, 137, 138, 176, 214; golden, 61, 193; *see also* ages
Gomorah, 20, 104, 105
good, 6, 7, 10, 19, 20, 21, 22, 24, 25, 26, 32, 35, 43, 44, 45, 54, 55, 66, 67, 72, 81, 82, 92, 95, 100, 101, 106, 118, 122, 125, 127, 134, 135, 147, 150, 153, 154, 162, 171, 172, 179, 189, 190, 207, 211, 214; goodness, 13, 17, 18, 70, 72
Gospel, the, 151, 153, 154, 155, 192, 194, 195, 208; *see also* Bible
Gothenburg, 197

government(s), 41, 137, 178, 202, 204; governors, 42, 168
Grace, 119, 133, 198
grave(s), 43, 82, 83, 195; grave goods, 43
Great Tartary, 67, 80, 81, 86, 106
Greece, 50, 68, 76, 77, 78, 87; Greek(s), 7, 33, 54, 75, 77, 87, 146, 196
groves, 74, 75, 159

Hadad, 134
Hagar, 134
Ham, 88
Haran, 121
Haydn, 203
heart(s), 20, 42, 48, 50, 52, 59, 81, 93, 97, 116, 125, 132, 146, 163, 167, 170, 173, 174, 184, 203
heathen, 161, 180, 202, 205, 208; *see also* gentile(s)
heaven(s), 8, 11, 17, 19, 22, 23, 25, 26, 27, 33, 34, 36, 38, 39, 40, 43, 45, 46, 49, 57, 59, 60, 68, 70, 74, 75, 76, 77, 82, 83, 84, 85, 86, 87, 88, 89, 92, 102, 103, 105, 106, 107, 108, 111, 114, 115, 121, 123, 125, 126, 128, 129, 131, 133, 136, 137, 141, 147, 148, 150, 151, 154, 156, 157, 158, 160, 161, 162, 163, 167, 168, 169, 170, 171, 173, 174, 176, 177, 178, 179, 183, 184, 187, 188, 189, 190, 192, 193, 194, 195, 196, 197, 198, 199, 202, 204, 206, 207, 208, 209, 210, 213, 214, 215; celestial, 8, 9, 127, 147; communication/links with, 17, 27, 33, 45, 55, 76, 103, 115, 162, 171, 189, 192, 193; false, 190, 213; New, 19, 183, 189, 190, 191, 192, 194, 197, 200, 203, 213, 214; third, 8, 9, 76
Heber, 6, 12, 65, 97, 98, 99
Hebrew (language), 50, 99, 126, 127, 136, 137, 146, 187
Hebron, 83
Helicon, 77, 78
hell(s), 19, 26, 82, 89, 120, 136, 147, 148, 149, 150, 162, 169, 174, 177, 178, 187, 188, 189, 190, 199, 202, 213

heresies, 52, 53, 155, 156, 158, 172
Heshbon, 78
Heth, 133, 134
hieroglyphic(s), 50, 79, 91; hieroglyphs, 50, 68, 80
Hindu(ism), 160, 161; Hindus, 7
history, 4, 5, 9, 10, 11, 12, 13, 25, 35, 51, 53, 54, 56, 69, 112, 113, 115, 121, 129, 130, 131, 132, 154, 155, 157, 191; historic(al), 3, 5, 10, 11, 69, 78, 90, 100, 102, 104, 106, 112, 116, 128, 130, 131, 132; historian(s), 4, 13, 98, 112, 191
Hittites, 56
Hivites, 56
Holland, 165, 200, 207; Dutch, 205, 206; Low Countries, 137; Netherlands, 197
Holy Spirit, 84, 150, 151, 169
Holy Supper, 24, 86
Homer, 204
Hungary, 165
hunter-gatherers, 35, 38, 42, 43, 56

idolatry, 93, 139, 159, 160, 161; idolatrous, 3, 23, 75, 88, 104, 116, 120, 123; idols, 88, 91, 105, 113, 133, 139, 140, 141, 159; idolaters, 104
image(s), 5, 25, 39, 68, 75, 76, 87, 114, 133, 139, 141, 159, 161, 192, 196
Imputation, 178, 198
India, 77; Indians, 161
Indies, the, 35, 67, 87, 165, 170
influx, 43, 45, 55, 147, 190, 203
Instruction of Amenemopet, 80
internal(s), 8, 23, 24, 26, 27, 32, 33, 34, 36, 44, 48, 49, 66, 73, 74, 84, 89, 101, 104, 113, 120, 123, 125, 129, 156, 174, 176, 189, 191; sense, 37, 51, 52, 53, 82, 116, 127, 129, 151, 152, 153, 193; respiration, 48, 49; *see also* spiritual sense
intuition, 46
Irad, 53
iron, 6, 13, 18, 138, 175, 176, 180; *see also* ages
Isaac, 105, 115, 117, 147

Ishmael, 134
Islam, 54, 159, 160, 161; Islamic, 14, 50; *see also* Mohammedan; Muslim
Israel, 6, 12, 23, 27, 65, 98, 99, 104, 117, 127, 137; Israelite(s), 3, 5, 78, 80, 100, 102, 106, 112, 116, 118, 119, 120, 121, 122, 125, 128, 131, 132; Children of, 60, 103, 114, 117, 118, 130; twelve tribes of, 112, 147, 150
Italy, 35, 77, 165; Italians, 87, 207

Jabal, 53
Jacob, 6, 56, 65, 104, 105, 111, 115, 116, 117, 121, 133, 147
James, 150, 151
Jared, 53
Jashar (book of), 80
Jehovah, 13, 32, 33, 60, 69, 70, 80, 89, 104, 105, 115, 121, 122, 123, 124, 125, 132, 147, 158, 195; The Wars of Jehovah, 78, 80, 102, 106
Jehovih, 19, 58, 60, 117
Jerome, 152, 153
Jerusalem, 8, 121, 129, 132, 153, 159, 183, 213; *see also* New Jerusalem
Jesus, 145, 148, 149, 152, 184, 192, 196, 212
Jetur, 134
Jew(s), 4, 8, 12, 22, 33, 90, 102, 111, 112, 113, 114, 119, 121, 122, 123, 125, 128, 129, 130, 132, 133, 135, 136, 137, 138, 147, 150, 153, 212; Jewish, 5, 7, 10, 18, 112, 113, 114, 116, 128, 130, 131, 136, 146, 152, 153, 154; diaspora, 137; Judaism, 201; *see also* church
John, 8, 9, 150, 151, 152, 191, 214
Jordan, 98, 104, 105
Joseph, 83, 105, 121
Joshua, 104, 105, 121, 131
Jubal, 53
Judah, 6, 23, 65, 112, 132
judgment, 19, 20, 22, 26, 118, 120, 125, 163, 168, 178, 179, 188, 202; *see also* Last Judgment
Jupiter, 38

justification, 172, 173, 198

Kedar, 134
Kedemah, 134
Keller, Helen, 212
Kenan, 53
king(s), 23, 41, 78, 83, 90, 120, 123, 130, 132, 140, 167, 192, 204; kingdom(s), 23, 42, 54, 68, 75, 76, 83, 87, 88, 97, 103, 106, 111, 120, 121, 122, 123, 136, 149, 150, 160, 165, 173, 174, 175, 192, 200
Koran, 50, 162

lamb(s), 39, 58, 68, 123, 159, 183, 193, 197, 214
Lamech, 53, 54, 55,
language, 47, 59, 86, 90, 99, 126, 127, 128, 130, 146, 154, 165, 171, 185, 187, 207, 212; *see also* speech
Lapps, the, 38
Last Judgment, 20, 188, 189, 190, 192, 194, 197, 200, 204, 205, 213; Judgment Day, 199
Latin, 4, 17, 46, 52, 153, 167, 196, 200, 207
Latter-Day Saints, 201
law(s), 105, 107, 116, 118, 123, 125, 130, 148, 161, 164, 165, 171, 177, 191; Law, the, 115, 118, 120, 145, 152; *see also* Ten Commandments
Leah, 133
Lebanon, 98, 131
Levant, the, 98
Liberia, 208
liberty, 25
library, libraries, 49, 50, 85, 86, 212
Lisbon earthquake, 201
Lord, the, 3, 4, 8, 9, 11, 17, 18, 19, 20, 21, 22, 23, 24, 25, 26, 27, 31, 32, 33, 34, 43, 44, 45, 46, 52, 57, 58, 60, 66, 69, 70, 72, 74, 81, 83, 86, 87, 89, 91, 101, 103, 111, 114, 115, 117, 118, 119, 120, 121, 122, 128, 129, 131, 134, 135, 136, 138, 142, 145, 146, 147, 148, 149, 150, 151, 152, 153, 154, 155, 156, 157, 158, 159, 160,

161, 162, 163, 164, 167, 168, 169, 170, 171, 172, 173, 174, 179, 180, 183, 184, 185, 186, 187, 189, 190, 192, 193, 194, 195, 197, 198, 199, 200, 201, 206, 208, 209, 210, 211, 212, 213, 214, 215; *see also* Creator; God
Loretto, 168
Louis XIV, 171
Louis XV, 204
love, 6, 7, 8, 18, 21, 22, 23, 24, 25, 26, 31, 32, 35, 39, 40, 42, 46, 52, 53, 57, 59, 60, 74, 79, 86, 92, 93, 101, 107, 114, 118, 122, 125, 127, 135, 137, 140, 141, 142, 148, 149, 150, 155, 156, 157, 163, 164, 166, 167, 173, 174, 179, 180, 190, 192, 206, 209, 210, 211, 214, 215
lungs, 48, 49, 59, 163, 170
Luther, Martin, 114, 152, 153, 171; Lutheran(s), 166, 174

Mahalalel, 53
Manchuria, 80; Manchu, 80
marriage, 40, 42, 43, 57, 59, 60, 90, 91, 92, 93, 100, 103, 105, 106, 107, 108, 140, 164, 171, 177, 178, 179, 209, 210; *see also* monogamy; polygamy
Mary, 158
Masoretes, 129
Massa, 134
Medebah, 79
Mediterranean, 56, 99, 102, 146
Mesolithic, 40
Mesopotamia(n), 67, 68, 76, 86, 89, 90, 97, 99, 103
Messiah, 122, 123
metals, 6, 9, 13, 18, 91, 101
Methodism, 201
Methusael, 53, 54
Methuselah, 53, 54
Mibsam, 134
Middle East, the, 36, 50, 68, 77, 88, 99, 102, 208
miracles, 122, 123, 174
Mishma, 134
Moab, 78

Mohammed, 7, 159, 160; Mohammedanism, 159; Mohammedan(s), 122, 160, 161, 170, 205, 208; *see also* Islamic; Muslim(s)
Mongolia, 80; Mongul, 80
monogamy, 161, 164; monogamous, 106, 107, 164; *see also* marriage
monotheism, 121, 122; monotheistic, 33, 121
Mormons, 201
Moses, 3, 60, 78, 79, 80, 102, 105, 106, 113, 114, 115, 116, 117, 118, 119, 120, 122, 123, 125, 130, 131, 146, 147, 151
mosques, 50
most ancients, 7, 18, 32, 33, 34, 36, 37, 38, 39, 40, 42, 43, 44, 45, 46, 47, 50, 57, 59, 79, 85, 102, 107, 121, 122; *see also* church
mountains, 8, 34, 39, 57, 58, 68, 74, 75, 77, 89, 90, 91, 106, 121, 132, 149, 159, 183, 190
Mozart, 204
mullahs, 50
Muses, 78, 203
music, 49, 203, 204, 209; blues, 209; jazz, 209
Muslim(s), 21, 161, 162; *see also* Islamic; Mohammedans
mystic(al), 38, 79
mythology, 7, 77; (Norse), 7; (Amerindian), 7; myths, 7, 53, 54, 68, 69, 77, 79, 83, 128, 129

Nahor, 104
Naphish, 134
Nash, Ogden, 113
natural, 6, 7, 8, 11, 12, 18, 44, 45, 46, 47, 50, 75, 92, 93, 101, 106, 107, 114, 117, 118, 123, 125, 126, 136, 139, 141, 147, 150, 157, 158, 162, 179, 180, 189, 191, 196, 198, 200, 203, 205, 206, 211; man, 11, 76
Nebaioth, 134
Nebuchadnezzar; dream, 3, 5, 18; statue, 9, 135, 138

neighbour, 20, 22, 24, 52, 74, 86, 107, 118, 135, 173, 174
neoclassical, 204
Neolithic, *see* ages
Neolithic Revolution, 53, 56
Netherlands, *see* Holland
New Church organizations, 212
New Jerusalem, 9, 138, 183, 194, 186, 189, 197, 200, 214
NewSearch, 49
New Sufi orders, 201
Nicene Council, *see* Council of Nicaea
Nile, 99
Nineveh, 54, 67, 86, 103
Noah, 5, 6, 10, 12, 53, 55, 66, 68, 71, 72, 73, 97, 117, 129; *see also* church
Nophah, 79
Norse, (mythology), 7; (Sagas), 50
nuclear family, *see* family

offspring, 43, 69, 211; *see also* children
Olympus, Mount, 34, 77
oracles, 84, 88
Oriental(s), 20, 21, 159, 160, 161
Ovid, 38, 39, 42, 77; *Metamorphoses*, 38, 77
oxygen, 48, 49

Palaeolithic, *see* ages
Panthéon, 204
Papacy, 167
Papal Bulls, 167
Papists, 88
Paradise, 129
parents, 39, 40, 41, 211; parental, 43, 211
Paris, 204
Parsee Theosophy, 201
Passover, 121
pastoralists, 39
patriarch(s), 6, 41, 54, 196
Pax Romana, 147
Pegasus, 77
perception, 32, 40, 42, 43, 44, 45, 46, 53, 54, 56, 76, 85, 92, 103, 151
Pergamum, 103

Perizzite, 100
Persian Gulf, 83
Persians, 7
Peter, 150, 151
Pharaoh, 105, 118, 119, 120
Pharisees, 22, 150
Philadelphia, 212
Philistia, 67, 86
Phoenicians, 99
pillars, 74
Pindus, 77, 78
Pluto, 168
Poland, 165
politics, 200; politic(al), 12, 99, 131, 147, 151, 156
polygamy, 164; polygamists, 107, 161; polygamous, 106, 140, 165, 177; *see also* marriage
polytheism, 122; polytheists, 33, 121
pope(s), 167, 168, 169, 171, 202; Sixtus V, 167, 168
Portugal, 137, 165
power(s), 7, 23,26, 76, 101, 107, 141, 149, 150, 158, 170, 180, 191, 194; *see also* dominion
Pre-adamites, 31
Prophecies, The, 78; *see also* Utterances, The
priest(s), 22, 26, 90, 100, 102, 118, 125, 167, 173, 178, 193, 202
printing, 50, 185, 186
Prophets, the, 3, 79, 103, 114, 117, 122, 124, 130, 131, 132, 145, 146, 147, 148, 151, 152, 184, 194, 195; prophet(s), 5, 123, 131, 133, 159; prophetic(al), 3, 78, 79, 102, 104, 106, 116, 132, 134; *see also* Bible, Word
proprium, 52
Protestant(s), 145, 153, 166, 171, 190; Protestantism, 207; *see also* church
providence, 20, 25, 38, 89, 90, 103, 115, 127, 128, 146, 151, 154, 157, 159, 160, 161, 163, 170, 185, 186
Prussia, 191
psychology, 32, 43, 56, 82; psychological(ly),

19, 68, 210
psycho-spiritual, 4, 11, 43, 81
Ptahhotep, 80
pygmies, 35
pyramids, 83

Rachael, 133
Red Sea, 105
Reformation, the, 170, 171, 185
Reformed, 165, 167, 169, 170, 171, 174, 185, 198, 205, 206; *see also* church
Regency style, 204
regeneration, 44, 71, 72, 130, 172, 207; regenerate(d), 24, 31, 71, 72, 118, 161
religion(s), 4, 14, 17, 20, 21, 22, 23, 25, 26, 32, 33, 34, 36, 54, 57, 73, 80, 87, 102, 117, 119, 122, 133, 135, 147, 156, 158, 159, 160, 161, 162, 165, 167, 168, 169, 170, 171, 172, 177, 178, 179, 208; religious, 26, 34, 69, 77, 90, 102, 117, 123, 161, 176, 178, 180, 201, 202, 213; *see also* church
remnants, 40, 55, 56, 90, 102, 117, 175
representations, 27, 46, 68, 132, 134; representatives, 23, 27, 74, 75, 92, 101, 103, 111, 116, 118, 120, 121, 123, 159; *see also* church; correspondences
respiration, 48, 49
resurrection, 20, 82, 83, 163
revelation, 19, 46, 54, 87, 127, 128, 129, 151, 185, 189, 193, 196, 199, 213
rituals, 27, 86, 102, 115, 125
Roberts, J M, 194
rococo, 204
Rome, 87, 151, 167, 207
Roman(s), 7, 75, 87, 90, 126, 137, 146; Empire, 146, 156; Emperors, 147
Roman Catholics, *see* Catholic(s)
Royal Academy, 204
Russia, 80, 165; Russian, 81

sabbaths, 118, 123
sacrifice(s), 97, 100, 101, 102, 118, 123, 124, 129, 159

Sadducees, 22, 136
Sagas, 50
saints, 168, 169
salvation, 17, 26, 161, 171, 172, 173, 198; saved, 25, 26, 118, 162, 173
Samuel, 114; *see also* Bible
Sarah, 134
Saturn (time of), 18
Scripture(s), 102, 103, 107, 108, 113, 122, 145, 146, 147, 152, 168, 202; *see also* Bible; Word
seasons, 4; autumn, 9; spring, 9, 10; summer, 9, 10; winter, 9, 10
Second Coming, 183, 194, 195, 196
self-love, 25, 42, 52, 149
service, 8, 85, 191
Seth, 53, 54
Seven Years War, 191, 201
sexual relations, 138, 175, 209, 210
shaman, 46
shrines, 74, 130, 139, 193
Sidon, 54, 67, 76, 86, 103
Sierra Leone, 208
Sihon, 78
silver, 6, 18, 92, 93, 94, 113, 137, 138, 176; *see also* ages
Sinai, Mount, 3, 60, 117, 118, 120
Sixtus V, Pope, 167, 168
Snowdon, 34
Sodom, 20, 104, 105
Sogdian, 80
Solomon, 22, 23, 27, 130, 131
soul(s), 24, 59, 60, 84, 85, 92, 93, 115, 140, 178, 188, 190, 199
South Africa, 13
South-East Asia, 87
space, 11, 139
Spain, 137, 165, 168; Spanish, 207
speech, 31, 47, 49, 119, 127; *see also* language
spirit(s), 8, 24, 26, 27, 33, 42, 44, 46, 49, 57, 80, 82, 84, 89, 91, 136, 150, 155, 162, 179, 183, 184, 185, 187, 188, 189, 190, 194, 196, 198, 199, 208, 213; (evil), 55, 57

spiritual, 6, 7, 8, 11, 12, 19, 34, 44, 46, 68, 73, 75, 77, 84, 86, 102, 107, 113, 115, 116, 117, 118, 126, 127, 128, 131, 136, 137, 139, 141, 151, 155, 156, 158, 170, 179, 180, 186, 189, 196, 197, 199, 202, 203, 206, 207, 209, 213, 214, 215; development, 12, 113, 147, 161; life, 10, 24, 26; love, 74, 75, 79, 155, 206; marriage, 92, 179, 211; matters, 68, 69, 115, 186, 202; meaning, 6, 75, 79; person/people, 8, 73, 114, 191; sense, 68, 113, 129, 130, 147, 150, 154, 174, 193, 194, 196, 198, 202, 214; things, 23, 27, 50, 74, 87, 101, 103, 120, 136, 159, 172; truth, 46, 91, 92, 119, 132, 139; world, 8, 46, 80, 139, 157, 160, 161, 162, 164, 174, 187, 188, 189, 191, 192, 200, 202, 203, 205; spiritually, 27, 56, 84, 180; spiritualty, 23, 141; *see also* internal sense; world of spirits

Stone Age, *see* ages

Strindberg, August, 212

Sumerian, 89, 90

sun, 9, 60, 68, 70, 71, 158, 159, 189; midnight sun, 10; worship, 70

superstition, 69, 167

Suphah, 78

Sutherland, Graham, 195

Swaminarayan Movement, 201

Sweden, 165, 197; Swede(s), 10, 205

Swedenborg; *Apocalypse Explained*, 4, 6, 18, 35, 36, 37, 131, 157, 161, 162, 170, 171, 173, 184, 203; *Apocalypse Revealed*, 6, 8, 145, 166, 169, 171, 184, 213, 214, 215; *Appendix to the White Horse*, 50; *Arcana Caelestia*, 4, 5, 6, 7, 8, 10, 12, 17, 18, 20, 22, 24, 27, 32, 33, 34, 35, 36, 37, 40, 41, 42, 43, 44, 45, 47, 48, 49, 50, 51, 52, 53, 54, 55, 56, 57, 65, 66, 67, 69, 70, 71, 72, 73, 74, 79, 82, 83, 84, 86, 87, 89, 90, 97, 98, 100, 101, 104, 111, 112, 113, 115, 116, 117, 118, 119, 120, 121, 122, 123, 124, 125, 129, 130, 131, 133, 134, 135, 136, 147, 149, 155, 156, 162, 174, 184, 185, 187, 188, 197, 203; *Athanasian Creed*, 70, 195; *The Brief Exposition*, 158; *Canons of the New Church*, 158; *Conjugial Love*, 4, 36, 39, 40, 57, 68, 85, 90, 103, 105, 112, 135, 138, 161, 164, 165, 175, 209, 210, 211; *De Conjugio*, 18, 43; *Continuation of the Last Judgment*, 189, 200, 206, 207; *The Coronis*, 5, 6, 7, 18, 19, 20, 53, 66, 67, 75, 87, 88, 105, 117, 118, 131, 132, 133, 154, 172, 174, 194; *Divine Providence*, 23, 25, 26, 27, 38, 39, 41, 111, 128, 154, 160, 161, 166; *The Divine Wisdom*, 121; *Doctrine of Faith*, 166; *Doctrine of Life*, 166; *Doctrine of the Lord*, 148, 191, 197; *Doctrine of the Sacred Scripture*, 20, 67, 87, 104, 169, 170, 171; *Heaven and Hell*, 4, 11, 12, 23, 46, 50, 87, 126, 127, 199, 210, 213; *Last Judgment*, 4, 20, 22, 26, 128, 150, 161, 189, 191, 196, 200, 201, 202, 205; *The Last Judgment (Posthumous)*, 136, 138, 200, 208; Letter(s) to Beyer, 187, 197, 198, 200; *The New Jerusalem*, 20, 21, 27, 152, 153, 171, 192, 211; *On the Sacred Scripture*, 8, 17, 38, 68, 77, 114, 136, 147, 165, 185; *The Spiritual Diary (Spiritual Experiences)*, 31, 50, 54, 84, 85, 113, 127, 128, 153, 163, 167, 187; *The True Christian Religion*, 3, 4, 10, 32, 36, 54, 76, 79, 80, 87, 117, 122, 146, 148, 151, 153, 155, 157, 158, 161, 167, 172, 184, 187, 192, 193, 194, 198, 199, 200; *Worlds in Space*, 48, 49

Swedenborg Concordance, The, 49

Swedenborgian(s), 19, 20, 80, 99, 204, 212

Swedenborg Society, 204

symbols, 9, 46, 50, 51, 71, 102, 121, 125; symbolism, 7, 13, 27, 37, 51, 69, 72, 100, 114, 129, 131; symbolic(ally), 12, 27, 46, 53, 74, 76, 83, 112, 113, 115, 121, 124, 126, 151, 204, 212, 215; symbolize, 6, 20, 22, 53, 54, 73, 75, 78, 88, 105, 115, 133, 147, 151, 166

Syria, 54, 67, 68, 76, 86, 97, 98, 99, 103

Index

Tabernacle, the, 60, 118, 124, 125, 131, 159, 183; *see also* tent(s)
tablets, 50, 51, 60, 86, 102, 103, 108, 115, 116, 120
telepathy, 48, 49
Tema, 134
temples, 75, 76, 92, 159; the (Solomon's) Temple, 23, 115, 131, 149, 159; Temple of Artemis, 75
temptation(s), 71, 114, 115, 128, 148, 149
Ten Commandments, 3, 117, 155, 162, 208; *see also* Decalogue,
tent(s), 35, 36, 37, 38, 58, 59, 60, 61, 125
Terah, 104
theology, 187, 200, 212; theological, 5, 146, 197, 207; theologians, 22, 173
Theosophy, 201
Thummim, 138
Tower of Babel, 89, 90, 213
Tree of Life, 7, 214, 215
tribes, 34, 35, 39, 40, 41, 43, 44, 73, 83, 112, 121, 132, 147, 150; tribal, 13, 40, 43
Trinity, 158, 172, 196
truth(s), 6, 13, 17, 18, 21, 25, 26, 32, 43, 44, 45, 46, 48, 54, 55, 66, 67, 70, 71, 72, 73, 74, 76, 77, 82, 85, 91, 92, 93, 100, 101, 102, 105, 106, 107, 118, 119, 122, 127, 128, 132, 134, 135, 137, 139, 150, 153, 154, 156, 157, 162, 168, 171, 172, 173, 175, 178, 179, 193, 197, 201, 202, 205, 207, 208, 214, 215
Tubal-Cain, 13, 53
turinga, 51
Turnbull, Colin, 34-5, 41; *The Forest People*, 41
twelve tribes of Israel, *see* Israel
Tyre, 54, 67, 76, 86, 103, 138

Ugarit, 99
Uluru, 34
understanding, 7, 25, 32, 33, 43, 44, 45, 48, 71, 72, 81, 82, 91, 118, 119, 150, 184, 193, 194, 196, 208, 209, 210, 212
Ungud, 33

Unitarians, 201
United States, 207; *see also* America
Uranus, 33
Ur, 89
Urim, 138
Utterances, The, 80, 102, 106; *see also* Prophecies, The

Van der Post, Laurens, 34
variety, 22, 66, 140, 151, 213, 215
vastation, 132; vastated, 54
Vatican, 167, 168
vineyard, 73, 132
visions, 4, 12, 46

Wadstrom, Charles, 208
Waheb, 78
walkabout, 37, 44
wandering, 36, 37, 38
war(s), 120, 191, 200, 201
Wars of Jehovah, The, 78, 80, 102, 106
washing, 125
wealth, 42, 163, 168, 215
Wedgwood, 204
West, 13, 157; Western, 13, 45, 151, 155, 208
West Africa, 161, 208
will, 7, 25, 32, 43, 44, 45, 71, 72, 81, 82, 140, 209, 210
wisdom, 6, 7, 8, 23, 25, 31, 32, 41, 56, 59, 60, 68, 69, 70, 74, 76, 85, 103, 107, 148, 163, 169
wise men, 9, 179, 198, 215
Word, the, 3, 4, 5, 6, 7, 8, 10, 11, 17, 19, 20, 21, 23, 32, 35, 37, 50, 55, 65, 66, 76, 77, 78, 80, 82, 98, 99, 102, 103, 104, 106, 111, 112, 114, 115, 116, 117, 118, 121, 122, 126, 127, 128, 129, 132, 134, 136, 137, 138, 139, 145, 147, 150, 151, 153, 154, 155, 156, 157, 159, 162, 163, 165, 167, 169, 170, 171, 172, 173, 174, 175, 183, 185, 187, 188, 193, 194, 196, 198, 200, 202, 209, 211, 212, 214, 215; *see also* Ancient Word; Bible; Sacred Scripture

world, 8, 9, 10, 11, 20, 21, 22, 23, 27, 32, 34, 35, 36, 42, 44, 45, 46, 47, 56, 58, 60, 66, 68, 69, 70, 76, 83, 85, 86, 87, 88, 91, 98, 103, 107, 113, 116, 121, 122, 126, 128, 129, 134, 135, 137, 138, 145, 147, 148, 149, 150, 151, 154, 157, 158, 159, 160, 163, 164, 165, 167, 168, 170, 173, 174, 177, 185, 188, 189, 190, 191, 192, 194, 195, 199, 200, 201, 202, 203, 204, 205, 207, 208, 209, 210, 211, 212, 213; *see also* earth

world of spirits, 26, 136, 162, 167, 189, 190, 205, 206, 207; *see also* spiritual world

worship, 23, 24, 25, 27, 33, 34, 35, 36, 37, 45, 60, 66, 69, 70, 73, 74, 75, 76, 80, 87, 89, 90, 97, 98, 100, 101, 102, 103, 104, 105, 115, 122, 123, 135, 138, 139, 141, 149, 159, 162, 163, 168, 170, 172, 196, 212

Yahweh, 33, 113
Yeats, William Butler, 212

Zeboiim, 104
Zeus, 203
ziggurat, 89, 90
Zion, 83
Zoroastrian, 71